The Pioneers of
Development Economics

The Pioneers of
Development Economics

Great Economists on Development

Edited by
JOMO K.S.

 Tulika Books

Zed Books
London and New York

First published in India in 2005 by
Tulika Books
35 A/1 (third floor), Shahpur Jat, New Delhi 110 049, India

First published outside South Asia in 2005 by
Zed Books
7 Cynthia Street, London N1 9JF, UK, and Room 400, 175 Fifth
Avenue, New York, NY 10010, USA. www.zedbooks.demon.co.uk

© Jomo K.S., 2005

The right of Jomo K.S., to be identified as the editor of this work has
been asserted by him in accordance with the Copyright, Designs and
Patents Act, 1988

ISBN (Tulika Books edition): 81-85229-99-6

ISBN (Zed Books edition): 1 84277 644 4 hb   1 84277 645 2 pb

A catalogue record for this book is available from the British Library.
US CIP data is available from the Library of Congress

Distributed in the USA exclusively by Palgrave, a division of
St. Martin's Press, LLC, 175 Fifth Avenue, New York 10010

Cover designed by Ram Rahman; typeset in Sabon and Univers at
Tulika Print Communication Services, New Delhi, India; printed and
bound at Chaman Enterprises, 1603 Pataudi House, Daryaganj, New
Delhi 110 002, India

Contents

Introduction

Jomo K.S.

The history of economic thought as acknowledged by the orthodoxy that currently dominates the economics profession amounts to little more than 'a total fixation on their own previous work'. Often, the intellectual legacy of earlier thinkers is reduced in stylized form to support the claims of contemporary economists. Thus, the history of economic ideas is depicted as a unique trajectory of progress towards an ever-superior understanding of economic reality. Other social insights are swept aside, except when susceptible to similarly formalistic expression.

Reconsidering the history of development economics provides a valuable opportunity to challenge this limited and limiting approach. While every branch of economic inquiry has generally suffered from the debilitating consequences of historical amnesia, development economics, thankfully, has been spared its worst effects. Its fundamental categories of analysis are necessarily linked to particular historical circumstances, including the transition from the colonialism of the imperial era to the 'post-colonial' era.

The pioneering generation of development economists not only reflected the more tolerant intellectual environment within the economics discipline in the post-war period, but have provided an enduring basis from which to challenge the neoclassical orthodoxy whose grip over economic inquiry has tightened in the recent period. Fortunately, substantial work exists on the history and legacy of this pioneering generation.

The task of reassessing the history of development economics is more urgent than ever today, not only because of its relevance to contemporary debates, but also for the light it casts on the discipline of economics as a whole. The 'pioneering generation' of the post-war decades reflected the diversity that still characterized economic thought at that time, before the vice of orthodoxy was firmly clamped, consigning its challengers to a 'heterodox' fringe. In the course of this process, development economics was first challenged and then overwhelmed by neoliberal dogma, which took the form of the 'Washington Consensus'.

Rich, varied and 'heterodox' though their legacy is, the contributions of the pioneering generation of development economists provided an inadequate defence against this assault. Like classical political economy, the work of this pioneering generation has been subjected to stylized abstraction, which often disregards the circumstances in which the theories, concepts and methods of development economics were first formed. The broader approach represented by the work of Meier and others (for example, Meier and Seers, eds 1984; Meier, ed. 1994) has been 'replaced' by more orthodox reformulations. The studies in the present volume as well as in two other companion volumes contribute to a critical response to such formalistic reductionism in development economics.

While appearing to concede much of this more historically oriented theoretical ground, the recent 'new' development economics continues the intellectual offensive against a development economics tradition that constitutes an alternative to the Washington Consensus. How this has been achieved, and how it affects current debates, is the remit of a companion volume on the 'new development economics', which contains a variety of studies on the transition from the Washington Consensus to the post-Washington Consensus (Jomo and Fine, eds 2005).

The other companion volume (Jomo and Reinert, eds 2005) shows that, historically, the study of economics has been principally concerned with economic development, rather than current fads such as 'equilibrium', etc. It considers how different schools of economics have addressed the challenges of development over the last five centuries. It surveys economic policy ideas associated with the Italian city-states, the developmental intent of mercantilism and the German historical school. It also considers the debates over the transition to capitalism, international trade, growth theory, and Latin American structuralism and dependency.

After an opening essay redefining the scope and purpose of development economics, the studies in this volume add depth and perspective to current debates in at least three ways. First, they emphasize the imperial origins of economic thought impinging on the discourse on contemporary development by critically considering the influence of William Petty and David Ricardo's international trade theory of comparative advantage. Second, they highlight the relevance of contributions by economists not normally seen as pioneers of development economics, including Friedrich List, Karl Marx, V.I. Lenin, Alfred Marshall, Michal Kalecki, John Maynard Keynes, Nicholas Kaldor, Karl Polanyi and Alexander Gerschenkron. Third, the principal heterodox economic implications of the major contributions of some pioneers of development economics – such as Arthur Lewis, Raul Prebisch and Hans Singer – are highlighted.

In the introductory chapter, Prabhat Patnaik emphasizes the wide-ranging implications for economic analysis of theories, frameworks and methodologies that continue to treat national economies as closed and self-contained, and which fail to consider the interactions between capitalist and non-capitalist sectors. Ignoring these interactions impoverishes not only theoretical analysis of the world economy, but is especially crucial for meaningful development economics.

He critically considers the flawed character of analyses associated with mainstream growth Theory, the so-called non-accelerating inflation rate of unemployment (NAIRU) and its monetarist variant, the natural rate of unemployment (NRU), as well as international trade theory. Suggesting that the contrived marginalization of development economics has impoverished economic analysis more generally, he suggests that there is no analytical justification for the Chinese wall that has come in between.

From Colonialism to International Trade Theory

The literature on the history of development economics is dominated by a perspective which assumes that Adam Smith's *Wealth of Nations* is the starting point of the discipline's intellectual ancestry. The idea of the Smithian ancestry of development economics is challenged by Hugh Goodacre who shows William Petty to be the earlier and more significant source of development economics. In fact, Petty applied his pioneering quantitative methods to coldly calculate the advantages to the imperial power of different colonial options.

Later, development economics was established as an academic subdiscipline at Oxford University, before World War II, as part of the 'Colonial Studies' training course for service in Britain's colonial empire. After the war, with decolonization clearly imminent, this purpose was superseded by the need to train replacements from among the nationals of countries gaining independence from the late 1940s. Recognizing and addressing the implications of its origins is urgent if development economics is to be capable of performing the analytical and policy tasks expected of it.

An outstanding example of how orthodox economic thought has been used to justify economic imperialism is provided by the Ricardian theory of comparative advantage in international trade. Utsa Patnaik's chapter critically exposes the fallacious assumptions on which it rests. David Ricardo's concept famously relies on what is now termed the transformation frontier between goods that can be produced at different costs in different countries. Yet, as Utsa Patnaik points out, a logical fallacy lies at the heart of his argument as one of the two goods cannot actually be produced in both countries – hence, no transformation frontier exists for comparison. The context of Ricardo's theory is shown to be a world of colonial trade and extra-economic compulsion, obscured by his theoretical subterfuge. Most alarmingly, economics textbooks have perpetuated and promoted Ricardo's logical fallacy to this day.

Forgotten Pioneers

The next chapter, by Mehdi Shafaeddin, approaches the issues of economic development and international trade from a perspective that has been neglected in the orthodox tradition – that of the mid-nineteenth-century 'latecomers' to capitalist development, Germany and the USA. The chapter provides a revealing analysis of the arguments for trade protection to develop new economic capacities and capabilities advanced by the German Friedrich List, at a time when the USA was the 'home' of this policy, thanks to the enduring influence of one of its founding fathers, US Treasury Secretary Alexander Hamilton. Shafaeddin shows how List developed the basic framework for the strategic trade theory and industrial or investment policy that has guided most subsequent policies for structural transformation, industrialization and development until the present day.

The work of Karl Marx and V.I. Lenin has also been very significant for the understanding of economic development. Marx used the term 'development' to refer to the development of capitalism, rather than its contemporary use in orthodox development economics to refer to development under capitalism. Prabhat Patnaik underscores Marx's original contributions to the understanding of capitalist development, distinguishing carefully between the development of market relations and the creation of conditions for capital accumulation. He emphasizes the significance of Marx's discussions of the 'primary' accumulation and centralization of capital for understanding development dichotomies. He also notes that Marx's analytical preoccupation with the prospects for European revolution was paralleled by a growing recognition of the prospects for revolution in the third world as well as his pioneering contribution to the analysis of surplus transfers from the South.

Inspired by Marx, and by contemporary Russian and European debates over revolutionary conditions, Lenin's careful analysis of the development of capitalism in Russia at the end of the nineteenth century may seem a surprising source for the contemporary study of economic development. Utsa Patnaik's chapter shows how Lenin analysed a range of development issues, including the effects of increasing production for the market, the 'differentiation' of the peasantry, the persistence of non-capitalist relations and the emergence of capitalist relations. Perhaps most importantly, she notes the origins of contemporary neoclassical analysis of the peasantry in the work of Chayanov, who was inspired by Russian populism. She also demonstrates that Lenin pioneered the statistical method for summarizing inequality, later known as the 'Lorenz curve'.

The following chapter by Renee Prendergast on Alfred Marshall returns the discussion of development to the mainstream of the history of economic thought. She shows how the liberal tradition of Mill, which provided the basis for Marshall's world view, resulted in an evolutionary view of the economy, rooted in the late Victorian idea of progress. Despite the central role of development in Marshall's vision of the economic process, this evolutionary developmental view was ironically marginalized by Marshall's marginalist analysis. The difficulty of incorporating development within his equilibrium framework manifested as a conflict between increasing returns and competition. Marshall recognized that the free play of market forces was not always beneficial; for him, societies had to restrain free enterprise to check excesses and to achieve greater gains in the medium term.

Next, Jayati Ghosh notes that although Michal Kalecki anticipated Keynes's seminal contribution to economic thought, this has been scantly recognized by most of the profession and in most histories of economic thought. Nonetheless, Kalecki's approach to economics remains especially significant for analysing development. While this approach was greatly influenced by his deep understanding of developed capitalist economies and socialist planning, he recognized critical features of developing economies that made them fundamentally different. Kalecki was always mindful of the macroeconomic and policy implications of different social, political and economic configurations, and historical processes. Ghosh also reviews his contributions on financing development and emphasizes that for Kalecki, economics was ultimately about politics, and that he was particularly concerned about the distributive implications of economic policy options.

While John Maynard Keynes had no direct influence on modern development economics, John Toye suggests indirect influences besides the contributions of Keynes's disciples and his own posthumous reputation. Keynes's seminal contribution on the macroeconomics of employment, his role in creating the Bretton Woods institutions and his proposal for commodity price stabilization continue to influence economic development. Much of Toye's chapter considers the possible significance of Keynes's lesser known writings. First, until around 1930, the then neo-Malthusian Keynes anticipated the isolation paradox and the North–South model as he maintained that industry's terms of trade faced a secular decline. Second, Keynes's critique of Soviet economic policy in the 1920s and 1930s anticipated contemporary neoliberal criticisms of the industrial policies of many post-war developing countries. Ironically, Toye notes, the self-professed 'anti-Keynesian' counter-revolution against development economics of the 1970s actually elaborated Keynes's ideas then.

In his assessment of the contributions of Keynes and Nicholas Kaldor to development economics, Amiya Kumar Bagchi emphasizes their contributions on macroeconomics and finance. While both believed that capitalism better delivered growth, they also recognized its inherent instability. Bagchi notes their analysis of the problem of stabilizing the prices of primary commodities. Keynes's analysis of stockmarkets is more relevant than ever in the face of recent financial liberalization, which has slowed growth and caused havoc in the global economy. Bagchi considers Kaldor the most worthy successor to Keynes, not only for his contribution to development economics, but also for elaborating a macroeconomic framework that could stimulate investment and growth, raise incomes and effective demand, and thus stabilize and stimulate the global economy. The counter-revolution against development economics in recent decades, in tandem with the trashing of Keynesianism, underscores the connection between the two.

Kari Polanyi Levitt suggests that previously it would have been unthinkable for her father to be considered a pioneer of development economics. For Karl Polanyi, *The Great Transformation*, originally entitled 'origins of our times', was the main cause of the world economic crisis, and of the demise of democracy in much of continental Europe that ended the long nineteenth century and eventually led to the major reforms after World War II. In multifarious ways, Polanyi's critique of the liberal economic order of 1870 to 1914 and its consequences anticipated contemporary critics of market fundamentalism and globalization. After his magnum opus, he studied economic life in 'primitive' and archaic societies to prove that profits and markets had never before been the central organizing principle of economic life. His research challenged the preconceptions of those who imposed – on pre-capitalist societies – concepts of scarcity and price-making markets based on the claim of mainstream economics to universal validity. His comparative and non-teleological perspective greatly enhanced understanding of the variety of responses to market expansion and economic incentives, so crucial to assumptions about what brings about economic development.

C.P. Chandrasekhar shows the relevance of Alexander Gerschenkron's study of economic history for economic development policy. Gerschenkron was primarily concerned with the historical processes by which Europe developed. This needed a developmental state capable of intervening effectively to help overcome obstacles to 'late industrialization'. He also emphasized the role of appropriate financial arrangements conducive to the developmental effort; these would necessarily be unlike the English financial system during Britain's industrialization. For him, economic development required specific financial arrangements and a financial system responsive to such needs. After all, there was little reason to expect that financial markets would ensure the most appropriate investment allocations, or even maximize the investment rate on their own.

Heterodox Pioneers

For Kari Polanyi Levitt, Raul Prebisch and W. Arthur Lewis define two central themes in development economics – the centre–periphery paradigm and the development of a modern capitalist sector in conditions of unlimited labour supplies. Both Prebisch and Lewis advocated industrialization, albeit for different reasons. Prebisch advocated industrialization to capture the gains of technological progress in view of the secular deterioration of the terms of trade of primary commodity exports. While labour shares productivity gains with capital in the centre, the weak bargaining position of labour in the periphery limits the adoption of labour-saving technology, and productivity gains in export production are transferred to the centre in the form of low prices. For Lewis, labour surplus countries have a comparative advantage in manufacturing, as wages in the modern capitalist sector are not determined by labour productivity but by its opportunity cost.

Finally, Kunibert Raffer's tribute to Hans Singer is a reminder of the hopes placed on Keynesian policies internationally in the post-war period. Raffer emphasizes Singer's humanity and the ethical basis of his commitment to egalitarian development at the world level. Singer was a co-author of the Singer–Prebisch thesis on the declining terms of trade faced by primary commodities. Raffer's survey shows that the thesis has stood up well to a barrage of criticism in the last half century. Singer went on to make important contributions on a variety of economic development issues, including trade policies. He was also a tireless advocate of soft finance, food aid and international institutional reform.

This volume clearly suggests that the way forward for development economics must involve rejection of its imperialist and 'nineteenth-century English liberal economic' origins. Instead, it must build on the many heterodox economic legacies that have contributed valuable insights which development economics has built upon. And the enduring contributions of the early development economists are decidedly heterodox in nature. Hence, rather than encourage development economics to be 'domesticated' and 'rehabilitated' by the orthodox mainstream, the economics of development needs to be recognized as offering a superior mode of economic analysis, as Prabhat Patnaik's introductory chapter suggests.

References

Jomo K.S. and Ben Fine, eds (2005), *The New Development Economics: After the Washington Consensus* (New Delhi: Tulika Books; London: Zed Books).

Jomo K.S. and Erik S. Reinert, eds (2005), *The Origins of Development Economics: How Schools of Economic Thought Have Addressed Development* (New Delhi: Tulika Books; London: Zed Books).

Meier, Gerald M., ed. (1994), *From Classical Economics to Development Economics* (London: Macmillan).

Meier, Gerald M. and Dudley Seers, eds (1984), *Pioneers in Development* (New York: Oxford University Press, for the World Bank).

Contributors

AMIYA KUMAR BAGCHI is Professor and Director, Institute of Development Studies, Kolkata.

C.P. CHANDRASEKHAR is Professor, Centre for Economic Studies and Planning, Jawaharlal Nehru University, New Delhi.

JAYATI GHOSH is Professor, Centre for Economic Studies and Planning, Jawaharlal Nehru University, New Delhi.

HUGH GOODACRE is Visiting Lecturer in Economics at City University, London.

JOMO K.S. was Professor in the Applied Economics Department, University of Malaya, Kuala Lumpur, and Senior Visiting Research Fellow at the Asia Research Institute, National University of Singapore, before joining the United Nations.

KARI POLANYI LEVITT is Professor Emerita, Department of Economics, McGill University, Montreal, and founding member and Honorary President of the Karl Polanyi Institute of Political Economy at Concordia University.

PRABHAT PATNAIK is Professor, Centre for Economic Studies and Planning, Jawaharlal Nehru University, New Delhi, and Editor, *Social Scientist*.

UTSA PATNAIK is Professor, Centre for Economic Studies and Planning, Jawaharlal Nehru University, New Delhi, a member of the International Advisory Board, *Journal of Agrarian Change* and of the Editorial Board, *Social Scientist*.

RENEE PRENDERGAST is Reader in Economics, School of Management and Economics, Queen's University, Belfast.

KUNIBERT RAFFER is Professor, Department of Economics, University of Vienna, and a Senior Associate of the New Economics Foundation, London.

MEHDI SHAFAEDDIN is Officer-in-Charge, Macroeconomic and Development Policies Branch, Division for Globalization and Development Strategies, UNCTAD.

JOHN TOYE is Professor, Department of Economics, University of Oxford. He was Chief of the Division for Globalization and Development Strategies, UNCTAD, and Director of the Institute for Development Studies, University of Sussex.

Why 'Development Economics'?

Prabhat Patnaik

When I was a student in the 1960s, we thought of economics as basically divided into two segments: there was 'economic theory' on the one side, and there was a whole mishmash of economic history, 'Indian economics' and 'development economics' on the other. Those who were very bright and mathematically competent (the two were taken as synonymous) did the former and were on a par with the most highbrow *sahibs,* while those who were less so did the latter (large chunks of which were sometimes pejoratively referred to as 'cowdung economics'). Nowadays, ever since a host of game theorists and other mathematically oriented economists invaded the domain of development economics, the absurd stigma attached to the latter has diminished somewhat, though it has by no means disappeared; but the basic dichotomy still persists, between 'economics' (or 'economic principles' if you like) and 'development economics'. In almost every university in the world, including every Indian university, there is a whole set of lectures on 'economic theory' that makes absolutely no reference to the developing countries or their problems. Then, there is a whole set of separate lectures on 'development economics' that deals exclusively with these problems, in which some of the tools of analysis learned in the first set of lectures are occasionally applied. The question arises: how can such a dichotomy be justified?

The most obvious answer to this question is probably as follows: developed economies and underdeveloped economies have very different institutions, notwithstanding the fact of an overlap of institutions between them. The former represent, by definition, a higher level of development than the latter. It follows that the institutions prevailing in the former must constitute the central focus of analysis from which a study of the latter economies – though necessarily separate because of their specificities – can still benefit, both because of the overlap referred to and because the former represent the ultimate goal. Looking at it differently, since developing countries are those that lag behind the developed ones along the road of development, there is an obvious rationale in studying the institutions of the former as the central focus, and then looking at the specific reasons as to why the laggards stay behind.

This perception, interestingly, is not confined to 'mainstream' thinking;

it is to be found even within the Marxian tradition. Marx's (1977: 91) remark that 'the country that is more developed industrially only shows, to the less developed, an image of its own future', which was made in the context of Britain and Germany, is often universalized to cover the case of even the underdeveloped economies, which are presumed to follow – quite spontaneously, in the normal course – the path traversed by Britain and the other developed countries. From this it follows that focusing on the analysis of these developed economies taken in isolation constitutes the first priority, while the reason why some others lag behind can be discussed subsequently. At any rate, the two inquiries are essentially separate according to this perception.

Of course, one can have an alternative, more sophisticated justification for this procedure within the Marxist tradition. One can argue that the laws of motion of a particular mode of production – whether capitalist or feudal, seen in its internal unity and as an 'ideal type' – must take precedence over, or form a prelude to, the 'concrete analysis of the concrete conditions' of economies caught in a process of transition, with admixtures of capitalist and pre-capitalist characteristics. On this reasoning, *whether or not the underdeveloped economies ever manage to make the transition to capitalism*, that is, whether or not they are only 'laggards' who will eventually 'catch up', there is a purely theoretical case for a dichotomy between the two areas, which we traditionally designate as 'theory' (focused primarily on, but not referring concretely to, the advanced countries) and 'development economics' (referring concretely to the underdeveloped countries).

There is, however, a basic flaw in this perception: it sees the developed economies, or 'capitalism' for that matter, in exclusive isolation. It is predicated upon the view that capitalism is a self-contained system that can therefore be legitimately analysed in isolation from its pre-capitalist environment. Indeed, the reason why 'mainstream' theory and certain tendencies within the Marxist tradition converge on this question of dichotomy is that they both view capitalism as a self-contained system, no matter how basic their differences about its nature. To be sure, the existence of trade relations is recognized, but 'mainstream' economics sees trade merely as enlarging the opportunities available to a country, *and not as essential for an economy's existence and growth*. In short, trade is seen to benefit every country and to constitute an additional bonus for all. Trade theory, though a part of 'economic theory' (indeed, a special case for the application of its basic conclusions), does not therefore enter the core of it.

Within the Marxist tradition, the scope for viewing capitalism in isolation, as being self-contained, arises, despite Marx's (1977) acute awareness of the phenomenon of colonial exploitation and his remarks about the 'primitive accumulation of capital' through colonial looting, because international trade scarcely figures in his model of capitalism. Whether this is a result of the imprint of classical political economy (especially Ricardo) on Marx or a reflection of the unfinished-ness of Marx's project, is beside the point. It makes possible the emergence of the above-mentioned theoretical dichotomy within the Marxist tradition, even though the literature on imperialism that came up within this tradition around World War I makes the tradition, as a whole, immune to the charge of upholding this dichotomy.

The result of this dichotomy, which 'mainstream' economics so assiduously cultivates, is to *impoverish both 'economic theory' and 'development economics'*. In other words, it does not merely detract from an understanding of the problems of development; it makes the so-called economic theory itself largely irrelevant. I shall cite three examples from economic theory to illustrate this point.

Growth Theory

My first example relates to 'mainstream' growth theory. I shall refer explicitly only to Solow's (1956) model, even though the commentary applies to growth theory in its other incarnations as well. The basic conclusion of the theory is that the rate of growth of a capitalist economy is tethered in the long run to the exogenously given rate of growth of its labour force in 'efficiency units' (in recent 'endogenous' growth theories, this rate of growth is not entirely exogenous, but the exogenous component nonetheless exercises a restraining effect on long-run accumulation[1]). This is because, unlike in the classical or Von Neumann models, labour here is a 'rent good'; it cannot be internally produced or acquired in adequate quantities at the going wage rate.

At first sight, this appears to be a plausible assumption. Even though the advanced countries may not have full employment, they have reserve armies of labour which can quickly get exhausted; and the very process of exhaustion would put pressure on the wage rate and lower the rate of accumulation (Goodwin 1967). What is wrong, then, in asserting that accumulation is constrained by the exogenously given rate of growth of the labour force?

The error is due to the belief that capital has only the labour force of its country of origin available to it. In fact, the entire labour force of the world is at its command, and the reserve army at the world level is so large that the constraint on accumulation cannot conceivably be attributed either to any absolute labour shortage or to any pressures on the wage rate arising from the process of its exhaustion.

This is no idle speculation. Throughout history, *capital accumulation by the metropolis, whether located in the metropolis itself or outside of it, has always drawn on world labour reserves (particularly located in India and China) whenever the need has arisen.* In the nineteenth century, there were two huge streams of migration: of European labour migrating to the temperate new regions of white settlement, occupying land by forcibly dispossessing the local population and having capital follow in its wake; and of tropical labour, mainly from India and China, migrating to other tropical lands to serve the needs of European capital in mines and plantations. The two streams were kept strictly separate by migration controls, and their incomes were vastly different (owing to the former's access to 'free land'). But each of these was a mighty stream, involving as many as 50 million persons.[2]

Similarly, in the post-World War II years, when Keynesian demand management lowered unemployment in the metropolis, substantial migration took place from less developed countries to the metropolis to serve the needs of capital – from Turkey to Germany, from Algeria to France, from the Indian subcontinent to the UK, from Mexico to the USA and so on. Given this enormous scale of migration that has unfailingly occurred historically to serve the needs of capital, to believe that capital meekly adjusts to the 'natural rate of growth' of the labour force within its country of origin, is nothing short of a travesty. As Nicholas Kaldor (1978) came to emphasize in his later writings, the one thing that capital accumulation has never been constrained by, is shortage of labour. The poverty of 'mainstream' theory here arises because it looks at the capitalist economy in isolation, as a self-contained entity, with no access to labour from other economies.

'Natural Rate of Unemployment'

The second example relates to the so-called non-accelerating inflation rate of unemployment (NAIRU).[3] The monetarist version of it is the natural rate of unemployment (NRU), which is nothing else but *de facto* full employment. Let us consider the monetarist version first. At the NRU, the supply price of labour equals the marginal product of labour. The level of employment can be increased beyond what is given by the NRU, but only if the workers do not anticipate inflation. Even in such a case, it can be *maintained* at this level only if expectations are adaptive and not rational, and then, too, only at the expense of accelerating inflation. The presumption underlying all this is that a given amount of labour is supplied only if a particular real wage is expected; if the expected real wage is lower, a smaller amount of labour would be supplied. Now, in third world economies saddled with massive labour reserves, this is patently untrue; even when real wages secularly decline, without any necessary divergence between the expected and the actual real wage, the labour supply never starts drying up. From this it follows that, in so far as commodities produced by third world labour enter the production process in the metropolis as inputs, talking of a natural rate of unemployment is meaningless.

Even if we take the more general concept of NAIRU, which is in no way linked to *de facto* full employment, the same question arises: as long as there are workers located within an ocean of labour reserves, whose *ex ante* wage claims are compressible in real terms, we cannot talk in terms of a NAIRU. If these workers are located outside the capitalist economy, so that their lower real wage rate expresses itself as lower terms of trade for the outside economy's product vis-à-vis that of the capitalist economy, we can talk of particular NAIRU levels within the capitalist economy, *associated with different terms of trade*. But since the real wage rate of these workers is *ex ante* compressible, that is, can be lowered without accelerating inflation, it follows that the terms of trade can always be turned against their products to the extent required to prevent accelerating inflation in the metropolis, *no matter what the level of employment*. In other words, the capitalist economy can settle at any level of employment without experiencing accelerating inflation, as long as labour reserves exist outside, in other economies. The fact that the contrary has been asserted and, on the basis of it, the possibility of Keynesian demand management has been denied, is only because the capitalist sector has been seen in isolation, as a self-contained entity.

International Trade Theory

My third example concerns international trade theory.[4] The following basic presumption underlying the theorems of trade theory is worth reiterating, if only because it is not always appreciated. All the propositions of trade theory – such as 'free trade is better than no trade', 'free trade is better than restricted trade', etc. – are propositions that are supposed to hold independently of what the actual post-trade income distribution is going to be. In other words, the term 'better' is given a specific meaning, namely, that the utility possibility curve associated with the supposedly 'better' option lies outside that associated with the 'worse' option. The only case where we can be sure of this happening is when a vector-wise larger bundle of goods becomes available through trade, as compared to the pre-trade situation. In other words, the proposition that trade will be unambiguously beneficial – that is, will increase 'potential welfare' (Samuelson 1950) – can hold only when it enlarges, vector-wise, the bundle of available goods, as compared to the pre-trade situation. This, in turn, can only happen when each country produces (in the simple two-goods case) both goods in the pre-trade situation. Thus, *'mainstream' trade theory – no matter whether we are looking at the Ricardian or the Heckscher–Ohlin version of it – necessarily assumes that each country can, and does, produce both commodities in the pre-trade situation.*

This, however, is obviously an erroneous presumption. Trade between the metropolitan countries and the tropical colonies was precisely of the sort where the former obtained, through trade, commodities from the latter that they themselves could not produce, such as tea, coffee, rubber, cocoa, sugar, fruits, cotton, etc. Indeed, Ricardo's famous example, of England and Portugal engaging in trade to mutual benefit, was a complete fudge, since the presumption that both England and Portugal could produce both commodities – wine and cloth – was wrong. England could certainly not produce wine, though Portugal could produce both wine and cloth. Likewise, the tropical colonies could produce both types of goods, the range of primary commodities mentioned above and a whole range of manufactured goods, while the metropolis could produce only manufactures. The motives for trade and the implications for trade under these circumstances – involving an asymmetry between the trading partners – are vastly different from what trade theory suggests.

If trade allows a country to get hold of goods that it otherwise could not have access to, then, surely, the motive for engaging in trade must be very different from what 'mainstream' theory suggests. Likewise, once we recognize that in certain lands, certain conditions can produce only certain things, and thereby jettison the production functions approach which assumes substitutability in the production of goods, it follows that trade, in any period, will not only necessarily reduce the availability of the exported good in the metropolis, but may also reduce the availability of the exported good in the tropical economy, which completely destroys the conclusions of 'mainstream' trade theory regarding the beneficial effects of trade for all economies. This naive (one may even call it ideological) view of trade, as beneficial for all, is sustained once again by a view of the capitalist metropolis as a self-sufficient, self-contained entity, for which engagement in trade is not essential, though it is beneficial.

Reintegrating Development Economics

To sum up, as the three examples cited above show, the view of capitalism as a self-contained entity makes for poor theory as much as for poor development economics. Indeed, each of the three examples constitutes a case where ignoring the interactions between the capitalist and non-capitalist segments impoverishes not only our theoretical understanding of capitalism, but also our understanding of the role and, hence, the problems of the underdeveloped world – the fact that it constitutes a source of labour reserves for the capitalist metropolis, the fact that it is necessary for providing stability to the capitalist system, and the fact that it is the source of otherwise unobtainable raw materials for capitalism. This is by no means an exhaustive list of its uses.

Under these conditions, the dichotomy that lies at the core of the economics discipline – between 'economics' and 'development economics' – must be rejected. Underdeveloped economies are not mere laggards waiting to catch up with developed countries. Their present predicament is a result not of their pristine pre-capitalist state but of their interaction (no doubt on the basis of their pre-existing structures) with metropolitan capitalism. In other words, developed and underdeveloped countries together constitute the totality of capitalism – which is not the same as saying, as Frank (1975) and others do, that underdeveloped countries are *ipso facto* capitalist. This totality must be the domain of analysis of economic theory, in which case there would be no separate 'development economics'.

We could, of course, still study the specific non-capitalist institutions existing in these societies, but this study would only be a part of the analytical totality, integrated into it, rather than constituting a separate domain. Putting it differently, we may study a set of topics that we may still conveniently refer to as 'development economics', but we can do this properly only when the current distinction between 'economics' and 'development economics' has been superseded by a study of the totality of the capitalist system. In such a situation, the topics studied under the rubric 'development economics' would constitute mediations in the analysis of this totality.

Let me give an example. We cannot study the Indian economy without

studying the prevailing agrarian relations, and, in that sense, the study of agrarian relations remains an integral part of 'development economics'. But the precise agrarian relations have been shaped by the economy's integration into the
capitalist system and these, though they differ from country to country, are not
merely reducible to some predetermined outcome of this integration; they must,
in turn, throw up contradictions for this process of integration. We may, for the
sake of convenience, look at these country differences, these historical specificities and these contradictions under a separate rubric called 'development economics', but this is still, theoretically, an integral part of the totality of 'economics', not a separate domain. What I am suggesting is an epistemological
integration of two domains that are currently dichotomized, though functional
demarcations may still continue for the sake of convenience.

Not resorting to such an epistemological integration would give rise to a
highly flawed understanding of important issues. Consider, for example, the
issue of rural poverty. The Bretton Woods institutions would have us believe that
the rural poverty ratio went down in India in the 1990s, and to the extent that it
did not, they would attribute the failure to what they call 'bad governance'. This
explanation is in line with the dichotomy we have been discussing, which postu-
lates that the problems of underdeveloped countries are specific to their own
conditions and are in no way caused by integration with metropolitan capitalism.

But even without going into the question of what happened to the rural
poverty ratio in the 1990s (which, by now, has become an ideologically charged
issue), we can safely say that 'rural distress' increased, at least in the sense that
per capita foodgrain availability in the 1990s declined drastically. Per capita
foodgrain availability, which had gone down from around 200 kilograms per
annum at the beginning of the twentieth century to around 150 kilograms by the
time of independence, had recovered to around 180 kilograms by the end of the
1980s (177 kilograms in the triennium centred on 1990–91). By 2000–01, however, it had gone down to around 151 kilograms. (It recovered marginally to
158.37 kilograms in 2001–02, and 157.69 kilograms in 2002–03, but even this
last figure was attained because of a host of drought relief operations.[5])

This decline was not because of the decline in per capita foodgrain output during the decade, though that happened, but because of an even more drastic decline in the purchasing power of the rural poor. This is confirmed by the
burgeoning foodgrain stocks with the government, which – prior to the drought
of 2002–03 (that led to some decline in inventories) and the massive food exports
(at subsidized prices) – amounted to over 60 million tonnes. Even on 1 July 2004,
the level of stocks with the government was over 30 million tonnes, which is at
least 6 million tonnes more than the total buffer and operational stocks considered necessary.[6]

The reason for this drastic squeeze in rural purchasing power *inter alia*
lies in the sharp fall in government rural development expenditure, as a
proportion of GDP. The latter, in turn, is part of the deflationary policy forced

upon governments all over the world by the emergence of a new form of globally mobile international finance capital. (Only the US government enjoys a degree of immunity from this pressure to deflate the economy because its currency – considered 'as good as gold' by most wealth-holders in the world – enjoys a special status.) In short, India's progressive – though by no means, as yet, total – integration into the vortex of globalized finance has exposed the government to pressures to deflate the economy. (Deflation is the favourite recipe of international finance capital, and it is no accident that even in the midst of massive unused food stocks, unutilized industrial capacity and burgeoning foreign exchange reserves – all of which characterize the Indian economy today – the most commonly heard refrain is for curtailment of the fiscal deficit, which would only succeed in exacerbating the demand constraint.)

Of course, the increase in rural distress is more general than the decline in per capita foodgrain availability (the growing incidence of farmers' suicides, for instance, though another fall-out of the process of 'globalization', has little to do with foodgrain availability). But this decline is an important factor contributing to the growth in rural distress in recent years; and it is a direct outcome of the economy's integration into the sphere of globalized finance. This integration, in turn, has been forced upon it by the emergence of a new and powerful actor in contemporary capitalism, international finance capital in a new form, whose interests are assiduously promoted by the Bretton Woods institutions.[7] Thus an issue, viz. rural distress, that is pervasively considered 'internal' to the country, turns out, on closer examination, to be an outcome of developments in world capitalism. Unless we are sensitive to these developments, and alter our understanding and teaching of 'development economics' to overcome the dichotomy between 'economics' and 'development economics', we will be unable to make any intervention for the betterment of our people, which, after all, is the objective of the study of economics.

Notes

[1] This is true of all 'endogenous' growth theories in which the attainment of an equilibrium is not dependent on a specific rate of labour force growth. In these models, the larger the rate of labour force growth, the higher is the rate of growth of capital stock and output in steady state. There are, however, some theories in which equilibrium can be attained only with a stagnant population (any positive rate of population growth makes the economy explode). In the case of these, the assertion in the text that the rate of accumulation would be higher for a higher growth rate of the exogenous component (viz. labour force) would not be justified. But these models, no matter what one thinks of their insights, must be considered structurally flawed in this respect.

[2] W. Arthur Lewis (1978: 14) wrote: 'The development of the agricultural countries in the second half of the nineteenth century was promoted by two vast streams of international migration. About fifty million people left Europe for the temperate settlements. . . . About the same number – fifty million people – left India and China to work mainly as indentured labourers in the tropics on plantations, in mines, or in construction projects'.

[3] The argument of this section has been developed at length in Prabhat Patnaik (1997).

[4] The argument in this paragraph is taken from Utsa Patnaik (2003b).

[5] These figures are taken from Utsa Patnaik (2003a).

[6] It is sometimes argued that the reason for the decline in per capita foodgrain consumption is a change in tastes occurring all over India with increased per capita income. This claim, however, is without any merit for two reasons. First, evidence from all over the world shows that as incomes increase, while the direct consumption of foodgrains does not increase (and may even decline), *direct-plus-indirect* consumption (the latter via animal feed and processed foods) increases as a result of dietary diversification, and there is no reason why India should be an exception to this general rule. Second, the decline in per capita foodgrain availability (and hence, by implication, in per capita foodgrain consumption) has also been accompanied by a decline in per capita calorie intake in rural India, during this period, of 13 per cent, which only confirms the hypothesis of growing rural distress. See Utsa Patnaik (2003a).

[7] Different aspects of this new form of international finance capital, as well as the implications of its emergence, are discussed in Prabhat Patnaik (2003).

References

Frank, A.G. (1975), *Capitalism and Underdevelopment in Latin America* (Harmondsworth: Penguin).

Goodwin, R.M. (1967), 'The Growth Cycle', in C.H. Feinstein, ed., *Socialism, Capitalism and Economic Growth: Essays Presented to Maurice Dobb* (Cambridge: Cambridge University Press).

Kaldor, Nicholas (1978), *Further Essays on Economic Theory* (London: Duckworth).

Lewis, W. Arthur (1978), *The Evolution of the International Economic Order* (Princeton: Princeton University Press).

Marx, Karl (1977), *Capital*, Volume I (New York: Vintage Books).

Patnaik, Prabhat (1997), *Accumulation and Stability under Capitalism* (Oxford: Clarendon Press).

—— (2003), *The Retreat to Unfreedom: Essays on the Emerging World Order* (New Delhi: Tulika Books).

Patnaik, Utsa (2003a), 'Foodstocks and Hunger', *Social Scientist*, July–August.

—— (2003b), 'On the Inverse Relation between Primary Exports and Food Absorption in Developing Countries under Liberalized Trade Regimes', in Jayati Ghosh and C.P. Chandrasekhar, eds, *Work and Well-being in the Age of Finance* (New Delhi: Tulika Books).

Samuelson, P.A. (1950), 'The Evaluation of Real National Income', *Oxford Economic Papers*, 2, January.

Solow, R.M. (1956), 'A Contribution to the Theory of Economic Growth', *Quarterly Journal of Economics*, LXX, February.

William Petty and Early Colonial Roots of Development Economics

Hugh Goodacre

The seventeenth-century English writer William Petty has been described by Amartya Sen as 'a founder of development economics' (Sen 1988: 10). Indeed, almost any branch of economics, or for that matter of any other social science, can find a good proportion of its aims and methods anticipated in one way or another in Petty's pioneering works of social and economic analysis. Yet, he seldom receives more than a passing mention in the development literature, a particularly disappointing omission, since even the most casual acquaintance with his writings is enough to show that it was he, particularly in his writings on Ireland, who first attempted to conceptualize many of the issues that remain central for the development economists of today. He clearly addressed, for example, such questions as the relation between the subsistence and commercial sectors of the economy, the relation of town to country and of manufacture to agriculture, as well as the obstacles to the consolidation of a wage-earning labour force in an agrarian context, and the influence on economic life of traditional society and culture. Above all, there is one feature of Petty's writings that, even on its own, would justify according him a prominent status in the intellectual ancestry of development economics, rather than being relegated, as he customarily is, to the status of a mere 'precursor of Adam Smith'. This salient feature is the explicitly colonial context in which his economic thought was forged.

For it was once again colonialism that, two-and-a-half centuries after Petty's death, provided the context in which development economics was first established as an academic sub-discipline. A prime example is the case of Oxford University, where it was introduced around the time of World War II as an element in the 'Colonial Studies' course for students being trained for service in Britain's colonial empire (Meier 1984: 8 and 1994b: 183–87). Barely had this new element in the curriculum been established, however, when the requirement for training such officials was overtaken by the policy of training replacements for them from among nationals of the countries emerging into independence from the 1950s and 1960s onwards. In the course of this reorientation, a further task assumed increasing importance, which was to contribute to the modification of attitudes prevailing within the colonial metropolis itself towards its colonies and ex-colonies; there was now clearly a need to accelerate the process in which 'areas that had been considered in the eighteenth century as "rude and barbarous", in the nineteenth century as "backward", and in the pre-war period as "underdeveloped", now became the "less developed countries" or "the poor countries" – and also the "emergent countries" and "developing economies"' (Meier and Rauch 2000: 69).

If, indeed, development economists have hitherto addressed these two principal aspects of their mission on a theoretical and methodological basis whose intellectual roots stretch back to Petty, then, some awkward questions arise as to the adequacy of their approach for the tasks they confront. For, in Petty's writings, the goal of development, to the extent that any anticipation of such an idea can be discerned there, is unequivocally given second place to motives of colonial conquest and repression, international rivalry and predatory warfare. Furthermore, no effort is made to disguise the explicit aim of utterly obliterating the social, cultural and intellectual traditions indigenous to the colonized society, which were assumed to constitute, by their very existence, a challenge to the unquestioned dominance of the colonial power.

In what follows, an attempt will be made to address these uncomfortable issues without the customary equivocation. To this end, the literature, such as it is, on the relevance of Petty's writings to developmental issues will first be critically reviewed, followed by an account of his biographical background in its historical context. His approach to some central issues in the intellectual ancestry of development economics will then be analysed – the emergence of a wage-earning labour force in an agrarian context, the ideology of a 'civilizing mission', the role of institutions in economic transformation and the political–economic status of the state in the colony. In each case, it will be shown that his writings provide a valuable historical vantage point from where to assess the extent to which development economics has, or has not, surmounted the intellectual legacy of colonialist thought and moved forward to the construction of a truly postcolonial perspective on economic development in the world today.

Petty, Smith and Development Economics

Such few passing references to Petty as may be gleaned from the writings on development economics and its history are predominantly found in writers of the pioneering period, including Colin Clark, Arthur Lewis and Amartya Sen, as well as the work of more recent authors who continue to adhere to the same general approach (for example, Yang 2003). Their comments, however, commonly amount to little more than an antiquarian flourish on more substantial discussion of Adam Smith, whose *Wealth of Nations* is widely regarded as the true starting point in tracing the sub-discipline's intellectual ancestry, this work being perceived as 'also an inquiry into the basic issues of development economics' (Sen 1988: 10). According to this view, the fate of the developmental approach to economic issues encapsulated in Smith's concept of the 'natural progress of opulence' was that 'in the neo-classical epoch, it was just put to bed' (Meier, ed. 1994: 7, citing Hicks), or was to 'almost die out' (Lewis 1988: 36), only to be reawoken or 'resurrected' (Meier 1994: 1) by the pioneers of today's development economics almost two centuries later (see also Meier 1984: 3–4).

Those elements of Smith's theoretical system adduced in support of this view are conventionally grouped in what is categorized collectively as his theory of economic growth, which is in turn sometimes cited as evidence of his orientation towards an ideal of social and economic progress; these elements are, most notably, his celebrated concept of the increase in the division of labour in response to the extension of the market, his discussions of the effects of increase of population and of capital ('stock'), his remarks on technological progress and his concept of a 'progressive state' of society (see, for example, Meier 1994a; Meier and Rauch 2000: 72–73; Yang 2003: 1).

The assumption that referring to Petty can somehow deepen the historical perspective on this theoretical heritage leads inevitably to a tendency among development economists to overestimate the extent to which his discussions of analogous subjects anticipate the Smithian theoretical system. In this they are by no means alone; for example, historians of economic thought have in general been inclined to exaggerate the extent to which Petty's discussions of division of labour – significant though these are – anticipate Smith's highly distinctive and far more elaborate theory (for an example in the development literature, see Yang 2003: 1, 31). With even less justification, Petty has been credited with the origination of the theory of economic growth, on the dubious basis of his contention, described as 'part of one of the earliest discussions of development economics', that 'the French grow too fast' (Sen 1988: 10, discussing *PA*: 242). A further assertion to be found in the development literature, whose inaccuracy will astonish anyone at all acquainted with Petty's writings, is that, in his time, 'economists are no longer occupied with military power' (Lewis 1988: 28). Clark stands alone in showing that he has actually studied Petty's writings, and in his seminal textbook first published in 1940, he not only makes use of Petty's statistical estimates of world trade but also attributes to him the 'brilliant and entirely correct generalization' – or 'what must be called, in all fairness, Petty's Law' – the idea that there is a long-term tendency for the working population to move 'from agriculture to manufacture, and from manufacture to commerce and services', or 'from primary production to secondary and tertiary' (Clark 1940: 448–49, 176–77, 341, citing *PA*: 256, 267; see also Clark 1984: 70). One commentator, who prefers the term 'Petty–Clark Law', also suggests that wider affinities exist between the methodologies of the two authors (Pyatt 1984: 79).

With the exception of Clark, then, references to Petty have largely been restricted to cursory and not always fully informed assertions by development economists who evidently presume that counting him in as a 'precursor' will, in some way, add historical depth to the thesis of the Smithian intellectual ancestry of their sub-discipline. This situation clearly indicates the need for a dedicated literature to clarify the issues involved; yet, there is, unfortunately, only one specialist study addressed explicitly to the subject of Petty's relevance to development economics, namely, Roncaglia (1988). This study does indeed provide a salutary corrective to a number of 'retrospective' distortions of the kind that currently prevail, taking as a case study the concept of a distinction (or 'dichotomy') between manufacture and agriculture.

Roncaglia argues that Petty did not represent these categories in terms of an inter-sectoral input–output system of the kind subsequently formulated by the physiocrats and further elaborated by Adam Smith;[1] rather, he argues, Petty perceived the relationship as one of 'vertical integration', a perception that would, moreover, have accorded with his own first-hand experience in establishing mining and other industrial ventures on his estate in rural Ireland.[2] Unfortunately, however, this study, while highly sensitive to the emergence of the fundamental categories of early modern political economy, includes only minimal engagement with the development literature it purports to address: all that is offered in this regard is a passing reference to Lewis (1954) in connection with 'the contrast between "natural" and market-oriented activities', and a rather pedantic criticism of Clark's use of the term 'Petty's Law'. It is not until the conclusion to his study that Roncaglia eventually raises the question of whether Petty's writings are relevant to the validity of the concepts used within the development literature today, but this is a question he raises only to leave unanswered.

Despite his useful critique of some retrospective distortions, Roncaglia's study nevertheless takes subsequent classical political economy as its reference point, and, moreover, totally ignores the colonial context of Petty's writings. The result is that the study ultimately has the effect of reducing Petty's status to that of a precursor of Smith, which, in turn, has the effect of implicitly endorsing the idea of the Smithian ancestry of development economics. However, this idea is not only open to question but has indeed come under criticism from a number of directions. It has long been pointed out, for example, that Smith's concept of the 'states of society' (progressive, stationary, declining) can by no means be assumed to embody unidirectional economic 'progress', such an optimistic idea being uneasily grafted by Smith on to what remains essentially a pessimistic cyclical theory inherited from ancient times – a point conspicuously absent from the arguments of those adhering to the 'Smithian origins' standpoint (see, for example, Meier 1994a), though familiar to other writers on the history of economic thought (see, for example, Cowen and Shenton 1995: 30–32, and, for the wider historical background, Perrotta 2003).

A more recent critique, which is also of more direct relevance in the present context, has been advanced by Michael Cowen and Robert Shenton. They argue that to identify Smith as the intellectual forbear of development economics is to misconstrue the motivation of the nineteenth-century writers who – whether under the banner of positivism, utilitarianism or imperial 'trusteeship' – began to advance the idea of economic development as it is now understood. They suggest that these nineteenth-century authors, far from being advocates of progress, were, on the contrary, searching for means to 'ameliorate the perceived chaos caused by progress' – the 'social disorder of rapid urbanization, poverty and unemployment'. They consequently criticize those who, in their attempts to 'legitimize' development economics, ignore this formative period and instead 'rummage through the writings of the Scottish Enlightenment, especially those of Adam Smith', to say nothing of even less historically minded writers who 'truncate development's historical domain' yet more drastically by confining their attention to the period since 1945 (Cowen and Shenton 1995: 29, 31). But while there is much of value in this critique, it is itself founded on another historical truncation, which, as the present study aims to demonstrate, has the consequence of eliding a previous, and even more profoundly relevant, field in which to seek an alternative to the idea of the Smithian roots of development theory.

In turning to Petty's writings on Ireland in this connection, the present study will accordingly be breaking with a number of other approaches to the question of the intellectual roots of development economics. First of all, it will break with the tradition, represented by Roncaglia, of centralizing the fundamental categories of political economy without reference to the colonial context in which they were first forged and set to work. Second, and by the same token, it will break with the centralization of Smithian 'growth theory'; for, though Smith frequently makes reference to colonies in this connection (almost exclusively the settler colonies of North America), his purpose is to explore general economic issues such as the effects of labour shortage and the plentiful supply of land, rather than to single out issues that are specifically colonial as such, in the sense of relating to the conquest and administration of subordinate territories. Third, there will also be a break with, or rather a reverse extension of, the critical theory advanced by Cowen and Shenton, whose analysis effectively discounts the relevance of the period prior to the more mature industrial and colonial theory of the nineteenth century.

One further study, though it makes no attempt to address the literature on development economics, nevertheless deserves mention in the present context. This study, Welch (1997), consists primarily of a correlation of aspects of Petty's writings on Ireland with Marx's theory of the role of colonialism in the primitive accumulation of capital. To this end, a selection of citations of relevant texts is discussed under three headings: 'brutality and religious factionalism', 'the supply of labour and the creation of markets', and 'public debt and taxation'. The outcome is that the study directs its focus unequivocally on to the realities of the colonial context in which Petty formulated his economic thought, something that none of the literature reviewed above has done.[3] It is to the task of continuing down the path thus opened up that much of the present study will be directed, widening the narrow base of the existing literature on the subject by incorporating insights developed within neighbouring fields of historical, social and literary research.

Petty and Ireland: Historical and Biographical Background[4]

William Petty (1623–1687) is described by the Irish nationalist historian John Mitchel (1873: 53) as 'the most successful land-pirate . . . and voracious land-shark who ever appeared in Western Europe'. Mitchel's allusion to piracy correctly reflects the fact that the particular colonial administration in which Petty served had been established on the basis of 'a land-based equivalent to a privateering expedition' (Braddick 2000: 213). This was the invasion of Ireland led by Oliver Cromwell in 1649 that restored the colonial rule which that country had succeeded in throwing off during the preceding period of civil wars in England. Far from making any attempt to gloss over the piratical basis on which they launched this enterprise, the English parliamentary authorities actively promoted the raising of a fund for the invasion by public subscription on the security of prospective shares in land to be expropriated from the Irish! (For an extensive study of these financial arrangements, see Bottigheimer 1971.)

Following this re-conquest, the English authorities initially declared their intention to undertake mass executions of Irish 'rebels' – defined sufficiently broadly to include the great majority of all adult males in the country – as well as deportations and enslavements, and the complete removal of the remaining Irish population from three of the country's four provinces to a kind of reservation in the west – the notorious policy encapsulated in the expression 'To Hell or Connaught!' (Gardiner 1899 remains the definitive study of this policy.) The army of occupation was to receive its arrears of pay in the form of entitlements to land thus expropriated, and would, it was hoped, form the core of a massive colonial immigration that would transform the Irish countryside into a replication of that of England – a landscape dominated by small-holdings cultivated by a peasant 'yeomanry', interspersed with larger manorial estates.[5]

Though neither the planned executions nor the 'transplantation' to Connaught were carried out on the mass scale originally envisaged, the expropriation and distribution of land went ahead; in this process, Petty's role was of pivotal importance, for it was to him that the army assigned the crucial task of surveying the expropriated land for distribution. The opportunities this position offered for bribery and corruption were bounded only by the shores of Ireland itself, and so fully did Petty exploit these opportunities that he soon became one of the foremost landowners in the country, alongside the wealthiest of the incumbent colonialists and other successful Cromwellian newcomers such as himself. These elements proceeded to buy out the bulk of the land entitlements of the rank-and-file soldiery, and, before long, Ireland had fallen into their hands. The outcome was a kind of neo-feudal situation, in which these large landowners were left lording it over the Irish population who remained effectively enserfed on the land they had formerly owned.

Following the collapse of the Cromwellian regime and the restoration of the monarchy in England in 1660, Petty succeeded in retaining most of the land he had seized, and for the rest of his days his lifestyle remained set in a neo-feudal mode. His London residence was described by a contemporary diarist as a 'splendid palace', while his fiefdom in county Kerry in southwest Ireland was run along the lines of a small principality, as is graphically illustrated in his correspondence with his family and agents. Much of his energy in the final decades of his life was devoted to fierce litigation to defend his title to these lands, as well as efforts to establish on them an iron foundry and a number of mining, fishery and forestry enterprises.[6]

Intermittently, when these preoccupations allowed, Petty also participated, as he had done from an early age, in the movement for the advancement of science and technology that was fashionable in his time, his own interests ranging widely from medicine (he was himself a qualified physician) to ship design.[7] But while his economic writings were undoubtedly influenced in their mode of analysis by this range of interests, it is another aspect of his biography that accounts for their motivation; this is the fact that, following the restoration of the monarchy, he never succeeded in relaunching his official career on the high-flying path it had followed during the Cromwellian period. It was this frustration of his ambitions that drove him to produce those works to which he owes his singular position in the history of economic thought – an unending series of schemes for fiscal, cadastral, administrative, naval and military initiatives, which he vainly hoped would be entrusted to him. It is in the text of these proposals, whose form varies all the way from extensive treatises to brief jottings, that much of the conceptual apparatus of subsequent economic analysis first began to emerge in primitive form, not least his 'political arithmetic', the precursor of all subsequent quantitative methodology in economic analysis.

The culmination of Petty's efforts to apply his new-fangled quantitative methodology was his notorious proposal to transfer the bulk of the population of Ireland to England. This scheme, which he continued to put forward in increasingly elaborate forms from the 1670s till the final weeks of his life in 1687, had a dual aim. On the one hand, it would increase the advantages of compactness of population in England – compactness being, in his view, the key to the advantages enjoyed by Holland, which was, in his time, not only Europe's most densely populated country, but also its most economically advanced (see, in particular, *PA*: Chapter 1).[8] On the other hand, the scheme would put an end to Ireland's national life and its associated anti-colonial traditions, and (in the final version of the scheme) would transform the whole country into a 'kind of factory' for rearing livestock for England – in other words, one vast cattle ranch. It would, in short, bring about a 'perpetual settlement' (or, in the term used prophetically by his editor in 1899, a 'final solution') that could at last 'cut up the roots of those evils' which 'have made Ireland for the most part a diminution and a burthen, not an advantage, to England' (*TI*: 560, 551, 546, 558).

Such is the biographical and historical background to the life and thought of this intellectually enterprising land-pirate, whose writings will now be scanned to assess whether he may also, as has been suggested, be accorded the additional epithet of 'a founder of development economics'.

Petty on Labour in Early Modern Ireland

Mainstream economics is singularly unsuited to the task of analysing the process of transition from one kind of socio-economic formation to another. Development economics, however, is inevitably concerned in the first instance with precisely such a process, and, for this reason, its pioneering practitioners, for all the profound differences between their respective approaches, have commonly been perceived as falling into the one broad category – very different from that of the mainstream – of theorists of structural change. (See, for example, Meier 1994b: 182.) Petty's writings on Ireland provide an opportunity to assess their efforts in this respect against his contemporary observations on an era of momentous significance for world history – an era when the world stood on the brink of the emergence of the capitalist system, and the 'great divergence' in fortunes between rich and poor countries to which that system gave rise.

It is hard to see where to begin this task if not from the phenomena that Marx associated with the primitive accumulation of capital, and which were the day-to-day reality reflected in Petty's life and thought – violence, social upheaval, the expropriation of cultivators from their land, the centrality of the state as the prime economic agent, and 'passions the most infamous, the most sordid, the pettiest, the most meanly odious' (Marx [1867] 1970: 762). What is far from clear, in contrast, is whether it is possible to identify in Petty's writings an awareness of the ultimately definitive element of that historical era – the process through which labour was brought into subjection to capital, so that capitalist accumulation could accordingly be set in train. His writings on Ireland are evidently relevant to this issue but are riven with inconsistencies, and need to be carefully situated in their biographical and historical context if their significance is to be adequately assessed. In particular, it is necessary to distinguish three successive, though overlapping, phases in his perspective on labour, each of which illustrates an aspect of the preliminary stages through which early modern political economy had to pass in its path towards a formulation of the concept of capitalist accumulation.

The first phase in Petty's perspective on labour in Ireland can readily be associated with the orientation he adopted with respect to the factional struggles within the colonial establishment in the Cromwellian period. These struggles centred on the fact that by the time he had risen to high office in the mid-1650s, the faction of large landowners into which he integrated had become increasingly opposed to the implementation of the 'transplantation' of the Irish *en masse*. They were naturally more than happy to see the 'rebel' landowners out of the way, but wanted the actual cultivators of the land to be left where they were. These cultivators constituted the population they aimed to enserf under their neo-feudal domination and they had no wish to see them swept out from under their feet; least of all did they want them replaced by the soldiery of the Cromwellian army of occupation, who were, from their point of view, factious and uncontrollable 'fanatics' who had performed the task of restoring colonial rule and were now best sent back to England as soon as possible.

The neo-feudalism of Petty and his fellow land magnates was far from being a mere reversion to 'true' feudalism as it had existed in the Middle Ages. On the contrary, as the enterprises which Petty subsequently established in his own fiefdom illustrated, a more commercial orientation differentiated such 'new seigneurs' as him from the feudal lords of the former epoch, just as the trade in grain surplus underlay the equivalent 'new feudalism' arising in areas of central and eastern Europe in the same period.[9] Nevertheless, from a conceptual point of view at least, Petty's standpoint towards labour at this stage shared more in common with feudalism than capitalism, in the sense that he advocated a situation in which labour was to be retained *in situ* as effectively an adjunct to the land.

A second phase in Petty's perspective on labour may be discerned following the restoration of the English monarchy in 1660. He then remained in England for a number of years, during which time his attention naturally focused more on English than on Irish affairs. In this phase, a contradiction opened out between his own continuing neo-feudal status and his increasing interest in the advance of the wage system. The idea that labour is, or should be, an adjunct to the land, in feudal style, now gave way in his writings to ideas and concepts that pointed forward to the world of emergent capitalism. Indeed, at the macro level, he ran ahead of the times in his celebrated formulation of a system of national accounts, in that he categorized the income of the entire labouring population purely and simply – and as yet utterly unrealistically – as 'wages' (see, for example, VS: Chapter 2). At the micro level, he discussed the motivation of labour in terms of the concept that was subsequently termed the 'backward-bending labour supply curve' – the idea that an excessive wage level or, in real terms, 'over-feeding of the people' results in 'indisposing them to their usual labour' (PA: 275).

Such simplifying assumptions and schematic concepts exemplify the manner in which Petty's thought prefigured what was eventually to become economics; they also, however, misrepresent the actual situation in England at the time. While dispossession of the peasantry was indeed far advanced, it by no means followed that the resulting dispossessed population had as yet become a wage-earning labour force, least of all a homogenous one. The reality was that the social dislocation, vagrancy and high mortality suffered by the dispossessed in the sixteenth century was to a large extent replaced only by the political and national upheaval, civil wars and high mortality of the seventeenth. If such was the case in England, it was incomparably more so in Ireland, and, when Petty returned to that country in 1666, his writings began to express increasing frustration over the problems involved in establishing a wage-earning labour force in the conditions prevailing there. The Irish socio-economic system, based as it still was on communal as well as individual patterns of land use, remained, even at that time, 'highly flexible and uniquely suited, in environmental terms', to its material circumstances (Morgan 1985: 278), and was fully capable of reabsorbing into itself those who might otherwise have constituted the demographic base for a wage-earning class. Petty rooted his comments on this situation in observation. The Irish, he stated,

are able to perform their husbandry with such harness and tackling as each man can make with his own hands, and living in such houses as almost every man can build; and every housewife being a spinner and dyer of wool and yarn, they can live and subsist after their present fashion, without the use of gold or silver money. (*PA*: 273)

Such being the case, the cash economy constituted, by his estimate, only a fifth of all their 'expense', the rest of their consumption being 'what their own family produceth' (*PAI*: 192); the principal exception was tobacco, which was evidently spearheading the introduction of cash transactions for consumption goods into the agrarian economy – the Coca Cola of its day. He furthermore asserted that the Irish are able to supply themselves with 'the necessities above-named without labouring two hours per diem' (*PA*: 273). He consequently asked:

> What need they to work, who can content themselves with potatoes, whereof the labour of one man can feed forty, and with milk, whereof one cow will in summertime give meat and drink enough for three men, when they can every-where gather cockles, oysters, muscles, crabs, etc., with boats, nets, angles or the art of fishing, [and] can build an house in three days? (*PAI*: 201)

Petty's discussions of how the Irish were to be 'kept to their labour' (*PAI*: 189) thus illustrated the obstacles to the subjection of labour to capital in conditions where they have the alternative of an independent livelihood on the land – conditions that were to remain characteristic of much of the colonial world in the following centuries (see Marx [1867] 1970: Chapter 33; and, for discussion: Rodriguez Braun 1987; Welch 1997: 164–65).

From frustration and oversimplification it is only a short step to fantasy, and it was to this mode of thought that Petty turned in what signalled a third and final phase in his changing perception of labour – his scheme for the wholesale transfer of the Irish population to England, which he initially put forward 'rather as a dream or reverie than a rational proposition' (*PA*: 285). The scheme nevertheless took on an increasingly realistic character, until it finally assumed a form whose elaborate statistical apparatus pioneered the entire genre of the economic policy proposal as it has existed ever since. Moreover, it then represented labour in yet another guise. Here Petty took forward his celebrated three-fold division of the macroeconomy into labour, capital and land – a division that unmistakably foreshadowed the subsequent concept of factors of production – and assigned to labour the role of what would, in today's spatial-economic analysis, be termed a 'mobile factor of production'.

However, to indulge in such retrospective analogies only highlights the limited extent to which Petty actually anticipated the 'factors of production' approach of subsequent economic theory, predicated as this was upon endorsement of capitalist competition in the market, an institution that he dismissed as a game of dice won 'rather by hit than wit' (*TTC*: 52–53; see also Aspromourgos 1996: 50–51 and Roncaglia 1988: 165–67). Rather, he turned spontaneously to the state as the sole force capable of imposing a solution to the problems of consolidating a wage-earning labour force in general, let alone implementing his own scheme.

Such was the long and complex process through which Petty's perspective on labour evolved from the neo-feudal standpoint of his Cromwellian years to the empirical and observational approach of the subsequent period, and, finally, to a more abstract approach that began to foreshadow – though only dimly and partially – the mature classical political economy of the following century and, beyond it, the economics that was to follow.

Petty, the Cromwellian Invasion of Ireland and the 'Civilizing Mission'

The tone of Petty's writings on Ireland, however harsh it may sound to modern ears, is restrained and dispassionate by comparison with the fulminations against all things Irish or Catholic that characterized much of the English political literature of the civil war period of the 1640s (Coughlan 1990: 216–17). This contrast might appear to accord with the complacent assumption still commonly found in the writings of English historians that Cromwell's invasion of Ireland coincided with a passing moment when fanatical forces temporally seized control of affairs of state in England; the ferocity of the accompanying anti-Irish hysteria was thus, according to this view, an aberration of English history, and was moreover soon rectified by more moderate counsels emanating from within the mainstream of the ruling establishment in England, in coordination with the supposedly paternalist neo-feudal land magnates in Ireland. This interpretation has, however, been challenged by the historian Norah Carlin, on the basis of her analysis of a body of propaganda material commissioned by the parliamentary authorities in support of the invasion. She points out that this propaganda explicitly delinks the invasion issue from matters of religion and, to a certain extent, also from the crudest forms of anti-Irish hysteria; rather, what marks it out as distinctive is its centralization and systematization of the argument that English colonial rule in Ireland could be justified by reference to 'Irish barbarism and the idea of an English civilizing mission' (Carlin 1993: 210). In other words, the ideology used to justify the invasion was not a manifestation of a passing wave of fanaticism but a systematic exposition of England's long-term colonial objectives, and was formulated not from within a political fringe but from within the mainstream of the ruling establishment of the time.

Petty shares with much of this literature a relatively dispassionate tone, and surpassed it all in his relentless efforts at theoretical systematization; his writings on Ireland are, in this sense, a continuation and further elaboration of the new wave of propaganda that originated in attempts to justify the Cromwellian invasion. Though he does not display direct acquaintance with the particular texts analysed by Carlin, he would undoubtedly have been aware of the substance of their argumentation, with which, as will now be shown, there is frequently resonance in his writings of the following decades.

For example, Petty castigated the Catholic priesthood for propagating rebellious aspirations among the Irish people, and for effectively constituting an 'internal and mystical government' that allowed Ireland to be 'governed indirectly by foreign power' (*PAI*: 199, 164). His comments were thus directed overwhelmingly towards political issues, and, while he was prepared to criticize certain aspects of Catholic religious practice that he considered 'peculiar to those Irish' (*PAI*: 198), he made it clear that he was in general not concerned to extend such discussion into issues relating to Catholic doctrine as such.

Besides delinking Irish political issues from the sphere of religion in this way, Petty also attempted to provide materialistic explanations for a range of other economic and social issues relating to Ireland and the Irish. For example, it has already been seen that he associated the supposed laziness of the Irish with their ready access to means of subsistence requiring only 'two hours per diem' for their production. He was also prepared to consider the possibility that the problem might lie in their physical make-up, though he concluded that this was not an adequate explanation: 'For their shape, stature, colour, and complexion, I see nothing in them inferior to any other people, nor any enormous predominance of any humour' (*PAI*: 201). It was not that he lacked crude notions in the field of physical anthropology, which he did not hesitate to apply to the 'several species of man' inhabiting other continents (Hodgen 1964: 419–22). Rather, his observation of Irish society was sufficiently close for him to prefer less fanciful explanations: 'Their lazing seems to me to proceed rather from want of employment and encouragement to work than from the natural abundance of phlegm in their bowels and blood' (*PAI*: 201).

But, while the intractability of Irish labour to subjection to capital could not thus be attributed to their physical characteristics, it was, he suggested, nonetheless deeply rooted in consequence of 'their ancient customs, which affect as well their consciences as their nature'; for,

> why should they desire to fare better, though with more labour, when they are
> taught that this way of living is more like the patriarchs of old and the saints of
> later times, by whose prayers and merits they are to be relieved, and whose
> examples they are therefore to follow? (PAI: 201–02)

Petty's secular explanatory framework, combined with reference to fashionable intellectual fads in what was retrospectively perceived as 'early modern science', accorded broadly with much of the propaganda justifying the 1649 invasion. A further range of correlations can also be identified with arguments commonly used in the period to justify rule by conquest (Carlin 1993: 219–20). Such arguments accorded with Petty's view that it was only by conquest that the Irish could be made to realize that ''tis their interest to join with them and follow their example who have brought arts, civility and freedom into their country' (*PAI*: 203).

In connection with the 'arts', a category that then included technology, Petty claimed that there were 'not ten iron furnaces' in the whole of Ireland (*PAI*: 209). That which he established on his own estate was manned primarily, if not exclusively, by colonists from England, and his experience in this and his other enterprises undoubtedly strengthened his prejudice that only colonialism could introduce technological progress into Ireland. An associated argument was that, left to themselves, the Irish would fail to develop the natural resources of their country. This argument was used to justify colonial rule in Ireland in a 1652 work by Gerard Boate, a writer who had frequented the same intellectual circles as Petty during the 1640s and whose work would surely have been known to him (quoted by Carlin 1993: 217; see also Coughlan 1990: 212–13. The same argument remained a familiar feature of colonialist writings throughout the subsequent era and was indeed one of the prime contexts in which the term 'economic development' first came into currency two centuries later (Arndt 1981: 460–62). A further common feature of this ideology of conquest is the denial that the colonized people had a history at all prior to the arrival of the invader. Petty enthusiastically embraced this idea:

> There is at this day no monument or real argument that, when the Irish were first invaded, they had any stone housing at all, any money, any foreign trade, nor any learning but the legends of the Saints, Psalters, Missals, Rituals, etc., viz. nor geometry, astronomy, anatomy, architecture, enginery, painting, carving, nor any mind of manufacture, nor the least use of navigation or the art military. (*PAI*: 154–55).

The ultimate insult in this connection was the assertion that the Irish were intruders in their own country, a common suggestion being that they were of 'Scythian' origin, which supposedly explained the apparently 'nomadic' (in fact, transhumant) aspect of Irish pastoral society.[10] Petty's own 'conjecture' was in fact less exotic, though perhaps intended to be no less wounding, suggesting as he did that Ireland's first inhabitants were likely to have come from Scotland, rather than being 'Phoenicians, Scythians, Biscayers, etc.' (*PAI*: 204).

The generally positive estimation that Petty receives from development economists for his contribution to their theoretical heritage is thus in contradiction with the assumption, which presumably most of them would share, that much of the impulse to the formative work of their pioneering representatives came from the perceived need to supersede the colonialist ideology of the 'civilizing mission' and provide a post-colonial alternative to it. Once it is taken into account, therefore, that Petty was in fact deeply engaged in an early, but crucial, stage of the formulation of this ideology, questions inevitably arise as to the level of self-awareness prevailing in the sub-discipline regarding the intellectual roots of the conceptual apparatus on which its practitioners continue to rely.

Petty on Institutions and Their Transformation

There is some remarkably close resonance with aspects of the development economics literature in Petty's comments on what would now be termed 'institutions', or, more specifically, the commercial and financial infrastructure, the legal institutions relating to the security of property rights, and the conditions for a culture of enterprise. Regarding commercial institutions, Petty posed the question: 'Why should they [that is, the Irish] raise more commodities, since there are not merchants sufficiently stocked to take them of them, nor provided with other more pleasing foreign commodities to give in exchange for them?' (*PAI*: 201). Moreover, commercial transactions are impeded by corresponding deficiencies in the financial institutions, in the form of 'difference, confusion and badness of coins, [and] exorbitant exchange and interest of money' (*PAI*: 196).

As for what are now termed property rights, Petty asked the question: 'Why should men endeavour to get estates, where the legislative power is not agreed upon, and where tricks and words destroy natural right and property?' (*PAI*: 202). This issue of secure land tenure was one with which he was deeply concerned throughout his career, first as both surveyor of Ireland and beneficiary of the Cromwellian confiscations, and subsequently in ongoing legal battles to retain possession of the lands he had seized. It is consequently no surprise that he repeatedly returned to this theme, calling for 'clear conditions' upon leases (*PAI*: 203) and, in the political sphere, 'certainty' over where ultimate legislative authority lay (*PAI*: 159–60). At the same time, he cautioned that laws might not be readily transferable between countries, since if 'first made and first fitted to thick-peopled countries', they might overload the more summary legal apparatus available in 'thin-peopled countries such as Ireland' (*PAI*: 202).

Against the background of such weak commercial, financial and legal institutions, it was no surprise that a culture of enterprise was failing to take root. Reflecting on the 'indisposition' of the Irish to take to maritime trade, he complained that 'the Irish had rather eat potatoes and milk on dry land than contest with the wind and waves with better food' (*PAI*: 208).

This entire range of discussion, based as it is on his own lifelong practical preoccupations and frustrations, gives Petty's writings on institutional matters a more concrete and immediate aspect than the rather unspecific and general observations on equivalent subjects that were propagated at the time of the 1649 invasion. He also strikes a more modern note than is subsequently to be found in Smith's discussions of colonialism, which, based as they are on second-hand information, are Olympian, academic and unrealistic by comparison.

This realism endows Petty's final proposal with a grimly practical character. Its virtue, in his eyes, was that it incorporated all the different means he had at various times considered for wiping out Ireland's national traditions – economic, social and cultural – which had proved so resilient to transformation in accordance with the requirements of colonialism and emergent capitalism. The English had never been able to muster sufficient colonists to swamp these traditions *in situ*; his scheme was, he argued, a more realistic means to achieving the same aim. It would, for example, facilitate eradication of the Irish language, along with replacement of 'those uncertain and unintelligible' Irish place names (*PAI*: 208). It would provide ample scope for cross marriages, in particular between Irish men and English women, so that the offspring would be reared in the language and culture of their mothers (*PAI*: 202–03). In short, 'the manners, habits, language and customs of the Irish . . . would all be transmuted into English' (*TI*: 573).

History is full of ironies, and by dismissing the market in favour of the blunter instrument of state action, Petty was in fact turning his back on precisely those forces that were ultimately to achieve what, for him, had been only a 'dream or reverie'. As the geographer Yann Morvran Goblet, writing in 1930, tellingly observed, Petty's scheme was grimly prophetic of what was actually to transpire in the two centuries that followed, when Ireland was indeed emptied of the majority of its inhabitants, many of them transported abroad as he had advocated, its language and traditional way of life fighting for survival, and much of the country's territory converted into one vast cattle ranch. This prompted Goblet to ask: 'What politician has ever put forward a plan, be it never so formal and official, which has been realized so comprehensively, point by point, as the "reverie" of Sir William Petty?' (Goblet 1930: 2, 305).

Petty and the State: Metropolitan and Colonial

As has been shown, what the tone of Petty's discussions lacks in fanatical invective is amply compensated by a clinical note that is, arguably, even more chilling. This reached its extreme in his use of anatomical imagery to justify his methodological approach to socio-economic analysis, and, in particular, his argument that Ireland presented an ideal opportunity for such 'political anatomy', just as 'students in medicine practise their inquiry upon cheap and common animals' (*PAI*: 129; for discussion, see Coughlan 1990: 213–20). The English state's experiments in this 'laboratory' of Ireland aimed at realizing a programme of social, political and religious transformation, encompassing 'governmental modernization, colonial expansion, religious reformation and identity formation all in process simultaneously' (Morgan 1999: 9). In the case of each of these processes, everything that constituted an advance from the English point of view necessarily entailed measures to suppress Ireland's cultural, political and religious life and annihilate its national identity: 'the development of "Englishness" depended on the negation of "Irishness"' (Hadfield and Maley 1993: 7). Petty's writings disingenuously reveal both sides of this equation with a frankness and clarity that contrast with the distorted perspective – all-too-common among historians of economic, social and political thought – which one-sidedly focuses on those aspects of his writings that are susceptible to being represented in a positive light, or even as socially progressive.[11]

The history of England's colonial policy in Ireland provides ample illustration of the paradoxical fact that the fundamental institutions of what is now perceived as capitalist private enterprise, such as the joint stock company and even corporate enterprise in general, first emerged in inseparable combination with state – usually military – activity (Bottigheimer 1971: 44; Morgan 1985: 262–67). It was in such a context, for which he elsewhere coined the term 'privato-public' (*TTC*: 65), that Petty made his fortune; in this, he exemplified the rise of neo-feudal upstarts of all kinds in the Europe of his time, a rise which, for all its local variation, had in common the fact that it was predicated on the strength of the state rather than, as in the 'true' feudalism of the medieval period, its weakness. It is therefore no surprise that Petty's economic writings are concerned above all with the tasks involved in furthering the development of what is now termed the 'fiscal–military state'. This term was originally coined with respect to the period following the 1688 revolution in England, but it is now widely acknowledged that it was the statesmen and writers of the preceding generation, not least Petty himself, who laid much of the ideological and intellectual groundwork for the subsequent reconstruction of the state along fiscal–military lines. Thus, the maximization of England's taxation revenue from Ireland dominated much of his writing on the latter country, and though he at times criticized the English authorities for imposing restraints on aspects of the Irish economy – particularly by restricting its cattle exports (see *PAI*: 160–61, with editorial note, and *PA*: 299) – this was unashamedly motivated by defence of the profits reaped by colonial landowners such as himself, rather than being an expression of sympathy with the idea of an independent economic life for Ireland, let alone an independent Irish nation-state.

The idea of economic planning by the state was, in Petty's time, strongly linked with utopian currents in social thought, not least in connection with colonial policy, Thomas More's *Utopia* having itself been described as marking 'a watershed in the development of colonial theory' (Morgan 1985: 269). One topical pamphlet in this genre emanated from the intellectual circles in which Petty had moved prior to his arrival in Ireland. It described a mythical kingdom named 'Macaria', whose 'excellent government' included a number of 'councils' handling the different aspects of state policy, one of these being a 'council for new plantations [that is, colonies]' (Webster 1979: 67–68). Petty greatly elaborated such ideas in his later writings; in his final scheme for the transformation of Ireland into a 'kind of factory', he outlined the tasks of a proposed 'council of fitting persons' in terms that vividly portray the transition from utopian speculation to the practicalities of administering a planned economy:

> pitching the number of each species of cattle, for every sort of land within the whole territory of Ireland; the same may pitch the number of cow-herds, shepherds, dairy-women, slaughter men and others, which are fit and sufficient to manage the trade of exported cattle, dead or alive, of hides, tallow, butter and cheese, wool and sea-fish, etc.; to appoint the foreign markets and ports where each commodity is to be shipped and sold, to provide shipping, and to keep account of the exportation above mentioned, and of the imported salt, tobacco, with a few other necessaries. (*TI*: 575)

The demography of the population remaining in Ireland was also to be placed under the control of this council, which may 'adjust' it in such a way as to pitch how many of them shall be English, or such as can speak English, and how many Irish, how many Catholics and how many others, without any other respect than the management of this trade, for the common good of all the owners of these lands and its stock indifferently (*TI*: 575).

This power of the council extended to 'managing the multiplication' of the population (*TI*: 605): since the entire population is to be 'all aged between 16 and 60 years' (*TI*: 563), the council would also be obliged to 'carry away children and superannuated persons'.

Despite the normally positive connotations that the term 'utopia' enjoys today, there has traditionally been, from Plato's *Republic* onwards, explicitly or implicitly, an associated 'dystopia' for those excluded from its highest privileges, and it is in this sense that Goblet described Petty's proposal as a system of 'twin utopias' (Goblet 1930: 2, 280–306). The polarity between the two comes across vividly in Petty's writings as a whole: on the one hand, the variety and luxury of the glittering colonial metropolis of London; on the other, the dour homogeneity of Petty's scheme for a 'new model Ireland' (*TI*: 567) – housing that reaches a standard of basic habitability (*TI*: 577), clothes that are 'uniform' (*TI*: 569), and a humble country diet of potatoes and dairy products, enlivened only by foraging (*PAI*: 201, as quoted above).

In view of this sharp distinction between the metropolitan and colonial worlds as they are depicted in Petty's writings, it is disappointing to note the lack of attention hitherto paid to the fact that he accorded the state a completely different political–economic status on either side of the divide; indeed, one otherwise perceptive study of his writings on government and administration totally omits any mention of colonies whatsoever (Mykkänen 1994), while Roncaglia (1988) is arguably even more remiss in succumbing to the same shortcoming in a study dedicated explicitly to Petty's relation to development economics. It is evidently necessary, therefore, to underline the fact that there is no assumption, in Petty's writings, of political, administrative or political–economic equivalence between the role of the state in the colonies and in the metropolis; in political economy, such a concept was to emerge only a century later, in the more universalistic theoretical system of Adam Smith, and then only in relation to the North American colonies (see, in particular, Smith [1776] 1976: 624–26). Petty's writings and practical involvements in state affairs thus usefully draw out the fact that his approach – especially as it concerns the issues now addressed by development economics – was based on the presumption of a dominant and subordinate status in all spheres of government, administration and political economy.

Conclusions

The conceptual resonance of Petty's mode of economic analysis with the economics of today never ceases to attract comment from historians of economic thought, and yet, as has been shown, the explicitly colonialist intent that motivated that analysis has been almost entirely ignored. This is despite the fact that only a few decades after his death, one of the world's most celebrated satirists, Jonathan Swift, author of *Gulliver's Travels*, drew attention to the appalling reality behind the clinical terms of Petty's 'political arithmetic' in a manner that would surely have been sufficiently forceful to impress the message indelibly on the minds of any less insensitive sector of the reading public. In his parody of

Petty, Swift (1729) put forward, in terms that imitated Petty's mode of expression with icy accuracy, a gruesome proposal for the breeding of Irish children as livestock, commenting that they would make 'excellent nutritious meat' – 'whether stewed, roasted, baked or boiled' – for sale to 'persons of quality and fortune'. This 'modest proposal for the public benefit' was advanced complete with Petty's characteristic panoply of statistical justification, covering the demographic aspects, the average weight of each carcass, the costs ('about two shillings per annum, rags included'), potential uses for the hides ('gloves for ladies, and summer boots for fine gentlemen'), the export potential, the implications for the revenue of the church, the numbers to be 'reserved for breed', and so on.

Both the unconcealed predatory intent and the reality of colonialist devastation that lay behind Petty's economic thought have been clear as day to writers as diverse as the Irish nationalist Mitchel, the French geographer Goblet and the satirist Swift. It is consequently mortifying to find that even adherents of the most critical perspectives within the social sciences today habitually fail to take account of this phase of the intellectual ancestry of their respective disciplines. Such a failure must be reckoned particularly reprehensible in the case of development economics, since this is the branch of economic thought most directly concerned with addressing the colonial experience and its aftermath.

In short, the search for the roots of the theoretical and methodological apparatus of today's development economics does not lead back, as is widely and complacently assumed, to the universalistic or progressive orientation commonly associated with the Enlightenment movement in eighteenth-century philosophy. Rather, the search for such roots leads back to Petty, who, applying his pioneering quantitative method, coldly calculated the advantages to the colonial power of the annihilation of the national life of the colonized people, their effective extinction as a demographic unit, and the imposition upon their territory of an intentionally dependent, single-export economy. The urgent, difficult and self-searching task of confronting and surmounting an intellectual heritage with roots in such an unbridled phase of colonialism must surely be prioritized by development economists, if they are to convincingly demonstrate that the conceptual apparatus prevailing in their sub-discipline is adequate for the progressive analytical tasks it claims to be capable of performing.

Notes

1 Kurz and Salvadori (2000: 156), in contrast, describe Petty as 'an important author in the genealogy of input–output analysis'.

2 The force of Roncaglia's argument is weakened by his failure, all too characteristic of economists, to take account of conspicuously relevant branches of literature in neighbouring fields, including research on the 'drift' of manufactures to the countryside as well as the entire debate over the concept of 'proto-industrialization', and, for that matter, also the substantial body of research by Barnard and others on Petty's own enterprises in Ireland (on which see further below).

3 The logical structure of Welch's argumentation can be obscure, and his application of Marxist terms and concepts is imprecise and sometimes questionable; this does not alter the fact, of course, that his study constitutes the main precedent for the present

one. Moreover, it certainly compares favourably with the analogous, but less focused, discussion in Perelman (2000: 125–29).

[4] It is over half a century since the publication of the last biographical monograph on Petty (Strauss 1954), but the following summary account reflects the fact that many aspects of his eventful life-story have continued to be explored within a variety of specialist historical fields.

[5] The case of Ireland thus breaches the neat distinction, which is current in some of the literature on the geography of development, between the 'new Englands' or 'neo-Europes' of colonial policy in the temperate zones, and the more oppressive 'extractive states' established in the tropics (see Goodacre 2004).

[6] These enterprises have been the subject of a number of detailed studies by the historian Toby Barnard (for references, see Barnard 2003: 431). Even in his notes on his estate affairs, Petty persisted in his relentless theorizing, as discussed by Aspromourgos (2000: 58–60).

[7] Despite the customary assumption that Petty was in the vanguard of scientific and technical progress, his supposed achievements in this regard have in fact received specialist assessment in only one field, that of surveying and cartography, where it has been shown that he lagged significantly behind the advanced practice of his time. See Andrews (1985: 65–66) and other studies by the same author.

[8] Petty's advocacy of the advantages of compactness has gone largely unnoticed in development economics, though Clark ([1940] 1957: 492–93) comments that it contrasts with the subsequent prevalence of 'Malthusian propaganda' (see also Pyatt 1984: 81). There is an oblique reference to the topic in Yang (2003: 1), where it is termed 'Petty's theory of urbanization'.

[9] It is disappointing that the debate among historians on the 'new feudalism' of the period has focused almost entirely on central and eastern Europe (see, for example, Brenner 1976: 50–60), despite the evident relevance of the situation in Ireland (as demonstrated by Morgan 1985: 274–78).

[10] This idea was given wide currency by the English poet Spenser (see Coughlan 1990: 207). See also Morgan (1985: 268). Carlin (1993: 221–22) compares this 'last twist of the knife' with 'white South African claims that the black majority are late arrivals in the area'.

[11] Once again, Colin Clark stands alone among development economists who have commented on Petty in at least alluding to the need for 'deploring his mercantile morality', as displayed in his inclusion, 'without a blush', of the proceeds of piracy and slavery in his estimate of England's import–export statistics (Clark 1940: 448–49, discussing PA: 296).

References

Writings of William Petty, with abbreviations

All page numbers for works of Petty refer to those in the following edition:

EW   Hull, Charles H., ed. (1899), The Economic Writings of Sir William Petty, 2 vols (Cambridge: Cambridge University Press).

The individual works of Petty, in the order in which they were written, are:

TTC   A Treatise of Taxes and Contributions, published 1662, in EW: 1–97.

VS   Verbum Sapienti, written 1665, first published 1691, in EW: 99–120.

PAI   The Political Anatomy of Ireland, written c. 1671, first published 1691, in EW: 121–231.

PA   Political Arithmetic, written c. 1671–72 and amended in subsequent years, first authorized edition published 1690, in EW: 233–313.

TI   A Treatise of Ireland, written 1687, first published 1899, in EW: 545–621.

Other References

Andrews, John H. (1985), Plantation Acres: An Historical Study of the Irish and Surveyor and His Maps (Omagh: Ulster Historical Foundation).

Arndt, Heinz W. (1981), 'Economic Development: A Semantic History', Economic Development and Cultural Change, 29: 456–66.

Aspromourgos, Tony (1996), *On the Origins of Classical Economics: Distribution and Value from William Petty to Adam Smith* (London: Routledge).

—— (2000), 'New Light on the Economics of William Petty (1623–1687): Some Findings from Previously Undisclosed Manuscripts', *Contributions to Political Economy*, 19: 53–70.

Barnard, Toby (2003), *A New Anatomy of Ireland: The Irish Protestants, 1649–1770* (New Haven: Yale University Press).

Bottigheimer, Karl S. (1971), *English Money and Irish Land: The 'Adventurers' in the Cromwellian Settlement of Ireland* (Oxford: Clarendon Press).

Braddick, Michael J. (2000), *State Formation in Early Modern England, c. 1550–1700* (Cambridge: Cambridge University Press).

Brenner, Robert (1976), 'Agrarian Class Structure and Economic Development in Pre-Industrial Europe', *Past and Present*, 70: 30–75.

Carlin, Norah (1993), 'Extreme or Mainstream?: The English Independents and the Cromwellian Reconquest of Ireland, 1649–1651', in Brendan Bradshaw, Andrew Hadfield and Willie Maley, eds, *Representing Ireland: Literature and the Origins of Conflict, 1534–1660* (Cambridge: Cambridge University Press): 209–26.

Clark, Colin G. (1940), *The Conditions of Economic Progress*, 1st edn; 2nd edn (1951): completely rewritten, 3rd edn (1957): largely rewritten (London: Macmillan).

—— (1984), 'Development Economics: The Early Years', in Gerald M. Meier and Dudley Seers, eds, *Pioneers in Development* (New York: Oxford University Press: for the World Bank), 59–83.

Coughlan, Patricia (1990), '"Cheap and Common Animals": The English Anatomy of Ireland in the Seventeenth Century', in Thomas Healy and Jonathan Sawday, eds, *Literature and the English Civil War* (Cambridge: Cambridge University Press): 205–23.

Cowen, Michael P. and Robert W. Shenton (1995), 'The Invention of Development', in Jonathan Crush, ed., *Power of Development* (London: Routledge): 27–43.

Gardiner, Samuel R. (1899), 'The Transplantation to Connaught', *English Historical Review*, 14: 700–34.

Goblet, Yann Morvran (1930), *La transformation de la géographie politique de l'Irelande au XVIIe siècle, dans les cartes et essais anthropogéographiques de Sir William Petty*, 2 vols (Paris: Berger–Levrault).

Goodacre, Hugh J. (2005), 'Development and Geography: Current Debates in Historical Perspective', in Jomo K.S. and Ben Fine, eds, *The New Development Economics: After the Washington Consensus* (New Delhi: Tulika Books; London: Zed Press).

Hadfield, Andrew and Willie Maley (1993), 'Irish Representations and English Alternatives', in Brendan Bradshaw, Andrew Hadfield and Willie Maley, eds, *Representing Ireland: Literature and the Origins of Conflict, 1534–1660* (Cambridge: Cambridge University Press): 1–23.

Hodgen, Margaret T. (1964), *Early Anthropology in the Sixteenth and Seventeenth Centuries* (Philadelphia: University of Pennsylvania Press).

Kurz, Heinz D. and Neri Salvadori (2000), '"Classical" Roots of Input–Output Analysis: A Short Account of Its Long Prehistory', *Economic Systems Research*, 12 (2): 153–79.

Lewis, William Arthur (1954), 'Economic Development with Unlimited Supplies of Labour', *The Manchester School*: 139–91.

—— (1988), 'The Roots of Development Theory', in Hollis Chenery and N. Srinavasan, eds, *Handbook of Development Economics*, Vol. I (Amsterdam and New York: Elsevier Science Publishers): 27–37.

Marx, Karl ([1867] 1970), *Capital: A Critique of Political Economy (Das Kapital: Kritik der politischen Oekonomie)* edited by Frederick Engels, trans. Samuel Moore and Edward Aveling, new edn (London: Lawrence and Wishart).

Meier, Gerald M. (1984), 'The Formative Period', in Gerald M. Meier and Dudley Seers, eds, *Pioneers in Development* (New York: Oxford University Press for the World Bank): 3–22.

—— (1994a), 'The "Progressive State" in Classical Economics', in Gerald M. Meier, ed., *From Classical Economics to Development Economics* (London: Macmillan): 5–27.

—— (1994b), 'From Colonial Economics to Development Economics', in Gerald M. Meier, ed., *From Classical Economics to Development Economics* (London: Macmillan): 173–96.

——, ed. (1994), *From Classical Economics to Development Economics* (London: Macmillan).

Meier, Gerald M. and James E. Rauch (2000), *Leading Issues in Economic Development*, 7th edn (New York: Oxford University Press).

Mitchel John (1873), *The Crusade of the Period; and Last Conquest of Ireland (perhaps)* (New York: Lynch, Cole and Meehan).

Morgan, Hiram (1985), 'The Colonial Venture of Sir Thomas Smith in Ulster, 1571–1575', *Historical Journal*, 28 (2): 261–78.

—— (1999), 'Beyond Spenser? A Historiographical Introduction to the Study of Political Ideas in Early Modern Ireland', in Hiram Morgan, ed., *Political Ideology in Ireland, 1541–1641* (Dublin: Four Courts Press): 9–21.

Mykkänen, Juri (1994), '"To Methodize and Regulate Them": William Petty's Governmental Science of Statistics', *History of the Human Sciences*, 7 (3): 65–88.

Perelman, Michael (2000), *The Invention of Capitalism: Classical Political Economy and the Secret History of Primitive Accumulation* (Durham, NC: Duke University Press).

Perrotta, Cosimo (2003), 'The Legacy of the Past: Ancient Economic Thought on Wealth and Development', *European Journal of the History of Economic Thought*, 10 (2): 177–229.

Pyatt, Graham (1984), 'Comment on Clark (1984)', in Gerald M. Meier and Dudley Seers, eds, *Pioneers in Development* (New York: Oxford University Press for the World Bank): 78–83.

Rodriguez Braun, Carlos (1987), 'Capital's Last Chapter', *History of Political Economy*, 19 (2): 299–310.

Roncaglia, Alessandro (1988), 'William Petty and the Conceptual Framework for the Analysis of Economic Development', in Kenneth J. Arrow, ed., *The Balance between Industry and Agriculture in Economic Development*, Vol. 1: Basic Issues: International Economic Association: 157–174.

Sen, Amartya K. (1988), 'The Concept of Development', in Hollis Chenery and N. Srinavasan, eds, *Handbook of Development Economics* (Amsterdam: Elsevier Science Publishers), Vol. I: 9–26.

Smith, Adam ([1776] 1976), *An Inquiry into the Nature and Causes of the Wealth of Nations*, edited by Roy H. Campbell, Alexander S. Skinner and William B. Todd (Oxford: Oxford University Press).

Strauss, Erich (1954), *Sir William Petty: Portrait of a Genius* (London: Bodley Head).

Swift, Jonathan (1729), *A modest proposal for preventing the children of poor people from being a burthen to their parents or country, and for making them beneficial to the public* (Dublin: S. Harding; London: J. Roberts).

Webster, Charles (1979), 'Utopian Planning and the Puritan Revolution: Gabriel Platte, Samuel Hartlib, and Macaria', Wellcome Unit for the History of Medicine. Research Publications 2, Oxford, with a facsimile reprint of *A description of the famous kingdome of Macaria*.

Welch, Patrick J. (1997), 'Cromwell's Occupation of Ireland as Judged from Petty's Observations and Marx's Theory of Colonialism', in James P. Henderson, ed., *The State of the History of Political Economy* (London: Routledge for the History of Economics Society): 157–72.

Yang, Xiaokai (2003), *Economic Development and the Division of Labour* (Oxford: Blackwell).

Ricardo's Fallacy

Mutual Benefit from Trade Based on Comparative Costs and Specialization?

Utsa Patnaik

The Ricardian theory of comparative advantage contains a logical fallacy when used to argue that mutual benefit necessarily results from trade. Ricardo's two-country, two-commodity model assumes that both goods can be produced in both countries. It is then shown that even if unit production cost is lower for both goods in one country compared to the other, provided the relative cost of production differs, it would be of mutual benefit for each country to specialize in the good in which it has lower relative cost and exchange with each other. The benefit arises from *an actual physical increase in total output owing to specialization*, such that for each country there is vector-wise improvement in the consumption of the two goods through exchange, that is, a higher level of one for at least the same level of the other, in the post-trade situation compared to the pre-trade one.

For example, taking the two goods as cloth and wine, following Ricardo's own famous example, let us assume that country *B* has higher unit cost than country *A* in both goods, for it requires 4 and 2.5 person-days respectively to produce a unit of cloth and a unit of wine, while country *A* requires only 2 and 1 person-days respectively to produce a unit of cloth and a unit of wine. Ricardo assumes full employment: the total available daily person-days in *A*, say, 200 person-days, can produce daily either a total of 100 units of cloth or a total of 200 units of wine, which defines the linear transformation frontier of cloth for wine, and every combination of these two goods on that frontier can be actually produced. Similarly *B*, with, say, 400 total person-days available, can produce daily either a total of 100 units of cloth or a total of 160 units of wine, with every combination on the frontier so defined also being producible. (*B* is assumed to have 400 person-days to *A*'s 200 so that the total output size in the two countries is roughly similar.)

In the initial pre-trade situation, if *A* produces, say, a combination of 50 units of cloth and 100 units of wine, and *B* produces a combination of 50 units of cloth and 80 units of wine, then, the total output taking both countries together is 100 units of cloth and 180 units of wine. (These particular numbers embodying the assumption that each country devotes half its resources to each good have no significance, and any other feasible combination would do equally well). *Relative disadvantage* is clearly less for *B* in producing cloth where it incurs double A's unit cost, while for wine it incurs more than double A's unit cost. A's relative advantage is greater in producing wine. Ricardo's cleverness lay in arguing that if B specialized completely in cloth, in which its relative disadvantage was less, and A specialized in wine, in which its relative advantage was more, *total output taking both countries would increase*, and this increased output could be shared through exchange making both countries better off. Thus, after specialization, B would produce 100 units of cloth alone and A would produce 200 units of wine alone, and total output of wine would be therefore higher by 20 units compared to 180 in the pre-trade situation, with total output of cloth unchanged. The extra 20 units of wine could be shared, say, with A retaining 110 units of wine and exchanging 90 units with B for 50 units of cloth. Thus each country after trade would have a higher level of consumption of wine, by 10 units, for the same level of consumption of cloth, 50 units, compared to the pre-specialization and trade situation (Table 1).

The exact ratio in which the sharing will take place has been the subject of much discussion, but need not detain us here. All we have to note is that *mutual benefit from sharing higher output* is put forward both as the reason that specialization and exchange is undertaken, and as the actual outcome of specialization and exchange. Ricardo put this forward *as a perfectly general argument for explaining all trade, and mentioned no exceptions whatsoever.* Extremely clever though it is, the argument is based on a fallacy, which relates to the sphere of applied logic.

A *fallacy* in an argument can arise either when the process of reasoning to draw an inference from the given premise is not correct, or when the assumption (the premise) of the argument is not true. Fallacies can be of various kinds – material fallacies arise from an incorrect statement of facts, verbal fallacies from an incorrect use of terms and formal fallacies from an incorrect process of inference. Ricardo's process of reasoning is valid, but a material fallacy arises because his assumption or premise is not true for a general theory of trade. There is a serious problem with the assumption, which is that both goods are producible and indeed are actually produced, in both countries. Only on this assumption can the shifting of resources from one good to the other, and hence the transformation of one good into the other, be postulated. Ricardo's argument is applicable only to countries with a similar production structure, where the assumption of the model holds – that both countries can produce both goods. It becomes an inapplicable argument when considering trade between temperate advanced countries and tropical developing countries, because such trade involves goods which cannot ever be produced at all in temperate regions, and for which cost of production and transformation frontiers cannot even be defined. This fallacy, which tacitly assumes a special case – both goods producible in both countries – and argues to a conclusion – mutual benefit – which is presented as being of general relevance, is a well-known type of material fallacy that, following Aristotle, has long been categorized by logicians as the 'converse fallacy of accident' under *secundum quid.* More fully:

TABLE 1   A Numerical Example Illustrating:

(A) 'Comparative advantage' when Ricardo's assumption is satisfied

(B) The undefinability of comparative advantage when Ricardo's assumption is not satisfied.

(A): Ricardo's assumption is satisfied and both countries A and B can produce good x (cloth) as well as good y (wine). A is assumed to have higher productivity in both goods than B, and total person-days available is assumed to be 200 in A and 400 in B.

Good	*Person-days per Unit Output*		*Pre-Trade Output/Consumption*		
	A	B	A	B	A + B
One unit cloth (x)	2	4	50	50	100
One unit wine (y)	1	2.5	100	80	180

	After Specialization Output in Units per Day			*Post-Trade Consumption*		
	A	B	A + B	A	B	A + B
Cloth (x)	0	100	100	50	50	100
Wine (y)	200	0	200	110	90	200

Result: Both countries are vector-wise better off in the post-trade situation.

(B) Ricardo's assumption is not satisfied. Country B cannot produce good y, only good x, while country A can produce both goods x and y.

Good	*Person-days per Unit Output*		*Pre-Trade Output/Consumption*		
	A	B	A	B	A + B
One unit cloth (x)	2	4	50	100	150
One unit wine (y)	1	...	100	0	100

	Output after Specialization by A			*Post-Trade Consumption*		
	A	B	A + B	A	B	A + B
Cloth (x)	0	100	100	50	50	100
Wine (y)	200	0	200	100	100	200

Result: Total output of the two commodities does not, and cannot, increase vector-wise, unlike in the previous case. Country B's consumption is diversified but the availability of commodities there does not, and cannot, increase vector-wise, unlike in the previous case. Country A is not necessarily better off vector-wise after specialization and trade (as the example shows), though it could be. (However, if land constraint prevails in A, it would (a) either prevent A from increasing sufficiently the output of y, such that A would necessarily experience unemployment created by x-displacing trade; or (b) if output of y is increased, given land constraint, that of non-traded crops like food would fall. As regards B, if Ricardo's assumption of initial full employment is not fulfilled, then, in the post-trade situation, the production and export of cloth by B in addition to its domestic consumption would increase employment there. B, in such a case, would have both diversified its consumption and increased its employment. All these asymmetric effects, however, are a far cry from the Ricardian picture of necessary mutual benefit from trade.

A *dicto simpliciter ad dictum secundum quid* or the fallacy of accident, when an argument applies a general rule to a case where some special circumstance ('accident') makes the rule inapplicable. . . . The converse fallacy of accident argues improperly from a special case to a general rule. The fact that a certain drug is beneficial to some sick persons does not imply that it is beneficial to all men. (*Encyclopaedia Britannica*: 11, 28)

What is the 'cost of production' in Germany of tea and coffee, or in the UK of natural rubber and sugarcane? How can the transformation frontier between machinery and coffee be defined for Germany, or that between cloth and natural rubber be defined for Britain? None of the tropical goods can be produced under field conditions in cold temperate countries; hence, neither costs nor transformation frontiers can be defined. Indeed, the specific example Ricardo himself gave, involving *cloth* and *wine* production in England and Portugal, is itself a highly problematic one. Warm temperate Portugal could produce not only wool for cloth but large supplies of grapes for making wine on a commercial basis, while cold temperate England could produce wool for cloth but not grapes (*vitis vinifra*) under field conditions. This was particularly true during the fourteenth to eighteenth centuries, when mean summer temperatures in Britain were lower than they are today and genetic modification of plants was unknown. The northern limit of grape-growing is defined by a mean July isotherm of 19 degrees Celsius or 66 degrees Fahrenheit. As Adam Smith had remarked, grapes could only be grown against artificially heated walls in Britain, and wine made from them at a preposterously higher unit cost compared to foreign imported wines (Smith 1776, I: 423–24). Grapes were not grown in Britain on a commercial basis for wine production – although sometimes, individual landed aristocrats showed off their great wealth by maintaining hot houses at enormous expense to supply their own tables with the fruit, as contemporary novels indicate (Austen 1992).

Ricardo fudges his argument in his chapter on trade, by failing to distinguish between *production* of the agricultural raw material and *processing* of the raw material. It is not possible that he did not know the distinction between the two. He says the following:

> Now suppose that England were to discover *a process for making wine*, so that it should become her interest to *grow it* rather than import it, she would naturally divert a portion of her capital from the foreign trade to the home trade; she would cease to manufacture cloth for exportation and would *grow wine* for herself. (Ricardo 1951: 137; emphasis added)

Ricardo goes on to say: 'If the *improvement in making wine* were of a very important description, it might become profitable for the two countries to exchange employments, for England to make all the wine and Portugal all the cloth consumed by them' (ibid.: 138; emphasis added).

The repeated use of the term 'grow wine' by Ricardo is highly significant. By using this phrase, the activity of *growing grapes* and the altogether different activity of *processing grapes into wine* are telescoped together into a single activity by Ricardo, and, thereby, the crucial distinction between these two activities is conceptually obliterated. *Growing* a crop is contingent on climate, whereas *processing* it is not. Indeed, the very first sentence quoted above suggests that, for Ricardo, 'a process for making wine' is the same as to 'grow wine'. Ricardo gets hopelessly enmeshed here in untenable concepts. An argument based on ambiguity of language is a verbal fallacy. The material fallacy (both countries produce both goods) is here supported and compounded by a verbal fallacy. The premise is stated by Ricardo in a verbally ambiguous form, which gives the misleading impression that it is a general premise – that 'growing wine', whatever that may mean, by England is as possible as 'growing wine' by Portugal. In fact, a country can no more 'grow wine' than it can 'grow cloth' or 'grow shoes'. It has to produce the raw material – grapes in the first case, wool in the second and leather in the third – before it can process the raw material into wine, cloth and shoes, respectively. While Portugal could both produce wool and produce grapes, and therefore could make both cloth and wine, England could produce wool but not grapes, and therefore could make cloth but not grape-wine. The transformation frontier of cloth to wine could be defined for Portugal but not for England.

Since the untenability of the Ricardian assumption is true even for a warm temperate primary good like grapes, it is true *a fortiori* for the purely tropical traded primary goods, such as cane sugar, coffee, tea, cocoa, jute, indigo, opium, rubber, tropical hardwoods like teak, mahogany and rosewood, cereals like rice, tropical fruits and vegetables, palm oil, and the many other goods which could never be produced under field conditions in cold temperate Europe or North America.

Joan Robinson was entirely correct in saying that Ricardo's model ruled out 'the whole of what Adam Smith regarded as the main sphere of trade – exchanges between town and country, that is, between manufactures and primary products' (Robinson 1975: 130). But she was surely not as correct when, pointing out that Ricardo's objective was to make a case against protection, she went on to say that: 'Modern exponents of free-trade theory do not hesitate to apply its dogmas *to producers of primary products, but in fact it has nothing to do with their problems*' (ibid.; emphasis added). On the contrary, it has everything to do with their problems: we know that the case against protection was actuated by Britain's imperative need to freely import precisely those vital *primary products, serving as wage-goods or as raw materials*, that it could not produce enough of (corn, hemp) or could not produce at all (tobacco, sugar, raw cotton, hardwoods, dyestuffs, etc.). It is no use trying to absolve Ricardo's theory of its link with trade based on extra-economic compulsion; the free trade agitation he championed was not other countries' freedom to export their manufactures (Ricardo is not on record as opposing existing high English tariffs on Asian textiles), but only Britain's freedom to import food and raw materials unhindered by local landlord interests or any other monopoly interests like the old chartered trading companies.

The 'free trade dogma' applied to dependent or colonized primary producers is not a modern invention, as Joan Robinson seems to suggest: it was Ricardo's theory that initiated the dogma, via his process of reasoning to a general conclusion using a specific premise without a word of qualification regarding that premise. The fallacious but convenient conclusion of necessary mutual benefit from free trade represented the interests of his country, the dominant trading and colonizing country of the time. We can visualize Ricardo, like any other civilized gentleman in England at that time, drinking a cup of Caribbean slave labour-produced coffee sweetened with cane sugar while smoking tobacco, with a carafe of grape wine at his side – none of these four goods being producible in Britain – and wearing a shirt made from cotton – a raw material not producible in his country – while engaged in writing at a polished mahogany table – a wood not producible in Britain – in order to formulate his allegedly 'general' model of trade which assumed that 'both goods are produced in both countries', with not a word of qualification regarding the limited domain of relevance of the assumption.

Wherever the Ricardian assumption does not hold, the Ricardian conclusion about mutual benefit from trade does not hold either. Where country B cannot domestically produce the good y it wishes to consume, then its exporting a part of the only good, x, that it can produce, to country A, which can produce both goods x and y but is made to specialize in y, *does not raise total output, does not raise consumption vector-wise in both countries, and mutual benefit does not follow.*

Continuing with the example in Table 1, suppose that country B (Britain) cannot produce grape wine, hence, in the pre-trade situation, it produces only cloth to the extent of 100 units by devoting all its available labour to it. Country A (Portugal), however, produces 50 units of cloth and 100 units of wine as before. Relative costs and hence relative advantage cannot be defined, for we have three cost terms but not the fourth. In the pre-trade situation, taking both countries, the total output of cloth is 150 units and the total output of wine is 100 units. Suppose by some extra-economic means (for there is no *a priori* economic reason for Portugal to specialize), Britain induces Portugal to stop producing 50 units of cloth and specialize entirely in producing 200 units of wine. Britain then trades 50 units of its own cloth output for, say, 100 units of wine from Portugal. In the post-specialization trade situation, taking both countries, total output of cloth has gone down by 50 units while total output of wine has gone up by 100 units, hence *there is no vector-wise increase* in *total output* – this is the crucial difference from the first case and it rules out mutual benefit.

Portugal is not necessarily better off: it may continue to consume 50 units of cloth and 100 units of wine, the same as its pre-trade combination, as shown in the example. Britain has diversified its consumption basket from one to two goods, while maintaining total cloth output at the pre-trade level. But

Britain too is not better off and cannot be better off as regards consumption in the Ricardian vector-wise sense (more of one good for no less of the other), for it does have to give up consuming 50 of its 100 units of cloth, in exchange for 100 units of wine, as long as the assumption of full employment is retained.

Suppose, however, we drop the assumption of full employment: in the pre-trade situation, Britain devotes only half its available daily person-days to produce 50 units of cloth because it can consume no more than 50 units, and the remaining 200 person-days remain unemployed. Then, if it induces Portugal to specialize in wine production, it can expand its own cloth output to 100 units and trade 50 units of these for 100 units of wine. This would mean a vector-wise improvement in output and consumption for Britain. If we postulate a land cons-traint in Portugal, then, total wine/grape output may not increase to the required extent and deindustrialization necessarily involves unemployment of cloth work-ers not fully absorbed into wine production; or, if wine output hence grape output does increase to absorb all labour displaced from cloth production, then, there is both deindustrialization and, given the land constraint, there might be decline in the output of non-traded crops like foodgrains.

Exchange of English woollen cloth for Portuguese wine had been actu-ally taking place for over a century before Ricardo wrote, but the reason did not lie in 'comparative advantage', which could not even be defined. In reality, a supply of Portuguese wine in partial exchange for English cloth was procured through Britain's successful mercantilist policies of attaining naval dominance, sealed by the 1703 Treaty of Methuen whose provisions established English trad-ers in Lisbon and Oporto with commercial privileges, and opened up 'the specta-cular increase in the importation of English cloth and other exports into Portu-gal, whence the bulk of them were re-exported to Brazil, and of Portuguese wines into Great Britain' (Boxer 1973: 170). There was a growing trade surplus for Britain vis-à-vis Portugal, settled by inflow of Luso–Brazilian gold, which glad-dened mercantilist hearts. In the post-trade situation, Portugal was deindustrialized to the extent of its mandatory cloth imports from Britain, while Britons diversi-fied their consumption basket by accessing wine they could not themselves pro-duce and, at the same time, increased their manufacturing output to the extent of exports, beyond domestic absorption. Improvement did not and could not take place for both countries, only for the one that was militarily and politically the more powerful. In fact, an actual welfare worsening is very much on the cards for the country that is obliged, owing to extra-economic pressures, to specialize as a primary goods exporter. To the extent that it faces a land constraint, increas-ing the output of primary traded crops very commonly has an adverse impact on availability of non-traded crops like domestically consumed foodgrains, and undermines nutrition levels of its population, as we have demonstrated elsewhere (Patnaik 2003). It would be interesting to investigate what happened to the non-traded foodgrains crops in Portugal as its wine exports increased.

It might be argued, from the quotations from Ricardo given earlier, in which he speaks of the 'process of making wine' and 'improvements in making wine' that might make it profitable for England to make wine, that Ricardo was stressing *technology leading to processing efficiency*, so that whether a country could actually grow the primary raw material or not was simply not relevant for him because, in his (implicit) view, it could always import the raw material and, provided it used superior technology, it would be able to process it at lower cost than the country of origin of the raw material. The obvious example is imported raw cotton processed into machine-made cloth in England and again exported. (Note that grapes, cited in the example of wine that Ricardo used, are too perishable for even this 'import-and-process' argument to hold.)

However, this technology argument with raw cotton and cloth raises its own deep problems: Britain only succeeded in making a technological breakthrough in cotton cloth production under a heavily protectionist regime, which was more prolonged than any protectionist regime ever seen in history. Beginning in 1700, for 75 years there was a legal blanket ban, enforced through heavy fines, on the sale and consumption of all pure cotton printed and painted fabrics that were wholly imported from India and Persia (Mantoux 1970: 200–01; Davis 1966, 1979). The lifting of this blanket ban on consumption followed Arkwright's successful application to Parliament in 1774 arguing that there should be no legal bar to sale and consumption of the new, domestically produced machine-made pure cotton goods (Mantoux 1970: 224–25). The granting of his demand by Parliament that amended the relevant Act, was combined with maintaining even more rigorously the barriers to importing printed cotton goods from Asia for domestic use.

'No protection could be more complete, for it gave the manufacturers a real monopoly of the home market' (ibid.: 256). Between 1787 and 1813, the import tariffs were raised from 16.5 per cent to 85 per cent *ad valorem* for calicoes, and from 18 per cent to 44 per cent for muslins, all during Ricardo's own lifetime, because many categories of these Asian handwoven fabrics stubbornly remained cheaper, even taking landed cost, than English machine-made cloth as late as 1813.[1] These duties were reduced over time as unit production costs of machine-made yarn and cloth fell further after 1820 (two tables of tariffs and duties on Asian cloth up to 1832 are given in Dutt 1970: 203)[2] but they still lasted for 70 years after 1775, the last tariffs not going until 1846. Conversely, the Asian colonies, like all other colonies, were compulsorily and completely trade liberalized throughout the period.

So abnormal was this prolonged, 150-year regime of metropolitan protectionism and colonial managed free trade, that one can hardly put it forward as an example of Ricardian 'neutral' technological advantage working quite independently of political power. Incidentally, most leading historians of Britain's Industrial Revolution (Deane and Cole 1969; Hobsbawm 1969) and historians of technical change in cotton textiles (Landes 1969) blandly ignore the economic effects of 150 years of protectionism in the form of import bans followed by high tariffs. Yet, the import ban on Asian textiles, lasting for three-quarters of a century must have greatly raised the profitability of potential import substitution, and provided the temporal climate conducive to the repeated, often abortive, experiments with technical innovations, which produced workable machines decades after they were first initiated (thirty years passed between the first experimental spinning jenny of 1735 and the Hargreaves jenny of 1765). The history of prolonged British protectionism against lower-cost Asian textiles is also ignored completely in their papers – there is not a single reference to the matter either in text or index – by the historians of Asia writing in the *Cambridge Economic History of India* (1984),[3] who imitatively follow their mentors' biased analysis of the subject. They attribute the decline of Indian cotton manufactures exports to Britain, followed by a rise in primary exports like raw cotton, to Ricardian 'comparative advantage' – fallaciously, as we have seen, since comparative cost could not be defined at all for Britain which could not produce raw cotton – and they make no reference at all to Britain's systematic commercial policy excluding competition from Asian manufactured goods. The Ricardian fallacy has cast a long shadow and continues to subvert correct analysis nearly two centuries after it was first formulated.

The 'technology' route for rescuing Ricardo does not work. The fatal flaw in his theory remains. Rather than confronting the fallacy in Ricardo's argument arising from its untenable assumption that both goods are produced in both countries, modern mainstream theory too has tried to hide it by ignoring it altogether. Paul Samuelson, in his paper titled 'Market Mechanisms and Maximization' (Samuelson 1970), discusses Ricardo's model of comparative cost in linear programming terms. Samuelson continues to treat it as a general theory and ignores its limited applicability arising from the crucial assumption of both countries producing both goods. Fudging the argument is continued but in a different manner. Without discussing his reason for doing so, Samuelson substitutes 'food' for the 'wine' of Ricardo's example in both the diagram and the text, while retaining unchanged the other good, cloth. Since 'food' can be produced in both England and Portugal, the immediate logical problem with Ricardo's own example is overcome.

But such silent fudging does not do away with the real-life problem, that a very large segment of world trade simply does not fit into the assumption of the model, which therefore is *not* a general theory of trade as is claimed. Having altered Ricardo's own example and thereby shown that he understood the problem, Samuelson should have mentioned why the comparative cost theory with its 'mutual benefit' conclusion could not be applied to trade between countries which have qualitatively different output vectors – in particular, to trade between advanced countries and developing tropical countries. But such a conclusion would go against the entire thrust of modern normative trade theory, whose proposition on 'free trade' being necessarily beneficial for all parties is such a useful rationalization for continuing to pursue trade policies that are in reality welfare-enhancing for advanced countries at the expense of welfare reduction for developing countries.

The longevity of the fallacious comparative advantage theory *as a general theory of trade* is to be understood, we believe, in terms of the important *apologetic function* it continues to play in the modern world. By positing necessary mutual benefit from all trade without exception – thereby tacitly including trade between advanced countries and developing countries – the theory helps to intellectually rationalize and justify all those past and present actually existing trade patterns that have been in fact the outcome of the asymmetric exercise of economic and political power, and which have served to widen the economic distance between nations. Generations of teachers of economics in both the advanced and the developing countries have taught an incorrect theory, and generations of intelligent students have uncritically reproduced this incorrect theory, in our assessment, largely owing to their subjection to the *intellectual hegemony* exercised by conservative Northern mainstream theory. These fallacious arguments have been criticized by a very few, individual exceptions to the rule of uncritical advocacy of generalized free trade.[4]

Notes

[1] E. Baines, *History of the Cotton Manufactures in Great Britain,* quoted in Mantoux (1970: 256, fn. 3).

[2] From the Minutes of Evidence & c., On the Affairs of the East India Company (1813: 153), quoted by H.H. Wilson in James Mill, *History of India, Wilson's Continuation Book 1,* Chapter 7.

[3] Notably, Morris D. Morris and K.N. Chaudhuri. For a brief critique of the analysis in the *Cambridge Economic History of India,* Vol. 2, see Patnaik (1984).

[4] Our list may not be complete, but writers since 1950 would include Ralph Davis (1979), Joan V. Robinson (1975), Paul Baran (1973) and Andre Gunder Frank (1971).

References

Austen, Jane (1992), *Pride and Prejudice* (London: Wordsworth Edition).

Baran, Paul (1973), *The Political Economy of Growth* (London: Pelican Books).

Boxer, Charles R. (1973), *The Portuguese Seaborne Empire, 1415–1825* (Harmondsworth: Pelican Books).

Chaudhuri, K.N. (1984), 'Foreign Trade and the Balance of Payments', in Kumar and Desai, eds, *The Cambridge Economic History of India,* Vol. 2.

Davis, Ralph (1966), 'The Rise of Protection in England 1689–1786', *Economic History Review,* 2nd Series, 19: 306–17.

――― (1979), *The Industrial Revolution and British Overseas Trade* (Leicester: Leicester University Press).

Deane, Phyliss and W.A. Cole (1969), *British Economic Growth 1688–1959: Trends and Structure,* 2nd edn (Cambridge: Cambridge University Press).

Hobsbawm, Eric. J. (1969), *Industry and Empire* (Harmondsworth: Penguin Books).

Kumar, Dharma and M. Desai, eds (1984), *The Cambridge Economic History of India,* Vol. 2, c.1757–c.1970 (Delhi: Orient Longman in association with Cambridge University Press).

Dutt, R.C. (1970), *The Economic History of India, Vol. I: Under Early British Rule 1757–1837* (New Delhi: Publications Division, Government of India); reprinted by Routledge and Kegan Paul, London.

Encyclopaedia Britannica (1984), Macropaedia, Vol. II.

Frank, A.G. (1971), *Capitalism and Underdevelopment in Latin America* (Harmondsworth: Pelican Books).

Landes, D.S. (1969), *The Unbound Prometheus: Technological Change and Industrial Development in Western Europe from 1750 to the Present* (Cambridge: Cambridge University Press).

Mantoux, Paul (1970), *The Industrial Revolution in the 18ᵗʰ Century* (London: Methuen); first published in Marjorie Vernon's English Translation in 1928 by Cape, London.

Morris, D.M. (1984), 'The Growth of Large Scale Industry to 1947', in Kumar and Desai, eds, *The Cambridge Economic History of India, Vol. 2*.

Patnaik, Utsa (1984), 'Tribute Transfer and the Balance of Payments in the *Cambridge Economic History of India*, Vol. II', *Social Scientist*, 12 (12); reprinted in Utsa Patnaik (1999), *The Long Transition: Essays on Political Economy* (New Delhi: Tulika Books).

———— (2003), 'On the Inverse Relation between Primary Exports and Food Absorption in Developing Countries under Liberalized Trade Regimes', in Jayati Ghosh and C.P. Chandrasekhar, eds, *Work and Well-being in the Age of Finance* (New Delhi: Tulika Books).

Ricardo, David ([1821] 1951), *On the Principles of Political Economy and Taxation*, edited by Pierro Sraffa with the collaboration of M.H. Dobb, in *The Works and Correspondence of David Ricardo*, Vol. 1 (Cambridge: Cambridge University Press).

Robinson, J.V. (1975), *Collected Economic Papers*, Vol. 5 (Oxford: Basil Blackwell).

Samuelson, P.A. (1970), 'Market Mechanisms and Maximization', in *The Collected Scientific Papers of P.A. Samuelson* (New Delhi: Oxford University Press).

Smith, Adam ([1776] 1922), *An Inquiry into the Nature and Causes of the Wealth of Nations*, edited by Edwin Cannan, 3ʳᵈ edn (London: Methuen).

Friedrich List and the Infant Industry Argument

Mehdi Shafaeddin

> . . . restrictions are but means, and liberty, in its proper sense, is an end.
>
> Friedrich List (1856: 64)

Schumpeter discussed the concept of development in the early twentieth century. His usage of the term was in the context of 'entrepreneurship' in microeconomics (Schumpeter 1961, particularly Chapter 2: 63–66, 74). However, the concept of economic development as used currently emerged after the World War II, following the publication of 'Problems of Industrialization of Eastern and South-Eastern Europe' by Rosenstein–Rodan (1943). For about a decade after the war, concepts such as 'underdevelopment' and 'underdeveloped countries' – as against 'advanced countries' and industrialized countries – were often used in the literature. During the 1950s, the concept of 'economic development' was advanced by such scholars as Hans Singer, Michal Kalecki, Arthur Lewis, Albert O. Hirschman, Gunnar Myrdal, Paul Streeten, Dudley Seers, Jacob Viner and Gottfried Haberler. Starting from the mid-1940s, industrialization of the 'late-comers', rather than 'economic development', was discussed by scholars interested in issues related to growth and catching up by countries dependent on agriculture and other primary commodities. Industrial countries were regarded as 'advanced', while 'progress' and development meant industrialization.

Friedrich List was the first to deal with the problems of industrialization of the late-comers in a comprehensive manner. He was not an economist by training, but a political scientist and journalist. Being concerned with industrialization of the 'late-comers' of his time, Germany and the USA, he developed and formulated the 'infant industry argument' as a significant challenge to the classical theory of international trade, that is, the theory of comparative (cost) advantage. His infant industry argument has been the basis of most new trade theories for the industrialization of developing countries. This argument has also been significant as a tool of policy-making. With the exception of Hong Kong, no country has developed its industrial base without resorting to infant industry protection. Both the early and newly industrialized countries applied the same principle, although to varying degrees and in different ways (Shafaeddin 1998; Chang 2002). Moreover, List's writings reveal that his theory was more than an 'infant industry argument', as he refers to the concept of 'productive power', which is close to what is currently regarded as the theory of 'economic development'.

List was strongly influenced by Alexander Hamilton, Henry Carey, Henry Clay and Daniel Raymon in the United States. He developed their ideas and presented them in the form of a theory. Yet, his contribution is largely ignored in the literature on the history of economic thought.[1] With this silence from eminent historians of economic thought, it is not altogether surprising that the writings of Friedrich List on infant industry have often been misinterpreted or misrepresented.

The infant industry literature is indeed replete with fallacies and confusion. It is sometimes regarded as being against free trade, or even international trade in general. It is often envisaged as synonymous with import substitution, which is, in turn, perceived as a strategy opposed to export orientation (for example, Little, Scitovsky and Scott 1970; Krueger 1978). Some limit the infant industry argument to production for the domestic market; others think that it should be applied across the board to the manufacturing sector as a whole, rather than on a selective basis (Greenaway and Milner 1993; Corden 1974: 260). Some others believe that List's infant industry argument is not applicable to small countries (Cronin 1980: 118). Finally, the failure of import substitution policies is often unjustifiably attributed to deficiencies in the theory of infant industry protection (Krueger 1978); as a result, many scholars and policy-makers argue that infant industry protection has failed and that the answer is the polar opposite – a policy of universal and across-the-board trade liberalization.

The purpose of this chapter is to clarify some of these issues by referring to List's original writings. After a brief review of the origins of the idea of infant industry protection that was initiated in the USA, we will discuss List's elaboration of those ideas which he presented to justify his theory of 'productive power' (economic development) as against the international trade theory of Adam Smith.

The modalities of implementation and the neglected features of List's theory – including his views on the importance of international trade, the ultimate goal of free trade and exports of manufactured goods – are discussed next. The subsequent section looks at the problems of industrialization of small economies before reviewing how List's theory was based on experience. The concluding remarks assert the applicability of List's infant industry argument in modern conditions.

Origins of the Argument: Alexander Hamilton, the Pioneer

The infant industry argument was a reaction to uneven industrial development following the first Industrial Revolution, when continental Europe and the United States of America fell behind Great Britain. According to List (1856: 69–70), 'the modern protectionist school of thought was actually born in the United States', and 'it was also the mother country and the bastion of modern protectionism'. The protectionist lobby was so strong in the USA in the nineteenth century that a Pennsylvania legislator referred to 'man' as 'an animal that makes tariff speeches' (Bairoch 1993: 23, 30). The first US Tariff Act to contain elements of protectionism was passed in 1789. The law imposed import duties on thirty-eight items, but raw materials were exempted and duty drawbacks were granted for all commodities re-exported within twelve months (Ashley 1920: 134–35). Whether or not that Tariff Act was protectionist in nature is disputed because, for over a century, between then and 1916, over twenty-five tariff Acts were passed for revenue purposes (ibid.: 138).[2]

The intellectual origin of the infant industry argument is attributable to Alexander Hamilton (1757–1804), the first US Secretary of Treasury (Hamilton 1791: 178–236). He initiated a debate on industrialization and argued for the protection of US industries vis-à-vis imports from Great Britain, when he made his famous *Report on Manufactures* to the US Congress in 1791. Hamilton maintained that international trade was not free; that Europe was more advanced in manufacturing and its industries enjoyed governmental support, and that such support destroys new industries in other countries (ibid.: 205). Hence, if the US pursued free trade, it would suffer from 'unequal exchange' because competition with established manufactures of other nations on equal terms would be impracticable (ibid.: 201, 204–05). Therefore, 'it is for the United States to consider by what means they can render themselves least dependent on the combinations, right or wrong, of foreign policy' (ibid.: 202).

Drawing on the successful experiences of other countries, Hamilton proposed a system of protective duties, prohibition and pecuniary bounties as a means of *temporary* infant industry protection (ibid.: 234–76). More importantly, he explicitly proposed a system of selective protection, that is, a system of premiums targeted at 'particular excellence or superiority, some extraordinary exertion or skill . . . in a small number of cases' (ibid.: 242–43). In such a system, imported inputs would be exempted from duties, except in a few cases. Further, the government would control the quality of goods produced and facilitate transportation. In selecting industries for protection, he proposed five criteria:

> The capacity of the country to furnish the raw materials; the degree in which the nature of the manufacture admits of a substitute for manual labour in machinery [allowing increases in labour productivity]; the facility of execution [technological access]; the extensiveness of the uses to which the articles can be applied [the extent of domestic market linkages]; its subserviency to other interests, particularly the great one of national defence [strategic nature of the product]. (ibid.: 249).

After proposing a list of such articles, Hamilton also drew attention to the need for government intervention in some other areas in the process of industrialization, particularly to encourage inventions and to promote institutions considered necessary for industrialization. In his view, the role of the government was complementary to that of the private sector, and significant at the early stages of industrialization when the financial capacity of the private sector is limited.[3]

It is true that Hamilton influenced politicians to favour protection. However, two main factors contributed to the practice of protection initiated later with the Tariff Act of 1816. One was the unification of the USA, which began in the late 1770s and was completed in 1800, making it possible to adopt unified trade policies vis-à-vis other countries. The other was the breaking out of war between France and Britain in the early nineteenth century, which reduced the supply and increased the price of imported manufactures to the USA (Kenwood and Lougheed 1994: 69). Further, the Anglo–American war of 1812–14 required a drastic increase in US government revenue. Hence import duties on most items were increased while imports of some items were prohibited. Such changes in trade policy stimulated domestic industry, particularly in the case of wool processing, cotton textiles, iron, glass and pottery (Ashley 1920: 140–44).

List, who lived in the United States between 1825 and 1830, was strongly influenced by the debate on protection at that time, and published his *Outlines of American Political Economy* in 1827. This book, which was a collection of his published articles in the American press, covered his basic ideas.[4] His more comprehensive argument for infant industry protection is contained in the book titled *National System of Political Economy*, published in German in 1841. Its first English translation appeared in 1856 in the USA. This later book was written in haste for the purpose of participating in a competition in France; therefore, he did not express his ideas well in it (Henderson 1983). Nevertheless, the outstanding and innovative aspect of List's infant industry argument, which distinguishes it from previous contributions to the debate, is that it was formulated in a wider context of development rather than as an instrument of trade policy. He vigorously used tools of economic analysis to develop his ideas (Schumpeter 1952). Thus, although many had argued in favour of protection before him, 'List offered his readers much more than a repetition of the familiar arguments put forward by these writers' (Henderson 1983: 158), as will be explained shortly.

As developed by List, the infant industry argument is based on the following principles.[5] First, countries go through five stages of development: (i) the savage stage; (ii) the pastoral stage; (iii) the agricultural stage; (iv) the agricultural and manufacturing stage; and (v) the agricultural, manufacturing and commercial [services] stage.[6] Second, in order to progress, countries must transit from stage (iii) to stages (iv) and (v). Third, such transitions do not take place automatically by relying on market forces. To do so, infant industry protection is necessary for countries at stage (iii) if some other countries are at higher stages of development. Fourth, protection should be temporary and confined to the manufacturing sector; agriculture should not be protected. Finally, List's theoretical perspective extends far beyond the infant industry argument as he considers infant industry protection as one of several instruments for promoting the 'productive power' – economic development – of a nation.

Justification: Productive Power versus Free Trade

To justify his theory as against Adam Smith's theory of comparative cost advantage, List emphasized the differences between national and universal interests, introduced the concept of 'productive power' vis-à-vis universal free trade, and concentrated on differences in the levels of industrialization of various countries. We will discuss each of these issues briefly.

National and Universal Interests

The main point of List's departure from Adam Smith's theory of international trade is philosophical. Smith (1776, Book II, Chapter V) does not make any distinction between the interests of individuals, nations and mankind at large. According to him, by seeking their own interests, individuals also preserve the interests of society as a whole. List, by contrast, considers the interests of mankind at three different levels: individual, national and universal. The economy of individuals is different from the national economy, which is, in turn, different from the cosmopolitan economy, that is, the economy of mankind. To List, the sum of individual interests is not necessarily equal to the national interest, that is, social interests may diverge from private interests (List 1856: 74, 245, 261).[7] Further, individuals may not take into account the security and defence of the nation, and, as a nation consists of successive generations, an individual's interest may not coincide with the interest of future generations (ibid.: 245–46).

Adam Smith overlooks the national interest by only arguing for the maximization of global welfare (ibid.: vi). For List, some nations may give more weight to their own welfare, rather than to the collective interest of humanity; if so, those nations would be more interested in the expansion of the productive forces of the country than in maximizing the welfare of humanity at large through free trade:

> As long as some nations will persist in regarding their special interests as of greater value to them than the collective interests of humanity, it must be folly to speak of unrestricted competition between individuals of different nations. The arguments of the School in favour of competition are then applicable only to the relations between inhabitants of the same country. (ibid. 261).

Adam Smith (1776) developed his universal theory of international trade (absolute comparative cost advantage) with the interests of Britain in mind, and advocated free trade.[8] List argued that free trade was in the interest of Britain after it had developed its industrial base through infant industry support:

> A country like England which is far in advance of all its competitors cannot better maintain and extend its manufacturing and commercial industry than by a trade as free as possible from all restrictions. For such a country, the cosmopolitan and the national principle are one and the same thing. This explains the favour with which the most enlightened economists of England regard free

trade, and the reluctance of the wise and prudent of other countries to adopt this principle in the actual state of the world.[9] (List 1856: 79)

Jacob Viner (1953: 4–5) correctly maintains that Smith and other classical economists took a cosmopolitan approach because they thought that what was in the interest of England was also in the interest of the world as a whole. But, Viner argues, what was relevant to their time and country may not necessarily be relevant for other times and other countries, and, in particular, may not be relevant for 'economically less advanced countries' at any time. Hence, 'it is today always necessary, as it was for the English classical economists, to be perfectly clear whether we are considering a problem, say, commercial policy, from a national or from a cosmopolitan point of view' (ibid.: 5).

Productive Power and Development

List was not, by any means, against universal association, but argued that although 'nature leads nations gradually to the highest degree of association . . . the association of nations, by means of trade, is even yet very imperfect'. Hence, 'to preserve, to develop, and to improve itself as a nation is consequently, at present, and ever must be, the principal object of a nation's efforts' (List 1856: 70–71).

> That insane doctrine [*laissez faire, laissez passer*] which sacrifices the interests of agriculture and manufacturing industry to the pretensions of commerce – to the claims of absolute free trade, is the natural offspring of a theory too fully occupied with values, and too little with productive power, and which regards the whole world as simply a republic of merchants, one and indivisible. (ibid.: 341)

Thus, considering the nature of human association at the national and cosmopolitan levels with different perspectives, List put forward his 'theory of productive power' (economic development). He proposed this theory for the development of the national economy as against the theory of interchangeable value (international trade) of Adam Smith, designed for the cosmopolitan economy. He emphasized that 'the objective [of a given nation] is not to increase directly by means of commercial restrictions the sum of exchangeable values in a country, but its productive power' (ibid.: 253).

List's theory of productive power goes far beyond international trade. In modern economic terms, this theory is similar to the theory of 'capability-building' in the context of state-directed economic development (Lall 1991). In fact, it is a multidisciplinary theory: the productive power of a nation depends not only on economic factors, but also on socio-economic, institutional, intellectual and moral factors, and on its independence and power as a nation.[10]

Interpreting List, Levi–Fauer (1997: 157) argues that three kinds of capital contribute to 'productive power': natural capital (natural resources), material capital (machinery, equipment, etc.) and mental capital ('human capital'). In contrast to Adam Smith, List believed that 'mental capital' (human capital) is more important than material capital. It is acquired through experience, education and training, and is the most important source of wealth. When a country exports a manufactured good in exchange for a (primary) commodity, the exporter country maximizes its productive power because it augments its mental capital (experience) while at the same time putting pressure on the productive power of the commodity exporter. In this sense protection is effectively an educational tax. Protection of some industrial products will eventually enable the primary commodity exporter to exchange mental capital for mental capital, not matter for matter, as it develops its industrial export capabilities (ibid.: 166).

According to List, mental capital is determined by 'social order', meaning a combination of socio-political and institutional factors such as a 'high moral culture among individuals, legal security of the citizens in their personal affairs and properties, free exercise of their moral and physical faculties' (List 1856: 211). It also involves regulating and facilitating trade, and suppressing all restraints upon industry, liberty, intelligence and morality, such as feudal institutions (ibid.: 76). Accumulation of discoveries, inventions and experience is the intellectual capital of the living race of man and a nation (ibid.: 223). List also refers to other sources of productive power, such as the importance of science, art (ibid.: 212), liberty of thought and conscience, transparency of judicial decisions, law enforcement, control of government by the public, local administration of towns (decentralization and participation), liberty of press, freedom of association (ibid.: 216–17), government policies (Senghaas 1989), large populations (see below), political power and division of labour (List 1856: 223).

List's theory of development is different from that of Smith not only in his wider definition of capital but also on the role of 'division of labour'. According to Smith, division of labour and accumulation of capital are two inter-related factors which are primary *causes* of development: accumulation of capital is a precondition for division of labour, and division of labour in turn leads to further capital accumulation and economic development. For List, in contrast, the direction of causation is the opposite: division of labour and accumulation of (material) capital are characteristic *results* of development, rather than its causes. Mental capital is the most important cause of development. Therefore, it is the role of the state to develop a system of education to educate and mobilize the masses (Levi–Fauer 1997: 158–60).

List further distinguishes between 'objective' and 'subjective' division of labour. In objective division of labour, a person allocates time to perform different tasks during a day. In subjective division of labour, a number of people work to produce an object. Division of labour – whether among individuals in a firm or among enterprises within the manufacturing sector – in a nation involves association of (cooperation among) different individuals or enterprises who work in combination, requiring cooperation and coordination (List 1856: 229–31).[11] List also discusses the need for association between sectors of the economy under one political power (ibid.: 232). National division of labour (for example, for agricultural production) requires a sophisticated system of communication, infrastructure and transport to exchange the surplus of each region with that of others. Hence, division of labour should be accompanied by a sense of national unity, independence, common goals and cooperation of productive forces, requiring involvement of the state in the process of development (ibid.: 74). However, List did not believe in over-regulation, arguing that when productive forces can 'better regulate themselves [through the market] and can be better promoted by private exertion', the government should avoid interference (Levi–Fauer 1997: 171).

Countries at Different Industrial Levels

For List, free trade was suitable for advanced countries such as England after it developed its industrial base, as mentioned earlier. By contrast, for countries not yet industrialized, industrialization would only become possible through free trade if all countries were at the same (low) level of development.[12] When countries are not at the same level of industrialization, protection of infant industries, List argued, is essential to enhance the *productive power* of a nation with a low industrial base (List 1856: 394). As put by Senghaas (1989), the existence of a 'competence gap' among nations would require infant industry protection by nations in inferior positions if they were to catch up. It was for this reason that List cast doubts on Adam Smith's doctrine of free trade:

> It [the principle of adopting free trade by a nation which has fallen behind in industrialization] seemed to me at first reasonable; but gradually I satisfied myself that the whole doctrine was applicable and sound only when adopted by all nations. Thus, I was led to the idea of nationality; I found that the theorists kept always in view mankind and man, never separate nations. It became then obvious to me that between two advanced nations, a free competition must necessarily be advantageous to both *if they were upon the same level of industrial progress*; and that a nation unhappily far behind as to industry, commerce and navigation must above everything put forth all its strength to sustain a *struggle with nations already in advance*. (List 1856: v–vi; emphasis added)

To support his infant industry argument, List provided a number of justifications, in the language of the time, in different parts of his book. His reasoning may be regarded as a basis for the modern theory of infant industry protection, in which more technical terms are applied, in at least in three respects. First, industrialization in countries with little or no experience in manufacturing will not take place according 'to the natural course of things' in the face of foreign competition (ibid.: 378, 394). In other words, the market fails to promote rapid industrialization in these countries.

Second, since the establishment of new industries involves great risk, the producer has to be provided with extra incentives to enter the industry. If the industry is open to foreign competition at the early stages of its development, it will be ruined (ibid.: 81, 248, 252, 378). Protection of domestic industry and the resulting monopoly would permit eventual reduction in costs and prices allowed by exploitation of the domestic market (ibid.: 378). Eventually, the gradual introduction of domestic competition would safeguard the interests of consumers (ibid.: 113). Although List does not use the term economies of scale, the concept is implied in the above argument.[13] Interestingly, he was also aware of the role of effective demand in realizing scale economies (ibid.: 383).

Third, List's emphasis on the importance of 'industrial training or education of the country as a whole' (ibid.: 68, 77–78) implies, in modern economic jargon, the role of dynamic external economies of learning in industrialization. In fact, while List does not specifically discuss externalities – understandably, because the term was not common in his time – this notion appears on several occasions in his writings. For example, he refers to experience, knowledge and relation (linkages) of certain industries with the rest of the economy as important criteria for choosing industries for protection (ibid.: 69). These are all externalities regarded as arguments for the modern version of infant industry protection, as already mentioned (see Corden 1974: Chapter 9).

Modalities of Implementation

Throughout his book, List emphasizes a few points on the modalities of protection, to which little attention has been paid by critics of the infant industry argument. These points may be grouped into seven categories, as follows. First, List regards regulation of import duties and subsidies as one but not the only means of government intervention in favour of industrialization.

Second, he recommends 'protection of manufacturing products on a selective and discriminatory rather than a universal basis'. He explicitly states that 'it is not necessary that *all branches of industry* be equally protected' (List 1856: 266; emphasis added). His reference to 'all branches of industry' might easily be misinterpreted but it is clear from the context of the argument that what List had in mind is all those branches of industry which are chosen for protection at a given moment in time. For example, he refers to certain industrial products for protection when he mentions the choice of industries that produce 'articles of general consumption' at the beginning of industrialization (ibid.: 388). Within this category, he specifies industries that 'require large capital . . . general knowledge, much dexterity and experience', and linkages with other industries. If he had meant general protection of all industries, he would not have specified individual industries.[14]

Third, List's theory is dynamic. Once the protected industries have been developed, others can be chosen for protection, and the degree of protection needed in their case could be lower. By 'other' industries, he does not mean just any industry but, rather, those with forward and backward linkages. 'When these [chosen industries] are suitably appreciated and developed, other branches of less importance grow up *round them* even with less protection' (ibid.: 267; emphasis added). List clearly excludes certain industries from protection in the early stages:

'Industries of luxury should not receive attention until in the last phase' (ibid.: 392).

To make his case for 'selectivity' at different points in time, List refers to the experience of England, explaining how this country started industrializing with the processing of domestically produced raw materials, flax, wool, cotton, silk, cloth and iron, and later deepened its industrial structure by moving to industries such as fisheries, metals, leather, etc. (ibid.: 112).[15]

Fourth, protection should not only be temporary, but its level should also not be excessive so as to eliminate competition from abroad or too low so as to kill the infant industry with foreign competition (ibid.: 79). As it often takes a long time to develop the industrial base of a country (ibid.: 373, 398), protective duties should be introduced in moderation and 'raised by degrees in proportion as intellectual and material capital, skill in the arts and the spirit of enterprise increase in the country' (ibid.: 266). 'All excessive and premature protection is expiated by a diminution of national prosperity' (ibid.: 78). List also advocates that the scale of protective duties should be determined in advance so that producers might be assured of 'safe business' (ibid.: 389).

Fifth, List holds that theory cannot determine the level of protection, and that no general rules for protection can be drawn. The specific conditions of the country concerned should be taken into account: 'everything depends on the circumstances and the relations between the less and the more advanced country' (ibid.: 390). Nevertheless, he advances some propositions on the minimum conditions necessary for the success of infant industry protection and the appropriate level of duties, and stresses that not all countries have the necessary conditions for industrialization.

> As a general rule, it may be said that a country in which a branch of manufacture cannot succeed with the aid of a protection of from forty to sixty per cent, at the beginning, and sustained itself afterwards with twenty or thirty, does not possess the essential conditions for development of a manufacturing industry. (ibid.: 79, 390)

He further suggests that there are a number of necessary conditions for industrialization: a certain level of development of the 'forces of production', a large population and moderate climate zones. States in hot zones 'ought to specialize in the provision of foodstuffs and agricultural raw materials' (Senghaas 1989: 65). His logic on climate is not clear, however, and recent experience of East Asian countries has shown that tropical countries have managed to industrialize successfully.

Sixth, List advocates that duties should either not be imposed on imports of raw material and intermediate goods or they should be subject to low duties. In the event they are imposed, he envisages a system of drawbacks for duties on raw materials or intermediate goods, giving the example of cotton yarn (List 1856: 392). He adds that few or no duties should be imposed on capital goods in the early stages of industrialization, when the country still lacks industrial capacity. Such duties could, however, be introduced later, when the 'country shall not be inferior in the construction of machines to the most skilful nation' (ibid.: 392).

Finally, List is well aware of the danger of 'monopoly' power arising from protection but maintains that it will decline, first with the gradual introduction of domestic competition and eventually with trade liberalization. He adds that absolute privilege should be provided 'neither for the benefit of producers nor for the detriment of consumers' by leaving a protected industry in the hands of monopolists (ibid.: 251–52, 460). Pressure should be applied on protected firms, through domestic competition, in exchange for incentives provided through protection – a policy that was later practised in Japan and East Asia (Amsden 1989). (The x-efficiency theory also advocated a similar policy towards firms, a century after *National System of Political Economy* was published.)

With respect to extending protection to the consumers, List argues that such costs should be incurred to obtain long-term benefits from protection in terms of higher productive capacity and lower prices. It was on the basis of this argument that Bastable (1903) presented his conditions for protection. According to him, the discounted social costs of protection during the initial period should be over-offset by its discounted social benefits in the subsequent period when protection is removed. In practice, of course, there are considerable problems of quantification in any attempt to measure such costs and benefits.

Neglected Features of List's Argument

List's infant industry argument has several features not appreciated, or misinterpreted, in the literature. We have discussed some of these in the previous pages. Nevertheless, it is worth putting together the neglected features of List's theory. First, he advocates temporary protection for any particular nation in the context of his proposal for a dynamic trade policy over time (List 1856: 133). At low levels of development free trade would contribute, *inter alia,* to the development of agriculture; at a later stage, import restrictions would give an impulse to manufacture and commerce; eventually, at some point in time, trade liberalization, and ultimately free trade, could be adopted.

> After having reached the highest degree of skill, wealth and power, by a *gradual return* to the principle of free trade and free competition in their own and foreign markets, they keep their agriculture from inaction, their manufactures and their merchants from indolence, and stimulate them to wholesome activity, [in order] that they maintain the supremacy which they have acquired. (ibid.: 188; emphasis added)

Second, in proposing a commercial policy one should, List asserts, take into account the particular situation of the nation and its industry, and prevailing conditions at each point in time (ibid.: 392). 'The measure it [political economy in matters of international commerce] advises must be appropriate to the want of our time, to special conditions of each people' (ibid.: 63). For example, it is not possible to draw a general rule as to whether one should apply a system of absolute (quantitative) prohibition of certain products, or of import duties, high or moderate (ibid.: 386). Similarly, the specific conditions of a country should be taken into account when choosing the type of goods to be protected, and the speed of protection or liberalization (ibid.: 389–92).

Third, List also strongly warns against premature and rapid liberalization of the import system (ibid.: 388). 'Every manufacture ruined by the [premature] reduction or withdrawal of protection, and specially by a governmental measure, is a dead body so exposed as to injure every living industry of the same kind' (ibid.: 69). In this context, he refers to the unfortunate experience of the United States, which had been induced, at one point, to prematurely open its ports to the manufactures of England after the country had experienced rapid growth under the protection system (ibid.: 62).[16] At the same time, he warns countries of the damage caused by prolonged and unnecessarily high levels of protection.

Fourth, for List, infant industry protection should eventually lead to massive exports of manufactured products. According to him, there are four phases in the development of international trade and industrialization. In the first phase, domestic agriculture is encouraged by imports of manufactured goods and exports of agricultural products. In the second phase, while imports of manufactured goods continue, domestic production of these products begins with the help of protection. In the third phase, home manufacturers supply the domestic market. In the final phase, exports of manufactured goods take place on a large scale. The entire process, however, is slow and gradual, since it involves 'industrial education' (ibid.: 77).

Fifth, and most importantly, List was not, by any means, against international trade or in favour of autarchy. On the contrary, his ideas on the importance of trade for development, by and large, were similar to those of Mill ([1948] 1965). 'International trade by rousing activity and energy, by the new wants it creates, by the propagation among nations of new ideas and discoveries, and by the diffusion of power, is one of the mightiest instruments of civilization, and one of the most powerful agencies in promoting national prosperity' (List 1856: 70–71). The distinguishing feature of his approach was his stress on the idea that trade is only an instrument – and not an end – of development. The ultimate end is progress, development and independence: 'To preserve, to develop, and to improve itself as a nation is consequently, at present, and ever must be, the principal object of a nation's effort' (ibid.: 70). It was in this context that he referred, for example, to the need for a domestic supply of machinery during war as a strategic consideration (ibid.: 392, 267–68).

The gist of List's argument is that restrictions are a means to development, independence and, ultimately, liberty and free trade: 'Restrictions are but means . . . and liberty in its proper sense is the end' (ibid.: 64). However, he stresses that 'liberty should not be reached without carrying human welfare with it' (ibid.: xi). 'The system of import duties is . . . a natural consequence of the tendency of nations to seek for guarantees of their existence and prosperity, and to establish and increase their weight in scale of national influence' (ibid.: 73). He claims that progress and development would lead to universal association, and free trade ultimately, in so far as nations have reached the same degree of culture and power (ibid.: 71).[17] Schumpeter later noted: 'List's argument about protection issues into free-trade argument: if this is not obvious, we can convince ourselves of it by noticing the fact that J.S. Mill accepted the infant industry theory (see below), evidently realizing that it ran within the free-trade logic' (Schumpeter 1952: 505).

Market Size

List was aware of the limitations of the infant industry argument in the case of small countries, owing to the small size of their markets. Nevertheless, he argued that, even for small countries, development of manufacturing was important if the surplus labour from agriculture was to be absorbed in order to prevent starvation of the expanding population (Yaffey 1998). In fact, he attributed the great Irish famine of the 1840s to mainly the lack of industrialization and over-population on small-holdings in the countryside (ibid.).

List proposed a number of ways in which a country could remedy the problem of size through alliance with other countries, small or large. For example, he argued in favour of the German *Zollverein*, a customs union of German-speaking cities. Referring to countries such as Belgium, Denmark, Holland and Hungary, he proposed 'the union of the interest of various states by means of free conventions' (ibid.: 99);[18] in other words, regional integration through customs union. Only if no solution could be found to resolve the size problem through alliance with other countries, 'did List prescribe that a country should give up hope of pursuing it [national system] and hope for the best in the world market' (ibid.: 98).

The issue of size as a limiting factor should not be exaggerated. Undoubtedly, large size is essential for industries that involve significant economies of scale. Nevertheless, unless the market is very small, the development of at least some efficient medium- or small-sized industries should be possible. This could include, for example, production of goods demanded by the public at large, such as food processing, clothing, etc. The experience of small countries like Switzerland indicate that industrialization of certain lines of production through initial protection is almost always feasible.

Theory and History

List was proud that his theory was primarily based on history and experience, rather than on unrealistic assumptions. He states that 'political economy in matters of international commerce must draw its lessons from experience' (ibid.: 63). To him, history does not provide justification for absolute freedom of international trade in all circumstances, as advocated by the classical school (ibid.: 394). In fact, he begins his first book by reviewing the history of the commercial policies of Italy, the Hanseatic cities, Flanders, Holland, Spain, Portugal, France, Germany, Russia, and, in particular, the United States and Britain. In the particular case of Britain, he argues that 'Great Britain borrowed from all the countries of the continent their special arts and gave them a home under the shelter of her protective system' (ibid.: 113); but that 'Theorists have since [early 1700] pretended that England has become rich and powerful, not on account, but in spite of, her commercial [protective] policy' (ibid.: 114). He adds that it was only after developing its industries under protection that England attempted to secure foreign markets through the Navigation Act, and advocated free trade for other countries (ibid.: 14–17).

In formulating his ideas on the merits of infant industry protection, it was above all the US experience that List saw as providing the most valuable lessons. There he was able to observe at first hand a country that was securing gradual industrialization and development under a system of regulation of foreign trade and government intervention in the economy: 'The best book on Political Economy in that country [the United States] is the volume of life; that book I have read earnestly and assiduously, and lessons drawn from it I have tried to compare and arrange with the results of my previous studies, experience, and reflections' (ibid.: xi–xii).

Before concluding this chapter, it is worth mentioning that among the classical economists, only J.S. Mill fully endorsed the infant industry argument. Alfred Marshall did not object to it but was not as supportive of it as Mill. In the following passage, though brief and lacking in detail, Mill is strikingly reminiscent of List's reasoning:

> The only case in which, on mere principles of political economy, protecting duties can be defensible, is when they are imposed temporarily (especially in a young and rising nation) in hopes of naturalizing a foreign industry, in itself perfectly suitable to the circumstances of the country. The superiority of one country over another in a branch of production often arises only from having begun it sooner. There may be no inherent advantage on one part, or disadvantage on the other, but only a present superiority of acquired skill and experience. A country which has this skill and experience yet to acquire, may in other respects be better adapted to the production than those which were earlier in the field: and besides, it is a just remark of Mr Rae, that nothing has a greater tendency to promote improvements in any branch of production than its trial under a new set of conditions. But it cannot be expected that individuals should, at their own risk, or rather to their certain loss, introduce a new manufacture, and bear the burden of carrying it on until the producers have been educated up to the level of those with whom the processes are traditional. A protecting duty, continued for a reasonable time, might sometimes be the least inconvenient mode in which the nation can tax itself for the support of such an experiment. (Mill [1948] 1965: 918–19)

This passage indicates that Mill, like List, was conscious of the need to compensate for the risk of establishing new manufacturing production in countries at early stages of industrialization and positive externalities related to training and skill development. Further, he adopted a similarly dynamic perspective on comparative advantage requiring active government policies. As put by William Cline over two centuries later, 'comparative advantage is made, not given' (Cline 1983: 155).

Alfred Marshall's view was that temporary protection of an industry lagging behind best practices abroad was not unreasonable because of lack of experience (Marshall [1923] 1966: 218–19). He nevertheless pointed out the risk of prolonged protection and consequent corruption based on the experience of the USA.[19] Marshall was not clear as to whether protection should be applied to all industries across the board or on a selective basis. At one point, he seems to advocate protection of the industrial sector as a whole, 'even though the [import] tax must inevitably do some hurt to those few of her industries which are manufacturing for exportation' (ibid.: 218). In another passage, however, he seems to prefer protecting specific industries.[20]

Although Marshall did not go into the details of what he meant by 'high-class progressive industries', he referred to the protection of industries that involve large economies of scale and 'learning effects', or what he called 'educative influence'. Further, he argued that these industries could act as leading industries whose 'energy' would 'spread over a great part of the industrial system' (ibid.: 219). In other words, in addition to scale economies, Marshall, like List, emphasized the importance of learning by doing, as well as linkages and externalities, although most of these terms did not exist at the time.

Concluding Remarks: The Relevance of List's Arguments Today

In this chapter we have reviewed List's contribution to the theory of economic development, especially his ideas on the infant industry argument, as there is some confusion about his views in the literature. List's point of departure from the classical theory of international trade was his distinction between 'universal association' and national interest, and recognition of the fact that different countries are at different levels of development. He was against neither international trade nor export expansion; indeed, he emphasized the importance of trade and the ultimate goal of free trade. His theory is clearly a dynamic one: infant industry protection becomes necessary for countries at the early stages of industrialization if some countries 'have outdistanced others in manufactures'; temporary protection was seen by him as an instrument for achieving development, export expansion and, ultimately, free trade.

Contrary to widely held belief, List did not recommend across-the-board protection of the whole manufacturing sector. When protection is applied, it should not only be temporary, but should also be selective or targeted and not excessive. To guard against the development of monopoly power, domestic competition should eventually be introduced, preceded by planned, gradual and targeted trade liberalization. List was aware of market size as a limiting factor for industrial development, but he argued that in most cases, this obstacle could be overcome through various types of alliances with other countries, large or small, including regional integration.

John Stuart Mill endorsed List's infant industry argument. Alfred Marshall did not object to it but was not as supportive as Mill, as he thought protection would prolong and lead to corruption.

Some have argued that the failure of import substitution strategies in many developing countries can be attributed to deficiencies in List's infant industry argument. This claim is unjust. In fact, the across-the-board import substitution that took place in many developing countries was often a reaction to balance of payments problems, rather than a result of clear industrial and trade policies. Reinert (2000)[21] has shown that the mode of protection that comes closest to infant industry protection is that of East Asia, which he labels it as 'good protection' – as against the 'bad protection' practised in Latin America.

Some also argue that the rules of the World Trade Organization (WTO) do not allow trade policies in line with the infant industry argument. But there is still some room for selective intervention within the framework of the WTO rules (Amsden 2000). Moreover, the existence of such rules is not an argument against infant industry protection. These rules can and need to be revised to achieve a fairer trading system, in which the different situations of countries at various stages of development are given greater consideration.

It should be stressed, however, that trade policy is not a universal panacea, and its role should not be exaggerated. Trade policy is only one element of a wider range of industrial and development policies. It was List who argued that the success of trade policy requires a host of other socio-economic factors, including the development of agriculture, infrastructure, institutions, organizations, science, know-how, research and development, entrepreneurship, predictable and efficient domestic policies, political and cultural factors, morality, a sense of national unity, and, above all, 'liberty'.

Finally, universal free trade is sometimes recommended on grounds of ease or convenience, as implementation of a dynamic, selective trade policy is difficult, particularly in many developing countries in the early stages of development where bureaucratic capacity is limited. However, 'ease' is not a substitute for 'soundness' in opting for a given trade and industrial policy.

It is worth noting that active, targeted industrial policy still prevails in various forms in most of the developed countries, including the United States, the most advanced industrial economy. For example, in 1997 alone, 58,000 US companies received subsidized finance from the government (for more details, see Reinert 2000 and Shafaeddin 2005). Joseph Stiglitz, former chairman of the Council of Economic Advisers to President Clinton's administration, has said: 'I found myself in the uncomfortable position of an American saying "do as we say, not as we do"' (cited in Reinert 2000: 16).

The infant industry argument as developed by List, in the context of his general theory of 'productive power' (or economic development), is still valid, if properly applied. One should not forget, however, that he emphasized that, beyond a point, trade should be liberalized selectively and gradually, aiming at the ultimate goal of free trade *when all nations will have reached the same level of development.*

The views expressed in this article are those of the author, and do not necessarily represent those of his employer, the United Nations Conference on Trade and Development.

Notes

1 For example, in *Economic Theory in Retrospect*, Blaug (1962) does not make a single reference to List's work. Similarly, in *The Origin of Economic Ideas*, Routh (1975) makes no mention of List. An important exception is Henderson (1983).

2 For more details about the history of industrial policy in the United States and Europe during the late eighteenth and early nineteenth centuries, see Shafaeddin (1998), Bairoch (1989, 1993), Goldstein (1993), Bairoch and Kozul–Wright (1996).

3 'In countries where there is great private wealth, much may be effected by the voluntary contributions of patriotic individuals; but in a community situated like that of the United States, the public purse must supply the *deficiency of private resources*. In what can it be useful, as in prompting and improving the efforts of industry?' (Hamilton 1791: 276; emphasis added).

4 In his writings in Germany, in the form of various memoranda during the period 1819–20, List argued for protection as a retaliatory measure, rather than for infant industry protection (Henderson 1983: 144–45).

5 See Hoselitz (1960: 197–205) and List (1856), particularly the introductory chapter.

6 The concept of economic stages was not new, as eighteenth-century economists had already referred to them. Adam Smith outlined a four-stage schema of economic development in *Lectures on Jurisprudence*. List made a minor variation on Smith's schema by inserting 'manufacturing' into a schema that originally moved from agriculture (stage iii) directly to commercial society (stage iv). I owe this point to John Toye.

7 'Social interests are known to differ immensely from the private interests of all the individuals of a nation, if each individual be taken separately and not as a member of the national association, if, as with Adam Smith and Say, individuals are regarded merely as producers and consumers, and not as citizens of a nation' (List 1856: 261).

8 It should be noted, however, that even Adam Smith regarded achievement of free trade as a utopia because of opposition from the private sector. Also, Smith was in favour of protecting defence industries, and approved the Navigation Acts to develop the English merchant navy to compete with Dutch commercial supremacy (Panic 1988: 125). Moreover, Smith recommended various sorts of government intervention in the domestic economy with their impacts on foreign trade. Goldsmith (1995) and Panic (1988) have argued that the classical theory of international trade is as sound as any theory based on assumptions. The problem is that its assumptions are unrealistic (see Shafaeddin 2000b).

9 Not surprisingly, List was seen by the British authorities 'as a dangerous enemy, on account of his endeavouring to rescue his country completely from the manufacturing monopoly of England' (List 1856: viii, translator's preface).

10 'The productive power of nations is not solely dependent on the labour, the saving, the morality, and the intelligence of individuals, or on the possession of natural advantage and material capital; it is dependent also upon institutions and law, social, political, and civil, but, above all, on the *securities of the duration*, their independence, and their power as nations. . . . Industrial production depends, *inter alia*, on the moral and material association of individuals for a common end' (List 1856: 74).

11 'A division of the operations, without the association of productive power of a common end, would be very little help in the production. That a favourable result may be obtained, it is necessary that the different individuals be united and cooperate in the work intellectually and bodily' (List 1856: 231).

12 'The elevation of an agricultural people to the condition of countries at once agricultural, manufacturing and commercial, can only be accomplished under the law of free trade, when the various nations engaged at the time in manufacturing industry shall be in the same degree of progress and civilization; when they shall place no obstacle in the way of the economical development of each other, and not impede their respective progress by war or adverse commercial legislation' (List 1856: 72–73).

13 In *Outlines of American Political Economy*, List provided a numerical example of a cloth factory working with different production scales, and showed the impact of change in the scale of production on average unit cost (Henderson 1983: 151). This example reflects his concern about static internal economies of scale. Nevertheless, List's argument on the impact of experience and learning over time on the cost of production indicates his view of what are called dynamic internal and external economies of learning (List 1856: 185).

14 List recommended the imposition of a general tariff on a country's industries in very exceptional circumstances (Henderson 1983: 161).

15 There is further evidence of his ideas on selective industrial protection in his book *Outline of American Political Economy*. In this book, he argues that the 'productive powers' of a new country, such as the United States, could best be stimulated by fostering only those industries 'which employ a number of labourers, and consume great quantities of agricultural produce and raw materials, which can be supported by machinery and by a great internal consumption . . . and which are not easy to be smuggled'. List considered that the first branches of manufacture to receive tariff protection should be the woollen, cotton, iron, earthenware and chemical industries. On the other hand, luxury goods did not require any protection at this stage of the economic development of the United States. 'Those articles of comfort and luxury, if imported cheaper than we can manufacture them, get in use among all labouring classes, and act as a stimulus in exciting the productive powers of the nation.' A few years later, List argued that 'there is no reason for the United States to encourage silk manufactures in competition with those of France, so long as France will not compel the Americans to do in regard to silk what, compelled by English restrictions, they would not avoid to do in regard to English cottons, woollens, and iron' (Henderson 1983: 148–49).

16 Despite advocacy of free trade by classical economists, Smith and Ricardo also warned against rapid trade liberalization when a country had developed its industrial base by protection. Retaining protection was regarded by them as the right policy 'if trade liberalization results in high unemployment and a drastic reduction in domestic income' (Panic 1988: 123–24).

17 In so far as List frequently referred to the role of protection in achieving independence and obtaining influence and power, his theory contains some elements of strategic trade policy.

18 Before List, Daniel Raymond (1786–1844) had argued for the development of a transport infrastructure to stimulate a dynamic relationship between the agricultural and manufacturing sectors in the United States, and for the removal of internal duties among various states (Yaffey 1998).

19 'Protection to a nascent industry in a country, whose capitalistic resources are scarce, is not necessarily unreasonable. But in fact the great part of such protection is commonly retained after the industry has already enjoyed a long and progressive life' (Marshall [1923] 1966: 218).

20 'The energy developed in a few "high-class progressive industries" may spread over a great part of the industrial system of the country; just as an iron screen, which concentrated the whole draught of a chimney on a small part of a nascent fire, may generate an intensive local heat, which precedes and pioneers the way for a broad strong fire' (Marshall [1923] 1966: 218).

21 Raul Prebisch, the theorist of 'import substitution strategy', was in fact the first to warn against 'bad protection' (Shafaeddin 2000a).

References

Amsden, Alice H. (1989), *Asia's Next Giant: South Korea and Late Industrialization* (New York: Oxford University Press).

—— (2000), 'Industrialization under New WTO Law', paper prepared for the UNCTAD High-level Round Table on 'Trade and Development Directions for the Twenty-first Century', Bangkok, 12 February.

Ashley, Percy (1920), *Modern Tariff History: Germany, United States, France*, third edn (London: John Murray).

Bairoch, Paul (1989), 'European Trade Policy, 1815–1914', in Peter Mathias and Sydney Pollard, eds, *The Cambridge Economic History of Europe, Vol. VIII: The Industrial Economies: The Development of Economic and Social Policies* (Cambridge: Cambridge University Press): 1–160.

—— (1993), *Economics and World History: Myths and Paradoxes* (Brighton: Wheatsheaf).

Bairoch and Kozul–Wright (1996), 'Globalization Myths: Some Historical Reflections on Integration, Industrialization and Growth in the World Economy', UNCTAD Discussion Papers, No. 113.

Bastable, Charles F. (1903), *The Theory of International Trade with Some of Its Applications to Economic Policy* (London: Macmillan).

Blaug, Mark (1962), *Economic Theory in Retrospect* (London: Heinemann).

Chang, Ha-Joon (2002), *Kicking Away the Ladder: Development Strategy in Historical Perspective* (London: Anthem).

Cline, William (1983), *Trade Policies in the 1980s* (Washington DC: Institute of International Economics).

Corden, W. Max (1974), *Trade Policy and Economic Welfare* (Oxford: Clarendon Press).

Cronin, Sean (1980), *Irish Nationalism: a History of Its Roots and Ideology* (Dublin: Academy Press).

Greenaway, David and Chris Milner (1993), *Trade and Industrial Policy in Developing Countries* (London: Macmillan).

Goldsmith, A.A. (1995), 'The State, the Market and Economic Development: A Second Look at Adam Smith in Theory and Practice', *Development and Change*, 26: 633–50.

Goldstein, Judith (1993), *Ideas, Interests and American Trade Policy* (Ithaca: Cornell University Press).

Hamilton, Alexander ([1791] 1934), 'Report on Manufactures', in Samuel McKee, ed., *Papers on Public Credit, Commerce and Finance* (New York: Columbia University Press): 175–276.

Henderson, O. William (1983), *Friedrich List: Economist and Visionary, 1789–1846* (London: Frank Cass).

Hoselitz, Bert F. (1960), 'Theories of Stages of Economic Growth', in Bert F. Hoselitz *et al.*, eds, *Theory of Economic Growth* (Glencoe: Free Press): 193–238.

Kenwood, Albert G. and Alan L. Lougheed (1994), *The Growth of the International Economy, 1820–90*, third edn (London: Routledge).

Krueger, Anne O. (1978), *Liberalization Attempts and Consequences* (Cambridge, Massachusetts: Ballinger, for the National Bureau of Economic Research).

Lall, Sanjaya (1991), *Building Industrial Competitiveness in Developing Countries* (Paris: OECD Development Centre).

Levi–Fauer, David (1997), 'Friedrich List and the Political Economy of the Nation-State', *Review of International Political Economy*, 4 (1): 154–78.

List, Friedrich (1827), *Outline of American Political Economy* (Philadelphia: Samuel Parker).

—— (1856), *The National System of Political Economy*, translated by George A. Matile (Philadelphia: J.B. Lippincott). (Translation of Friedrich List [1841], *Das nationale System der Politischen Oekonomie.*)

Little, Ian M.D., Tibor Scitovsky and Maurice Scott (1970), *Industry and Trade in Some Developing Countries* (Oxford: Oxford University Press).

Marshall, Alfred ([1923] 1966), *Money, Credit and Commerce* (London: Macmillan).

Mill, John Stuart ([1948] 1965), *Principles of Political Economy*, in *Collected Works of John Stuart Mill*, Vols. 2–3 (Toronto: University of Toronto Press).

Panic, Misha (1988), *National Management of the International Economy* (London: Macmillan).

Reinert, Erik (2000), 'The Other Canon: The Other Canon and the History of Economic Policy', (Oslo: Norsk Investor Forum and SVN, Centre for Development and Environment, University of Oslo).

Rosenstein–Rodan, P.N. (1943), 'Problems of Industrialization of Eastern and South-Eastern Europe', *The Economic Journal*, June–September. (Reprinted in A.N. Agarwala and S.P. Singh [1958], *The Economics of Underdevelopment* [Oxford: Oxford University Press]: 245–56).

Routh, Guy (1975), *The Origin of Economic Ideas* (London: Macmillan).

Schumpeter, Joseph A. (1952), *History of Economic Analysis* (London: Allen and Unwin).

—— (1961), *The Theory of Economic Development* translated by Redvers Opie from the German edition (1926) (Cambridge, Mass.: Harvard University Press).

Senghaas, Dieter (1989), 'Friedrich List and the Basic Problems of Modern Development', *Economics*, 40: 62–76.

Shafaeddin, Mehdi (1998), 'How did Developed Countries Industrialize? The History of Trade and Industrial Policy: The Case of Great Britain and the USA', UNCTAD Discussion Paper 139, UNCTAD, Geneva.

—— (2000a), 'What did Friedrich List Actually Say? Some Clarifications on the Infant Industry Argument', UNCTAD Discussion Paper 149, UNCTAD, Geneva.

—— (2000b), 'Free Trade or Fair Trade? Fallacies Surrounding the Theory of Trade Liberalization and Protection and Contradictions in International Trade Rules: An Inquiry into the Causes of Failure in the Recent Trade Negotiations', UNCTAD Discussion Paper 153, UNCTAD, Geneva.

—— (2005), *Trade Policy at the Crossroads: Recent Experiences of Developing Countries in Trade Liberalization* (London: Palgrave).

Smith, Adam ([1776] 1937), *An Inquiry into the Nature and Cause of the Wealth of Nations* (New York: Modern Library).

Viner, Jacob (1953), *International Trade and Economic Development* (Oxford: Clarendon Press).

Yaffey, Michael (1998), 'Friedrich List and the Causes of Irish Hunger', in Helen O'Neill and John Toye, eds, *A World without Famine? New Approaches to Aid and Development* (New York: St. Martin's Press): 84–106.

Karl Marx as a Development Economist

Prabhat Patnaik

Karl Marx was perhaps the first development economist, using the term for any one who studies not only development *under* capitalism, but also development *of* capitalism. Classical political economy, which did not see history beyond capitalism, was also less concerned about history before capitalism, that is, about the historical conditions for the emergence of capitalism itself, notwithstanding the several deep historical insights contained in Adam Smith's work. Its preoccupation was with arguing for the removal of the feudal–mercantilist restrictions that the emerging bourgeois order was hemmed in by, so that it gave the impression that if only these restrictions were removed, development would follow as a matter of 'natural' course. By contrast, Marx, whose emphasis was to locate capitalism within a historical context, was for that reason much more sensitive to the conditions for the emergence of capitalism, and hence, to the conditions that mark the transition from the relative stagnation of the feudal era to the 'development' characteristic of the bourgeois epoch – a transition that by no means could be expected to occur 'naturally' if the restrictions of the earlier era were removed.

Commodity Production and the Transition to Capitalism

Two issues raised by Marx on this problem of transition have attracted much discussion. The first concerns the role of the introduction of commodity production, and of merchant capital in general, in the transition from feudalism to capitalism, which became a matter of intense debate, known as the 'Transition Debate', among Dobb, Sweezy, Takahashi, Hilton, Lefebvre and Hill (Hilton *et al.* 1976). Dobb's position was that merchant capital, while it may have a dissolving effect on the feudal mode of production, does not, by itself, give rise to capitalism. (In certain circumstances, like in Eastern Europe for instance, the introduction of commodity production was responsible for the emergence of a 'second serfdom'.) The emergence of capitalism in Western Europe required a long process of differentiation among the petty producers who had been liberated from the feudal straitjacket (through the commutation of feudal rents, for instance); while the dissolving influence of merchant capital was undoubtedly behind this liberation, it cannot be considered the progenitor of capitalism *per se*. (Marx talked of merchants' and usurers' capital as being 'antediluvian' forms of capital, distinct from productive capital, which could flourish even in situations where the latter remained underdeveloped.)

The second issue arose out of Marx's puzzlement over the fact that countries like India and China, which had been quite advanced in earlier centuries, never succeeded in developing capitalism, while capitalism developed instead in regions that had been comparatively backward then. Marx's provisional answer to this puzzle was to advance the concept of an 'Asiatic mode of production', a variant of feudalism prevailing in the east, which had the peculiar property of remaining stagnant. His views on what precisely were the features of the Asiatic mode of production kept changing. At different times, he emphasized different properties as constituting its *differentia specifica,* but the list included: the absence of private property (sometimes he talked of communal property, at other times of all land belonging to the king), a self-sufficient village community, the unity of agriculture and industry and the absence of class differentiation in society (other than the king and his nobles extracting surplus from the producers). Almost every one of these particular traits has been shown to have been absent in India in the pre-colonial period (Habib 1963).

The point about the Asiatic mode of production, however, is not its historical veracity but the light it throws on Marx's understanding of the emergence of capitalism. Clearly, while commodity production and merchant capital were not sufficient conditions for capitalism, they were necessary. And Marx felt that the atomistic, self-sufficient village community, with its unity of agriculture and industry, precluded their development to a point where new impulses for change could be generated. (An important theoretical point implicit in this is that the division of labour and exchange of goods – as under the *jajmani* system in an Indian village – does not constitute commodity production, since it does not represent a complete separation of use-value from exchange value (Kautsky 1887–1903). Whether or not this characterized India or China historically, the understanding gleaned from it is of considerable value.

The flowering of capitalism, it followed, was not just a matter of removing feudal fetters and introducing a set of *laissez-faire* policies. It required very specific historical conditions. The trajectory of movement of any society, according to Marx, was determined by the manner of use of its surplus. But this manner of use itself was determined by the class configuration of that society, viz. to whom the surplus accrued and how they were predisposed towards using it. The class configuration necessary for the launching of capitalism was the result of a long and rather specific historical process.

The process of differentiation of petty producers, however, was not enough for achieving this class configuration. The task of throwing up a class of capitalists at one end, and a class of impoverished producers willing to work for a wage at the other, could not be entrusted solely to the process of differentiation of petty producers. This process was both painfully slow and hopelessly inadequate –

slow because it took, even according to Dobb, several centuries (and would have taken several more to bring about, if ever it could, the *requisite* degree of polarization of society); inadequate because the dominance of capitalism requires control over world trade, which this prolonged process of differentiation alone would not have ensured. The emergence of capitalism, given this background of change that was occurring, owed much to another process that was superimposed upon it, a process of 'primary accumulation of capital'.

'Primary' Capital Accumulation

The concept of 'primary accumulation of capital', though inspired by Adam Smith's 'original accumulation of capital', is an integral part of Marx's overall schema, and fits perfectly into his unique analysis of capitalist categories as embodying not just *things*, but also a set of *relations* (so that each category has a *dual* character, a physical and a social – for example, product/commodity, concrete labour/abstract labour, production process/value-creating process and so on). As Marx put it:

> In themselves money and commodities are no more capital than are the means of production and of subsistence. They want transforming into capital. But this transformation itself can only take place under certain circumstances that centre in this, viz., that two very different kinds of commodity-possessors must come face to face and into contact; on the one hand, the owners of money, means of production, means of subsistence, who are eager to increase the sum of values they possess; on the other hand, free labourers, the sellers of their own labour-power, and therefore the sellers of labour. Free labourers, in the double sense that neither they themselves form part and parcel of the means of production, as in the case of slaves, bondsmen, &c., nor do the means of production belong to them, as in the case of peasant-proprietors; they are, therefore, free from, unencumbered by, any means of production of their own. (Marx 1974a: 668)

Marx argued that this relationship between the 'two very different kinds of commodity-possessors' spontaneously perpetuates itself through the accumulation process under capitalism. But the question arises: how did it come into being in the first place? For this, Marx developed the concept of 'primary accumulation of capital', an original process of separation of producers, through the use of extra-economic coercion, from their means of production, and their conversion into free wage labourers, even as the means of production get concentrated in a few hands, a process that sets the capitalist mode of production on its feet. 'The primary accumulation plays in Political Economy about the same part as original sin in theology' (ibid.: 667).

'Primary accumulation' can be visualized as a single integral process, with the different moments of it coalesced together: if there is, say, a group of twenty peasants cultivating twenty different plots of land, and if they are ousted from their plots, which pass into the hands of a single owner who employs all twenty of them (or a fewer number) as labourers to cultivate the same land, then, not only do we have a forcible conversion of petty production into capitalist production, but also a ready market available for capitalism which is nothing else but the market taken over from the petty producers. (If the peasants were producing earlier entirely for subsistence, the surplus extracted from them now, which is in excess of what the capitalist consumes out of it, will have to be realized through investment; otherwise, as Rosa Luxemburg [1963] was to argue later, there would be a problem of 'realization'.)

But the different moments of primary accumulation need not always appear coalesced together; they may appear scattered, each element occurring at a different time and place. Place here includes not only the domestic economy but 'outlying regions' as well. 'Primary accumulation' therefore occurs over the globe, through plunder and colonial extraction of wealth (and surplus); and it occurs with its different moments scattered and dispersed, not always coalesced into an integral whole. Thus, since in a capitalist economy, *any* sum of value can act as capital, the extraction of colonial wealth, which constitutes such a sum of value, is an act of primary accumulation, *even if this extraction per se cannot be said to have provided a work force or a market for the metropolis.* Marx's discussion of the 'primary accumulation of capital' will not be intelligible (since he appears to lump together a number of dissimilar things) unless we keep in mind the global character and dispersed nature of the process.

The concept of 'primary accumulation of capital' has profound implications for development economics (defined in the broader sense of including within its corpus the development *of* capitalism as well). Economies at whose expense 'primary accumulation of capital' occurs become impoverished by the process; their chances of developing an autonomous capitalism become slimmer on account of their being accumulated *from*; and whatever displacement of petty producers occurs as a result of the 'primary accumulation' going on in their economies does not get offset by any absorption of the displaced producers into the capitalist work force. These displaced producers remain a vast pauperized mass. By contrast, precisely the opposite happens in the case of economies that are the beneficiaries of primary accumulation of capital. 'Primary accumulation' through colonialism (and other processes of wealth extraction from the third world) is therefore the progenitor of the development–underdevelopment dichotomy.

Centralization of Capital

There is a second process emphasized by Marx that also works towards reinforcing this dichotomy, and this is the process of 'centralization of capital' as an integral part of the accumulation process in a capitalist universe that has already come into being. Accumulation of capital does not take the form of a mere proliferation of units of existing sizes; it necessarily entails an enlargement of the scale of production. But it is not as if each bloc of capital becomes larger and larger at a uniform rate; some become larger at a rapid rate, while others dwindle into insignificance. In other words, the process of enlargement of blocs of capital leaves fewer and fewer blocs in business. (As Lenin was to emphasize later, this gives rise to monopoly capitalism.)

There are two mechanisms for centralization discussed by Marx. The first is centralization through fusion. Banks, stockmarkets, etc. – which gather numerous tiny units of capital and fuse them together into one gigantic bloc under the control of a particular directing agency, that is, capitalist – are the instruments of such centralization through fusion. Mergers and take-overs are the other obvious examples. 'The world would still be without railroads if it had been obliged to wait until accumulation would have enabled a few individual capitals to undertake the construction of a railroad. Centralization on the other hand accomplished this by a turn of the hand through stock companies' (Marx 1974a: 588).

The second mechanism of centralization is through the destruction of smaller capitals and the occupation of that space by capital of larger size, which, since it is a continuous process, leaves fewer and fewer blocs of capital, of ever-increasing size, in business over time. Marx summed up this process with the remark: 'One capitalist always kills many' (ibid.: 714). The mechanism through which this occurs is as follows.

The introduction of new technology that – at existing prices of inputs and output, entails a larger profit – requires, at any point in time, a certain minimum size of investment to embody it, a minimum that keeps rising over time. Larger capital, at any time therefore, is in a better position to introduce it, compared to smaller capital. Since labour productivity rises with the introduction of new technology, and workers bargain for higher wages on account of productivity increases, there is an increase in the wage rate. This eventually pushes smaller capitals out of business, since they are forced to pay higher wages even though they have not been able to introduce the new technology. As this is a continuous process (with the minimum scale of investment that can embody the new technology rising over time), the process of centralization is a continuous one. Indeed, since large capitals drive out small ones in this Darwinian struggle, there is external coercive pressure on capitalists to ensure that they do not remain small, which forms the driving force for capital accumulation. Capital accumulation for Marx is not a matter of volition for capitalists; it is necessary for their survival. This necessity is imposed upon them by the Darwinian struggle they are objectively caught up in.

Now, if we are talking of a capitalist universe – where capitals from different countries are competing against one another because of the absence of protectionism (so that there is free movement of goods across national boundaries) – then, the same process should be manifesting itself on a world scale. Since blocs of capital in established capitalist countries would generally be larger than in those countries that come late to capitalism (and that too under the aegis of a state that does not protect them against international competition, typically a colonial state), the process of centralization on the world scale takes the form of elimination of capitals of less developed countries by those of more developed countries. The tendency towards uneven development, arising from the process of primary accumulation of capital, would be reinforced by the unevenness of development arising from the process of centralization, even after domestic capitalist production has begun in the less developed country.

Marx himself saw a continuity between the process of primary accumulation of capital and the process of centralization of capital.

> As soon as this process of transformation has sufficiently decomposed the old society from top to bottom, as soon as the labourers are turned into proletarians, their means of labour into capital, as soon as the capitalist mode of production stands on its own feet, then the further socialization of labour and further transformation of land and other means of production into socially exploited and, therefore, common means of production, as well as the further expropriation of private proprietors, takes a new form. That which is now to be expropriated is no longer the labourer working for himself, but the capitalist exploiting many labourers. This expropriation is accomplished by the action of the immanent laws of capitalistic production itself, by the centralization of capital. (Marx 1974a: 714)

This continuous process of expropriation of the many by the few, this continuous process of centralization (taking 'primary accumulation' itself as one particular gigantic episode of centralization), necessarily has a *spatial* dimension as well: while the expropriation is spread over a larger universe, the employment of labour for capitalist production proper occurs over a smaller area, confined only to the metropolitan countries, leaving a vast pauperized mass outside in the 'outlying regions'. This remains true even though there is some employment of labour in the 'outlying regions' *indirectly* (that is, as petty producers) for metropolitan capitalism in primary producing activities. *Embedded within Marx's basic analysis of capitalism, therefore, is a dichotomy between the developed and the underdeveloped segments of the world.* Paradoxically, however, Marx never systematically drew attention to it. There are stray references in his work to this dichotomy produced by capitalist development but no elaborate discussion of it. An obvious question is: why?

Preoccupation with European Revolution

I argue below that in Marx, one finds two different perspectives – one in his main works, and the other in his letters and lesser writings – which are not temporally separate; these perspectives apparently coexisted at the same time. Marx had a more complex set of possibilities in mind which came through in his lesser writings, of which he expressed only one sub-set in his main works. The reason why this is the case, indeed the reason why Marx never systematically drew attention to the tendency of capitalist development to produce a dichotomy between developed and underdeveloped regions in his main works despite its being embedded in his basic argument, was his preoccupation with a European revolution.

This was not just because a European revolution was on the historical agenda, in his view, and still less because Marx was, in some sense, 'Eurocentric'. Rather, he saw quite clearly that a successful transition to socialism was possible only on the basis of a revolution in the advanced centres of capitalism, which meant a European revolution. Even after the prospects of a European revolution had receded, when Marx's interest shifted to Russia as a possible revolutionary theatre, he wrote to Vera Zasulich that while a direct transition from the Russian system of communal property to socialism was possible, it could occur only if aided by a European revolution. My point about this letter is not the argument about the possibility of such a direct transition – which was an extremely uncharacteristic argument for Marx, and was subsequently rejected by Engels as well as by Russian Marxists (Hobsbawm 1964: 49–50) – but his emphasis on a European revolution as an aid to the transition to socialism elsewhere.

It is this perspective that underlay his famous remark: 'The country that is more developed industrially only shows to the less developed the image of its own future' (Marx 1974a: 19). The terms 'more developed' and 'less developed' here refer exclusively to the metropolitan countries, almost as if the other countries – which, *under the prevailing arrangements* (that is, colonialism, etc.), could never spontaneously achieve the same 'future' – did not exist. The reason for not recognizing them was because Marx was addressing a very different audience, and was particularly interested in this audience, because it was only this audience that could work for a European revolution.

Another Marx

Meanwhile, in a number of lesser writings (in the sense of journalistic writings, which were nonetheless stunningly brilliant), Marx was setting out a more complex understanding. In 1953, a full fourteen years before the publication of *Capital*, Volume I, but roughly around the time that he was working out the basic ideas of his *magnum opus*, Marx wrote a series of eight articles on British rule in India for the *New York Daily Tribune*, where he touched upon a vast array of subjects having a bearing on 'development economics'.

He argued that British rule in India had a 'destructive' and a 'regenerative' effect. The destructiveness consisted in the fact that, unlike all previous invasions in India, it destroyed the 'self-sufficient village community', with its unity of agriculture and industry. It therefore broke the basis of the stagnation of Indian society. It did so through a number of measures: the charging of extraordinarily high rents; the introduction of modern, legally negotiable property rights; and, above all, the destruction of traditional industry owing to competition from cheap imported manufactured goods. Of course, 'England, it is true, in causing a social revolution in Hindoostan, was actuated only by the vilest interests, and was stupid in her manner of enforcing them. But that is not the question' (Marx and Engels 2001: 65–66).

The process of 'regeneration' – which, Marx felt, had begun – consisted mainly of the 'transformation of India into a reproductive country', that is, into a source of raw materials to export in exchange for imported manufactured goods. This necessitated the development of roads, irrigation and, above all, railways. Marx argued: 'when you have once introduced machinery into the locomotion of a country, which possesses iron and coal, you are unable to withhold it from its fabrication. The railway system will therefore become in India truly the forerunner of modern industry' (ibid.: 73).

But he went on to add:

> All the English bourgeoisie may be forced to do will neither emancipate nor materially mend the social condition of the mass of the people, depending not only on the development of the productive power, but on their appropriation by the people. But what they will not fail to do is to lay down the material premises for both. . . . The Indians will not reap the fruits of the new elements of society scattered among them by the British bourgeoisie till in Great Britain itself the now ruling classes shall have been supplanted by the industrial proletariat, or till the Hindoos themselves shall have grown strong enough to throw off the English yoke altogether. (Ibid.)

This passage is remarkable for a number of reasons. First, there is a very clear recognition in it that a revolution in India – consisting of the 'Hindoos' throwing off the colonial yoke altogether – could even precede a proletarian revolution in Britain. In other words, even as Marx was focusing all his theoretical energies on the European revolution, he could visualize a non-European revolution preceding it,[1] which is an example of what was mentioned earlier, namely, that his main work focused only on a sub-set of a more complex set of possibilities that he had in mind.

Second, Marx is talking not of colonialism *developing* the periphery, but only of colonialism 'scattering the new elements of society', 'laying down the material premises' for the 'development of productive power'. There is a very clear recognition here of the dichotomous effect of capitalist development in the metropolis: while it causes the development of productive forces in the metropolis, in the 'outlying regions' all it does is to lay down the material premises for such development but not carry out actual development of the same sort.

Third, when Marx talks about the 'Hindoos' throwing off the colonial yoke, he is clearly referring not to any proletarian revolution in India but to a bourgeois revolution. It is, of course, intriguing why he does not say so explicitly, and why he thinks of 'the Hindoos' as a single collective subject, undifferentiated not only by any class distinctions but even by any class aspirations.[2] But there can be little doubt that he is talking of a successful anti-colonial struggle by the 'Hindoo' elite, which cannot but have the character of a bourgeois revolution. In other words, Marx visualizes that, given the material premises laid down by colonialism, an anti-colonial bourgeois revolution in India (and hence, by inference, in other third world countries) can unleash the development of productive forces and thereby play a progressive role not only in the Indian context, but (as argued below) also in the world context.

In a letter to Engels in 1858, Marx had asked:

> The weighty question for us now is this: On the Continent the revolution is imminent and will from the first take on a socialist character. But will it not inevitably be crushed in this small corner, since the movement of bourgeois society is still ascendant on a far wider area?

Even though this question did bother Marx, his implicit answer to it, given five years earlier in the last of his India articles, was that a bourgeois revolution, in the 'outlying regions' at any rate, posed no threat to a socialist revolution in Europe. From this remark and from his letter to Vera Zasulich, one can piece together Marx's position on revolutions in non-European societies as follows: any socialist revolution in these societies, if at all possible, cannot succeed without a socialist revolution in Europe; but a bourgeois revolution, if at all possible, can move forward on its own, and a European socialist revolution has nothing to fear from it.

The idea of a third world anti-colonial (bourgeois) revolution – predating the European proletarian revolution and being a progressive force – remained with Marx and Engels till the end, and was expressed by the latter in a letter to Kautsky on 12 September 1882:

> India will perhaps, indeed very probably, produce a revolution, and as the proletariat emancipating itself cannot conduct any colonial wars, this would have to be given full scope; it would not pass off without all sorts of destruction, of course, but that sort of thing is inseparable from all revolutions. The same thing might also take place elsewhere, for example, in Algiers and Egypt, and would certainly be the best thing *for us*. (Marx and Engels 1978: 342).

Surplus Drain

As many scholars have noted, Marx's view of (metropolitan) capitalism underwent change over time. A part of it had to do with his increasing sense of revulsion: 'It seems probable that Marx who had earlier welcomed the impact of Western capitalism as an inhuman but historically progressive force on the stagnant pre-capitalist economies, found himself increasingly appalled by this inhumanity' (Hobsbawm 1964: 50). But a part had to do with his greater familiarity with the conditions prevailing in colonies like India.

With the possible exception of Dadabhai Naoroji, the intellectual founding father of Indian nationalism, Marx was the first to talk of a unilateral transfer of surplus value without any *quid pro quo* from India to Britain because of the colonial arrangement (what Naoroji was to call 'the drain of wealth' from India to Britain). He published careful calculations in an article in the *New York Daily Tribune* in 1858; and in *Capital*, Volume III (which, though published posthu-

mously, must have been prepared around this time), he had the following paragraph: 'India alone has to pay £5 million in tribute for "good government",
interest and dividends of British capital, etc., not counting the sums sent home
annually by officials as savings of their salaries or by English merchants as a
part of their profit in order to be invested in England' (Marx 1974b: 590).

Marx retained this perception of the 'drain' of surplus value till the end.
In a letter to N.F. Danielson on 19 February 1881, he wrote:

> What the English take from them annually in the form of rent, dividends for
> railways useless to the Hindus; pensions for military and civil servicemen, for
> Afghanistan and other wars, etc., etc. – what they take from them *without any*
> *equivalent* and *quite apart* from what they appropriate to themselves annually
> *within* India – speaking only of the *value of the commodities* the Indians have
> gratuitously and annually to *send over* to England – it amounts to *more than*
> *the total sum of income of the 60 millions of agricultural and industrial labourers*
> *of India!* This is a bleeding process with a vengeance![3]

This passage is important for a number of reasons (quite apart from the
fact that Marx, who had seen the railways as being harbingers of modern industry in India in 1853, talks here of railways as being 'useless to the Hindus'). First,
analytically, there are two alternative measures of 'drain', both of which are
stated here, the second one for the first time. The first measure looks at the
'heads' under which 'drain' may appear. The second measure looks at 'unrequited exports'. The two need not be identical since some of the surplus appropriated under the 'heads' that constitute 'drain' may not immediately translate
itself into an equivalent amount of unrequited exports of commodities (a fact
noted by Marx himself in this passage).[4]

Second, since a 'drain' of surplus value through colonial plunder must
be counted as part of the 'primary accumulation' of capital, this passage (as well
as Marx's earlier references to the process) clearly indicates that Marx recognized the fact of 'primary accumulation' not being confined to the genesis of
capitalism but being a continuing process even after capitalism had stood on its
feet – a point made by Rosa Luxemburg (1963) later. What is more, with such
'primary accumulation' resulting in a 'drain' of an amount exceeding the total
incomes of 60 million agricultural and industrial workers of India, clearly, the
prospects of capitalist development within India (and again, by inference, in the
whole of the third world subject to such 'drain') would have been severely damaged. In other words, the 'regenerating' effects of colonialism could only be seen
at a very general level, in creating the most elementary prerequisites (which,
once capitalism had developed in the west, could, in principle, even have been
created through local upheavals and local imitation, as in Japan).

In terms of actual structural arrangements, Marx's writings, especially
outside his main works, clearly show an awareness that capitalist development
in the metropolis was accompanied by a process of extraction of huge amounts of
surplus value on a continuing basis from the colonies and semi-colonies. This is

remarkably perceptive and has a modern ring about it, even though there is no mention of 'unequal exchange' (with which Marx would have had theoretical problems[5]), or of the problem of terms of trade (whose adverse movement for third world primary producers relates to a period that is effectively post-Marx), or of deflation (which becomes a systemic phenomenon only with the coming of finance capital).

Marx's Relevance

Development economics is so wide-ranging a subject that almost the whole of economics can be subsumed under it. Marx's views on development *under* a capitalist mode of production are well known, and have not been discussed in this chapter. Its concern has been with the problem of economic development of the underdeveloped countries, or, to be more precise, with the possibilities of progress in pre-capitalist social formations that have been penetrated and dominated by capitalism. Even under this rubric, there is so much of Marx that is relevant to the issue that including all of it would enlarge the scope of this chapter unmanageably. Our concern therefore has been simply to outline Marx's *perspective* on the issue.

Even though Marx's main analysis in *Capital* has much that is of direct and profound relevance to such economies, intriguingly, Marx says very little directly on this issue in his *magnum opus*. But the *magnum opus* itself rests on an overall understanding, of which we get glimpses in his lesser writings. The perspective one gets from these anticipates much that is valuable in current discussions on development problems. To think that Marx had come to these conclusions as early as the mid-nineteenth century is quite astounding.[6]

Notes

[1] See Habib (1995) for a similar interpretation.

[2] In an article date-lined 22 January 1858, in the *New York Daily Tribune*, Marx explicitly uses the term 'Indian capitalists'. See Habib (1995).

[3] There are reasons to believe that Marx's figures were actually taken from Naoroji, with whom he had a common friend in H.M. Hyndman, the English socialist (Habib 1995: 57).

[4] The subject of alternative measures of 'drain' has occupied India scholars for a long time. See Ganguli (1965); for a recent and rigorous exposition, see Utsa Patnaik (2006). Development economists have also emphasized the 'drain of surplus' from the underdeveloped to the developed countries, but their focus has been much more on 'drain' through 'unequal exchange'.

[5] In this chapter, I have not discussed the possible contrasts between Marx's theoretical positions and those of other development economists. My exclusive concern has been with culling out a *general* perspective on third world development problems from Marx's writings.

[6] As Habib (1995: 58) puts it: 'In 1853 to set colonial emancipation . . . as an objective of the European socialist movement; and, still more, to look forward to a national liberation . . . attained through their struggle by the Indian people, as an event that might even precede the emancipation of the European working class – such insight and vision could belong to Marx alone.'

References

Ganguli, B.N. (1965), *Dadabhai Naoroji and the Drain Theory* (Bombay: Asia Publishing House).

Habib, Irfan (1963), *The Agrarian System of Mughal India* (New Delhi: Oxford University Press).

—— (1995), *Essays in Indian History: Towards a Marxist Perception* (New Delhi: Tulika Books).

Hilton, Rodney *et al.* (1976), *The Transition from Feudalism to Capitalism* (London: New Left Books).

Hobsbawm, Eric J., ed. (1964), *Pre-Capitalist Economic Formations by Karl Marx* (London: Lawrence and Wishart).

Jomo K.S., ed. (2006), *Economic Globalization, Hegemony and World Economy* (New Delhi: Oxford University Press).

Kautsky, Karl (1887–1903), *The Economic Doctrines of Karl Marx* (London: N.C.L.C. Publishing Society).

Luxemburg, Rosa (1963), *The Accumulation of Capital* (London: Routledge).

Marx, Karl (1974a), *Capital*, Volume I (Moscow: Progress Publishers).

—— (1974b), *Capital*, Volume III (Moscow: Progress Publishers).

Marx, Karl and Friedrich Engels (1978), *On Colonialism* (Moscow: Progress Publishers).

—— (2001), *On the National and Colonial Question: Selected Writings*, edited with an Introduction by Aijaz Ahmad (New Delhi: LeftWord Books).

Patnaik, Utsa (2006), 'The Free Lunch: Transfers from the Tropical Colonies and Their Role in Capital Formation in Britain during the Industrial Revolution', in Jomo, ed., *Economic Globalization, Hegemony and World Economy*.

Lenin and the Agrarian Question

Utsa Patnaik

In developing his analysis of the agrarian question in general and of the growth of capitalist production in Russia in particular, Lenin drew upon and integrated three main sources of theory and empirical analysis. The first source was Marx's writings on *pre-capitalist relationships* including forms of landed property and surplus extraction, and that aspect of the primary accumulation of capital which related to the formation of a property-less labour force. It also included the question of the very different roles played by usury and merchant's capital in the transition to capitalist agriculture. The second source drew upon the *Marxist theory of ground rent*, in particular understanding and applying the crucial distinction made by Marx between Adam Smith's concept of rent, which Marx had termed *absolute ground rent*, and Ricardo's concept of 'rent', which he had termed *differential rent*. The third source was the voluminous Russian literature based on the *zemstvo*[1] statistical data; Lenin directly analysed these data from a Marxist perspective to delineate the process of capitalist development in agriculture, and the ongoing process of the formation of a class of capitalist producers at one pole and of wage-paid workers at the other.

By integrating these three sources into his analysis of the agrarian question, Lenin formulated a definitive theoretical perspective on an entire gamut of issues, ranging from the forms in which feudal relations both persisted and merged into capitalist ones in the era after the formal abolition of serfdom, to the effects of increasing production for the market on the process of economic and social 'differentiation' of the peasantry, to the forms in which capitalist relations were developing even within the landlord economy. His classic work dealing with these issues was *The Development of Capitalism in Russia* (Lenin 1899a). Lenin published a short review of Karl Kautsky's book, *Die Agrarfrage* (The Agrarian Question), in which he warmly endorsed its theoretical perspective and analysis (Lenin 1899b); this was followed by a long article defending Kautsky against the critics of his Marxist method (Lenin 1899c).

Lenin's analysis of the dynamics of agrarian change involved a continuous theoretical engagement with and refutation of the influential Russian Narodnik (populist) views. One of the most interesting parts of Lenin's analysis for the present author lies in his cogent critique of the treatment of statistics by the

Narodnik authors: his own analysis used a different method of aggregation of the very same statistics that the Narodniks used, in order to bring out the dynamic processes of change taking place in the agrarian economy, and thereby reached radically different conclusions.

In *The Development of Capitalism in Russia*, Lenin also pioneered the statistical method of summarizing inequality, which later came to be known as the 'Lorenz curve'. Lorenz published his article in an academic journal in 1905, while Lenin had already used the essence of the method in his book by 1899, in order to compare inequality in the distribution of land, livestock and assets among peasants, across the seventeen *gubernias* (districts) covered by the *zemstvo* (rural government) data that he analysed. Lenin's interest in the question of what statistical methods were appropriate for the analysis of agriculture was maintained throughout his life, and on the eve of the Revolution of 1917, he took the trouble to study and re-analyse the 1910 Census in the USA, which had extensive data on agriculture, and published a most penetrating piece based on his re-analysis, entitled 'New Data on the Laws Governing the Development of Capitalism in Agriculture' (Lenin 1915). The editors of the *Collected Works* refer to a fragmentary piece – tantalizingly titled 'Statistics and Sociology' – which was never completed.

Lenin's objective in undertaking a detailed study of agrarian relations and the process of growth of capitalism in agriculture was not, of course, purely academic: a correct analysis was vital for formulation of the strategic and tactical understanding informing the agrarian programme of the Russian Social Democratic Labour Party (RSDLP). It was Lenin's analysis that formed the bedrock on which the agrarian programme of the Party rested, which called for seizure of landlords' estates and nationalization of the land. It was Lenin's changed perspective after integrating the experience of the first 1905–07 revolution, again, which led to a significant alteration in the Party's programmatic understanding: recognition of 'peasant agrarian revolution' and, in addition to nationalization of land, provision for redistribution of seized land among the peasantry as private property. 'The Agrarian Programme of Social Democracy in the First Russian Revolution, 1905–1907' (Lenin 1908a) discussed these issues in detail.

The Development of Capitalism in Russia

Lenin consulted more than five hundred books, monographs, papers and data sources in the course of writing his *tour de force* while in Siberian exile. While both agriculture and industry are discussed in *The Development of Capitalism in Russia*, the sections on agriculture have attracted the most attention and are also more extensive, making up more than half the volume. The first chapter starts with the theoretical question of the formation of an internal market or 'home market' for capitalism, where he questions the Narodnik view that since the mass of the population was poor, and much capital went into the unproductive activities of usury and trade, growth of capitalism could not take place owing to the lack of an expanding home market.

The discussion of agrarian relations in Russia was treated by Lenin in two parts – the economy of the peasantry, and the economy of the landlords – with the links between the two being established through relations of land lease and labour hire. After the legal abolition of serfdom in Russia in 1861, the former serfs' economic situation improved little. First, they were required to pay cash in order to be declared free (redemption payments). Second, the common resources – by way of woods, forests and pastures – to which they had access earlier were appropriated by the landlords so that these lands were 'cut off' from the peasants, and they had to pay rent – in labour, kind or cash – in order to obtain their use. Since the 'cut-off' lands were essential for maintenance of the small peasant economy in particular, the majority of the peasants continued to be linked to landlords through modified relations of labour service (*barschina, otrabotki*) and half-crop share tenancy. Until 1881, it was not even obligatory for landlords to accept redemption payments from ex-serfs, so that many remained 'temporarily bound' peasants of their lords, in practice little better than serfs.

Lenin gives the information for 1883–87, that the private owners' estates in the 50 *gubernias* of European Russia comprised 16.472 million *desyatina*[2] of land, which they cultivated with a combination of peasant labour services, share tenants and hired labour. The peasantry cultivated land given as allotments from the village commune or *mir*, and they additionally cultivated land leased in from each other and from the landlords. The better-off section of the peasantry also purchased a considerable amount of land from the landlords, which they culti-vated in addition to the allotted and leased-in land. Lenin does not mention the total peasant land held under allotment tenure, but from the data in Watters (1968) for two dates, by linear interpolation, we can estimate that the allotment area amounted to 146.1 million *desyatina* by the turn of the century *circa* 1900, while leased-in (non-allotment) land under peasant cultivation was 38 million *desyatina* and land purchased amounted to 20.6 million *desyatina*, giving a total of 205 million *desyatina* cultivated by the peasantry.

There was a specific feature of Russian peasant land tenure that demar-cated it from other serf–lord systems, where all land was divided into lord's demesne and peasant farms – the former cultivated with the labour and instru-ments of enserfed peasants, and the latter cultivated by the same peasants to obtain their subsistence. This specific feature was the persistence – even after the abolition of serfdom – of the village commune, termed *mir* or *obschina*, which prevailed over most of European Russia. The *mir* followed the ancient principle of communal ownership and egalitarian distribution as far as peasant subsist-ence plots were concerned, and allotted land for farming to peasant households on the basis of family size so as to maintain a roughly equal per capita distribu-tion. The *mir* was absent, however, in the western provinces of Ukraine and White Russia, where heritable household tenures were the rule, accounting for 22 per cent of the total area of Russia (Owen 1937). There were periodic redistributions of the allotment area carried out by the *mir* as the size of families in relation to land changed.[3] The penetration of market relations certainly undermined the *mir*, and Owen (1937) tells us that, by the turn of the century, the practice of periodic redistributions had ceased or become infrequent on about 20 per cent of the allotment area.

Establishing Differentiation of the Peasantry to Combat Narodnik Views

The economy of the peasantry cultivating their own farms is analysed by Lenin in Chapter 11, titled 'The Differentiation of the Peasantry', which uses two rich data sources – the *zemstvo* statistics and the army horse census[4] on the distribution of land, livestock and equipment with the peasants. The one hundred-odd pages of the chapter are divided into thirteen sections, eleven of which present these detailed *zemstvo* statistics on peasant asset holding by individual *gubernias* with a summary, while the remaining sections present the results of the army horse census and *zemstvo* data on peasant budgets, with a concluding overall summary of the analysis in the chapter.

This chapter perhaps remains the most illuminating part of the entire book, because it deals *inter alia* with a number of issues of theory and data analysis that are of lasting relevance for all scholars studying agrarian relations in developing countries, and trying to use the appropriate statistical methods for doing so. Lenin was engaged in a continuous debate with and refutation of influential populist theories and conclusions, and he did so by putting forward a radically different Marxist perspective and statistical analysis of the same agrarian phenomena the populists talked of.

In countries with a substantial peasantry, to this day, populism of some variety is often highly influential as an intellectual trend. Populism here refers to that trend of theorizing which: (i) tends to view 'the peasantry' as a *homogeneous* entity in economic terms, or, if not homogeneous, where differing land and resource ownership plays no role in promoting variations; (ii) believes there is a peasant economy regulated by its own *egalitarian economic laws*, quite distinct from the feudal economy or capitalist economy; and (iii) stresses the *flexibility, efficiency and viability of peasant production* relative to capitalist production in agriculture.

Not all these ideas may be present in all populist thinking regarding agriculture everywhere, but there is a substantial similarity in the basic populist positions in all countries with large peasantries. In India, for example, we find that neoclassical models of peasant equilibrium and tenancy are directly in the populist tradition,[5] while much of what passes in economics for 'Marxist' analysis of the peasantry tends to be not Marxist at all but neo-populist, since such analysis also assumes initial peasant homogeneity (in the Russian populist tradition and in direct contrast to the Leninist method) and that peasant production is efficient relative to capitalist production. Further, an entire theory and school of thought among historians has been built up recently regarding the homogeneous 'peasant community' as a vehicle of spontaneous resistance to state oppression. There is a definite impetus that has been given to populist theory in economics by the use of the utility calculus applied to peasant equilibrium, pioneered by the neo-populist scholar A.V. Chayanov ([1915] 1966) in Russia, which enjoys a widespread contemporary revival in mainstream economics dealing with the peasantry and with tenancy (though its present-day practitioners are, by and large, unaware of the theoretical lineage they represent).

Populism in Russia as a theoretical trend was expressed by the theories of the Narodniki. A special impetus was given to populist thought on the egalitarian nature of peasant agriculture by the continued survival and functioning of the *mir* or village commune outside European Russia, to which we have already referred. The early Narodniki were greatly respected by the Marxists, for they were revolutionaries who dreamed of overthrowing the Czarist autocracy; but the Marxists differed on the question of the Narodnik belief that it was possible to achieve a transition to an egalitarian distribution based on the *mir*, bypassing the stage of formation of a landless labour force and of capitalism entirely. Vera Zasulich, the revolutionary Narodnik, had written a letter to Karl Marx regarding this possibility given the special character of the institution of the village commune, and Marx, who had been learning Russian and studying the history of that country, had responded at that time by not entirely ruling out the possibility in his brief initial remarks, while discussing at length the improbable nature of such an outcome:

> In appropriating the positive results of the capitalist mode of production, (Russia) is capable of developing and transforming the archaic form of its village community, instead of destroying it. . . . I now come to the crux of the question. We cannot overlook the fact that the archaic type, to which the Russian commune belongs, conceals an internal dualism, which may under certain historic circumstances lead to its ruin. Property in land is communal, but each peasant cultivates and manages his plot on his own account, in a way recalling the small peasant of the West. Common ownership, divided petty cultivation: this combination which was useful in remoter periods, becomes dangerous in ours. On the one hand mobile property, an element which plays an increasing part even in agriculture, gradually leads to differentiation of wealth among the members of the community, and therefore makes it possible for conflicts of interest to arise, particularly under the fiscal pressure of the state. On the other hand the economic superiority of communal ownership, as the basis of cooperative and combined labour, is lost. (From the Second Draft of Marx's letter to Vera Zasulich, dated 8 March 1881, Marx 1964)

Marx's prescient remarks on differentiation among communal property-holders owing to individual petty production were taken up by Lenin. By the early 1890s, the Marxists in Russia regarded the idea of a transition to socialism bypassing capitalism as an unrealistic and utopian one, given the reality of the rapid disintegration of the *mir*, the growth of commercial agriculture and the westward migration of labour to newly developing areas. All this was being stimulated by the hot-house development of railways and large-scale industry (financed largely by foreign capital inflows), and by rapid urbanization providing a growing market for commodities, which resulted from the Czarist regime's late drive for modernization of the backward Russian economy. The growth of the working class was rapid and, owing to a high degree of concentration of workers in large-scale units, the political movement of the working class also grew extremely fast. The Narodniks' continued harping on the support they claimed Marx had given much earlier to the 'direct transition' thesis, at a time when there was neither a developed proletariat nor a revolutionary Marxist political party, had to be handled circumspectly by Lenin, since it was Marx's authority that was being invoked. While no direct reference was made by him to it, all his writings on the development of capitalism constituted a critique of the thesis, on the basis of and by further developing Marx's own remarks on differentiation.

Lenin consistently attacked the Narodnik view that the peasantry operated on the basis of 'the labour principle' or 'the equalization principle'. According to the Narodnik scholars, peasants were not profit-makers but were interested simply in getting a customary level of consumption for their families, so they wished to cultivate only as much land as was warranted by their capacity to work and by their consumption requirements. Operating just enough land on the basis of 'the labour principle' led to an effective equality of command over resources when normalized for the size of the family; in short, 'the equalization principle' was satisfied. A.V. Chayanov was to develop these very same ideas more rigorously a decade or so later, by putting forward what has come to be known as a theory of 'demographic differentiation', in which the law of the peasant economy was stated to be that family size determined farm size, and that observed differences in farm size were a function of differences in family size. The peasant family workers' days worked rose as the 'pressure of consumption demand' rose, being a function of the size of the family and the ratio of consumers to workers (Chayanov [1915] 1966).

Lenin vigorously and repeatedly criticized the Narodnik scholars' practice of using overall averages, which masked the great variation in asset ownership, income and living standards within the peasantry, even though the basic data permitted analysis of variation. He pointed out that the Narodnik writers always used the allotment area alone to support their arguments, ignoring the rest of the area cultivated by the peasants, which included purchased area and net area rented in. The allotment area was redistributed by the *mir* precisely on the principle of egalitarianism, so it was hardly surprising that selectively picking out the allotment area 'proved' the Narodnik contention of equal distribution. While questioning the Narodnik argument based on classifying households according to allotment area alone, Lenin remarked:

> This argument ignores a fundamental feature of Russian life, namely, the un-
> free character of allotment land tenure, in that by force of law, it bears an
> equalitarian character, and that the purchase and sale of allotment area is hin-
> dered in the extreme. The whole process of the differentiation of the peasantry

is one of real life evading these legal bounds. In classifying the peasants according to allotment, we lump together the poor peasant who leases out land and
the rich peasant who rents or buys land; the poor peasant who abandons the
land and the rich peasant who 'gathers' land; the poor peasant who runs his
most wretched farm with an insignificant number of animals and the rich peasant who owns many animals, fertilizes his soil, introduces improvements, etc.,
etc. In other words we lump together the rural proletarian and the members of
the rural bourgeoisie. The 'averages' thus obtained obscure the differentiation.
. . . As the reader has probably observed, we reject *a limine* any classification
according to allotment and exclusively employ classification according to economic strength. (Lenin 1899a: 102–03)

While the purchase and sale of allotment area faced hindrances, and
although in principle it was not supposed to be even leased in and out amongst
the peasantry, in practice, such mutual leasing was on the increase. The correct
indicator, as regards land, of 'the economic strength' of peasant households,
would be the area they actually cultivated, the 'land in use' obtained by summing allotment area, purchased area and area leased in while deducting area
leased out. (This definition given by Lenin of 'land in use', or the technical units
in which land is cultivated, is actually followed in all statistical tabulations
relating to land in modern times – Indian sources, like the National Sample
Survey, give data on land-holding both by 'owned area' and by 'operated area',
the latter being defined as Lenin had defined 'land in use'.)

When land in use was considered for every *gubernia*, it was found to be
concentrated in the hands of a minority of well-to-do peasants, while, at the other
pole, the majority of peasants held much less land than their numbers warranted.
This happened because the poorer peasants leased out their allotment land (possibly owing to lack of the means to cultivate it) to a larger extent than others,
while the bulk of the leasing in of land (either allotment area or landlord land)
was done by the richer peasants who, with their better resources, also accounted
for the major part of outright land purchase. Most people tend to believe, on *a
priori* grounds, that in any society with a large peasantry, poor peasant households would be the main lessees since they would wish to augment their inadequate owned area, while well-to-do households would be the main lessors.
Russian data showed the converse – most of the total land leased out was done so
by the poorer households, and most of the total area leased in was done so by the
better-off households. Indian data half a century later also showed exactly the
same pattern.

Table 1 reproduces, in summary, the calculations made by Lenin for two
regions, Taurida and Saratov, out of the seventeen *gubernias* he analysed. The
allotment area is seen to be the most equally distributed, with not much difference for each size-group between that size-group's share of the total number of
persons and its share of the total allotment area. The story with regard to net
leased land and purchased land, however, is very different. Purchased land was

TABLE 1   *Distribution of land by type of tenure over households ranked by sown area*

Area sown Desyatina	No. of house- holds	Persons of both sexes	Allot- ment area	Pur- chased area	Rented area	Leased- out area	Land in use
(Three *uyezds* [sub-divisions])							
TAURIDA							
1. Up to 10	39.9	32.6	25.5	6.0	6.0	65.5	12.4
2. 10–25	41.7	42.2	46.5	16.0	35.0	25.3	41.2
3. Over 25	18.4	25.2	28.0	78.0	59.0	9.2	46.4
SARATOV							
1. Up to 5	40.5	31.3	28.3	—	7.0	67.0	12.3
2. 5–20	49.4	54.0	54.3	—	49.6	29.8	52.6
3. Over 20	10.1	14.7	17.4	—	43.4	3.2	35.1

Source: Lenin (1899a: 89, 107).

heavily concentrated in the hands of the top size-group (78 per cent of the total in Taurida, with no data available for Saratov), while leased-in land, termed rented area, was also mainly with this group. A high share of the land leased out was on account of the smallest group in each case. The 'land in use' for each group – obtained by summing allotment, purchased and rented-in area and subtracting area leased out – thus turned out to be far more unequally distributed than the distribution of allotment area alone.

Apart from land, the distribution of draught animals and improved imple-ments as well as the use of hired labour was positively associated with land in use. All these indicators showed such variation as to support the proposition that the peasantry was economically quite highly differentiated, with elements of a labour-hiring peasant bourgeoisie being formed at one end and semi-proletarians hiring out family labour for wages at the other, and the self-employed peasantry proper in the middle did not constitute the majority of households in many areas.

Having analysed the data on inequality and differentiation for selected *uyezds* in seventeen *gubernias* taken separately, the question was to summarize it. Direct comparison of the extent of inequality and hence economic differen-tiation across the regions was not possible since the *zemstvo* statistics gave the data by non-uniform size-groups of holdings (compare Taurida and Saratov in Table 1). Lenin got rid of this problem of non-commensurable groups by deriving the characteristics of the same *proportions* or *fractiles* of households in each region (Table 2). He thus developed the simple but useful principle of what later came to be known as the Lorenz curve of concentration, but which should be termed the Lenin–Lorenz measure of inequality (Lorenz published in 1905, six years after Lenin did).

Lenin formed two groups of cultivators ranked by sown area, in each region – the lowest 50 per cent and the top 20 per cent, and thereby the middle 30 per cent was defined. However, he used a linear interpolation procedure, as opposed to drawing a free-hand curve:

TABLE 2   *Economic characteristics of the same percentiles of households ranked by sown area in different regions*

Household percentile	Population	Allotment	Leased-out area	Rented in area	Purchased area	Land in use	Draught animals	Employment of	
								Farm labourers	Improved implements
TAURIDA									
Lowest 50%	41.8	33.2	72.7	13.8	12.8	23.8	26.6	15.6	3.6
Top 20%	27.0	36.7	9.7	61.9	78.8	49.0	42.3	62.9	85.2
Middle 30%	31.2	30.1	17.6	24.3	8.4	27.2	31.1	21.5	11.2
	100	100	100	100	100	100	100	100	100
SARATOV									
Lowest 50%	36.6	33	71.5	9.8	—	18.6	9.6	7.5	—
Top 20%	30.3	34.1	11.7	59	—	47.0	57.4	65.9	—
Middle 30%	33.1	32.9	16.8	31.2	—	34.4	33	26.6	—
	100	100	100	100	—	100	100	100	—

Note: Values for the middle 30 per cent have been derived as a residual (deducting from 100 the sum for the two groups).
Source: Lenin (1899a: 130–33).

In order to compare and combine the above quoted data on the differentiation of the peasantry, we obviously cannot take absolute figures. . . . We can only compare and juxtapose the relation of the top to the bottom groups as regards possession of land, animals, implements etc. . . . But the sizes of the groups in the different uyezds and gubernias are not equal. And so, we have to *split up* the groups to take in each locality an *equal percentage of households*. Let us agree to take 20 per cent of the households for the well-to-do peasants and 50 per cent for the poor. . . . Suppose we have five groups of the following proportions, from the bottom to the top: 30 per cent, 25 per cent, 20 per cent, 15 per cent and 10 per cent of the households (S=100). To form a bottom group we take the first group and 4/5 of the second group (30+25[4/5] = 50 per cent), and to form a top group we take the last group and 2/3 of the penultimate group (10+ 15[2/3] = 20 per cent), the percentages of area under crops, animals, implements, etc. being determined of course in the same way. (Lenin 1899a: 127–28; emphases in the original)

Lenin also explained that this linear procedure slightly understated the extent of resources with the top 20 per cent and slightly overstated the resources with the bottom 50 per cent:

This method involves a slight error, as a consequence of which the differentiation of the peasantry appears to be less than it actually is. Namely, to the top group are added average, and not the top members of the next group; to the bottom group are added average, and not the bottom members of the next group. Clearly the error becomes greater as the groups become larger and the number of groups smaller. (ibid.: fn. to 128)

Inspecting Table 2 makes it clear that the area allotted by the *mir* was relatively more equally distributed in Saratov where the share of each fractile group in the population is very close to its share in allotment area, while in Taurida, the best off top two deciles of households had managed a larger share even of the allotment area than their numbers warranted, depriving the lowest group. However, participation in the markets in land purchase and in land lease altered the picture drastically, for not only did the well-to-do top two deciles account for nearly four-fifths of all the purchased land in Taurida, in both regions the same top deciles were also net renters of land to the extent of three-fifths or more of the total land rented in. The bulk of total land leased out (over seven-tenths in both regions), however, was on account of the poorer farmers. Thus, despite the relative equality of the allotment component, the poor half of the peasantry ended up with a share of total land in use that was only a fifth to a quarter, far below its share in the population, while, conversely, the top group acquired control over land to the extent of nearly half of the total land in use. The use of improved implements and the employment of farm labourers were heavily concentrated with the top group.

No lesson appears to have been learnt by the Narodnik scholars from Lenin's analysis or his valid strictures on the inadmissibility of selective use of allotment area. In 1915, A.V. Chayanov published his 'Peasant Farm Organization', in which he put forward the same arguments about the 'equalization principle' and 'labour principle' in slightly different language, arguing that peasant households strove to maintain an 'optimum' ratio of land to number of family workers and to family size at any given point of time, and hence, over time, as the family size grew, so did the farm size. Chayanov (1966) presented data on allotment area (which he called 'repartitional commune area') alone to support his propositions, ignoring all of the rest of peasant-cultivated area, and ignoring the fact that allotment area itself was the result of a specific institution. The translation and revival of Chayanov's writings in the mid-1960s was an occasion for a number of evaluations of his work by scholars, in which Chayanov's table on land distribution over peasant households was reprinted but with no mention that it referred to repartitional commune area alone (which, by 1900, amounted to only 42 per cent of total peasant-cultivated area – see Patnaik 1979).

The analysis of peasant and labourers' budgets by Lenin also yielded very interesting findings, which can be compared with similar findings in contemporary economies with large peasantries. The daily-hire, wage-paid workers were found to obtain total earnings over the year that exceeded the total income of the small and poor peasants, and their daily wage rate was higher than the earnings per day worked of the latter. The same phenomenon is observed in countries like India today, which have both a large peasantry and hired agricultural workers: in effect, hired workers are subject to the uncertainty of finding enough work to make a living, while poor peasants trade off the certainty of getting some livelihood by operating their holdings, whether owned or leased, against a lower daily return to their labour than the market wage rate.

In the third chapter entitled 'The Landlords' Transition from Corvée to Capitalist Economy', Lenin analysed the way in which the formal abolition of serfdom in Russia barely four decades earlier, in 1861, had preserved important elements of feudal relations while paving the way for the development of landlords into capitalists through transitional forms. Feudal relations are described succinctly in the following words, which form a good introduction to the system:

> As our starting point in examining the present system of landlord economy we must take the system of that economy which prevailed in the epoch of serfdom. The essence of the economic system of those days was that the entire land of a given unit of agrarian economy, that is, of a given estate, was divided into the lord's and the peasants' land; the latter was distributed in allotments among the peasants who cultivated it with their own labour and their own implements, and obtained their livelihood from it. The product of this peasants' labour constituted the necessary product, to employ the terminology of theoretical political economy: necessary – for the peasants in providing them with the means of subsistence, and for the landlord in providing him with hands; in exactly the same way as the product which replaces the variable part of the value of capital is a necessary product in capitalist society. The peasants' surplus labour, on the other hand, consisted in their cultivation, with *the same* implements, of the landlord's land; the product of that labour went to the landlord. Hence, the surplus labour was separated in space from the necessary labour: for the landlord they cultivated his land, for themselves their allotments; for the landlord they worked some days of the week and for themselves others. It is this system of economy which we call corvée (Russian: *barshchina*). (Lenin 1899a: 191–92)

With the formal abolition of serfdom, the corvée system was undermined but not destroyed. Peasants had to make redemption payments to their lords for their freedom, and the acceptance of redemption payments was not even made mandatory until 1881. Free access to woods, pastures and common lands was denied to the peasantry, these being the lands that were 'cut off' by the lords who allowed their use by the peasants only against various forms of payment in labour service (*barschina, otrabotki*, etc.) or half-share kind rent or combinations of these along with some payment of money (ibid.: 198–202). Lenin pointed out that labour service of the old feudal type 'could only be performed by the peasant farmer who owns draught animals and implements'. But side by side with this was found the use of the labour of the proletarian with no draught animals or implements, which, although also termed 'labour service', had a different economic content in representing growing capitalist relations (ibid.: 206). A detailed discussion followed of the growing significance of hired labour in agriculture and the growth not only of commercial farming but also of agro-processing industries, as indicators of the capitalist relations developing in rural areas.

Two Paths of Transition to Capitalism

Lenin made repeated use in his writings of Marx's idea of 'two paths' of transition to capitalism – the revolutionary, democratic path involving the break-up of feudal landed property with peasant capitalism developing from below, versus the conservative path of preserving land monopoly, where feudal landlords themselves developed into capitalists while using their erstwhile serfs as hired labour. In history, the first path was illustrated by France after the revolution as well as North American developments, while the second path was identified with Prussian 'Junker' capitalism.

The agrarian programme Lenin espoused was the revolutionary break-up of feudal landed property with the subsequent development of peasant capitalism from below, as the only path that would both break the personal relations of labour service and promote the maximum development of productive forces. Using available data, he pointed out:

> Thus, *landlords' lands* cultivated on a feudal fashion (on a metayer basis and rented out in small lots) produce *smaller* yields than allotment lands! . . . No credit, no land reclamation, no 'aid' to the peasant, none of the measures of 'assistance' beloved of the bureaucrats and liberals, will yield results of any importance so long as there remains the yoke of the feudal latifundia, traditions, and systems of economy. On the other hand, an agrarian revolution which abolishes landlordism and breaks up the old medieval village commune (the nationalization of the land, for example, will break it up, not in the police and bureaucratic manner[6]), would unfailingly serve as the basis for remarkably rapid and really wide progress. (Lenin 1908b: 89)

The quotation above is from 'The Agrarian Question in Russia towards the Close of the Nineteenth Century', written a decade after *The Development of Capitalism in Russia*. This can be read both as a summary and as a supplement to the earlier work, and contains useful material on the concentration of land in feudal hands. We are given the total land under private ownership in 1877 and 1905, and its break-up at both dates in terms of the land owned by the nobility, peasants and other social estates (see Table 3).

The dominant land owners remained the nobility, with nearly 62 per cent of the total area in 1905, compared to 80 per cent in 1877. The share of total area owned by peasants had gone up considerably, from 6.3 per cent to 15.4 per cent, but other classes, like 'merchants and notable citizens', had also gained. However, as Lenin pointed out, land ownership remained very highly concentrated even in 1905, with only about 700 of the largest properties (average size: 30,000 *desyatina*) accounting for one-fifth of the total area, while, at the other pole, some 620,000 small-holders (average size: 10.5 *desyatina*) accounted for only one-twelfth of the total area (Lenin 1908b: 72; the largest size-group was compared with the two smallest groups – see Table 3). Working out the percentage distributions of numbers and area from the data given (Table 4) and using Lenin's own method of linear interpolation for comparing the top two deciles

TABLE 3   *Change in the distribution of privately owned land in Russia by social group, 1877, 1905*

	Per cent of total area	
Social estate of owners	1877	1905
Nobility	79.9	61.9
Clergy	0.2	0.4
Merchants and notable citizens	10.7	15.0
Urban petty bourgeoisie	2.1	4.4
Peasants	6.3	15.4
Other social estates and foreign subjects	0.8	2.9
Total	100.0	100.0
Absolute area	91.5 m. des.	85.9 m. des.

Source: Lenin (1908b: 73).

TABLE 4 *Distribution of Privately Owned Land by Size of Property in European Russia, 1905*

Size-class (desyatina)	Number of properties (000)	Area of properties (million des.)	Percentage number (%)	Distribution area (%)	Average size (desyatina)
Up to 10	409.864	1.62523	54.44	1.89	3.9
10 –50	209.119	4.89103	27.77	5.70	23.4
50 –500	106.065	17.32649	14.09	20.19	163.3
500–2,000	21.748	20.59071	2.89	23.99	947.0
2000–10,000	5.386	20.60211	0.72	24.00	3,825.0
> 10,000	0.699	20.79850	0.09	24.23	29,754.6
Total	752.881	85.83407	100.00	100.00	114.0

Source: Lenin (1908b: 74).

with the lowest five deciles, we find that the top one-fifth of all land owners had 93 per cent of the area while the lowest half of all land owners had less than 2 per cent of the total area – surely one of the most highly concentrated land ownership structures in history.

Allotment land was not included in the statistics of privately owned land and amounted to 139 million *desyatina*. This was itself not entirely subject to egalitarian distribution, as Lenin demonstrated by working out the per capita allotment.

Class Differentiation and Displacement of Small Farms by Large Farms

The discussion by Lenin of the *size of farms as economic enterprises*, the question of investment by larger farms and the displacement of 'small' farms by 'large' farms, is one of the most interesting elements of his analysis of the agrarian question for this author, for it remains of great relevance at the present time for analysis of the agrarian sector of developing economies. Narodnik scholars in Russia had long maintained that small family labour-based farms were more viable and efficient compared to large capitalist farms run with hired labour, and could in fact better survive the vagaries of fluctuating market prices or harvest failure. This was, according to them, because of the family labour farm's flexibility as an economic unit – it did not have to run after profit as the capitalist farm did, it was argued, since its objective was simply to get a composite family income for the purpose of consumption; hence, there was no question of it making 'losses' or going out of business, for example, when the market price of output fell such that the capitalist farm could no longer cover the wage bill and incurred loss.

Chayanov, who wrote in Lenin's own lifetime, reiterated the earlier Narodnik positions more rigorously, specifically giving a numerical example to illustrate the above case of a large fall in agricultural crop price (after the crop had been produced), bankrupting the capitalist employing hired labour while the peasant farmer was allegedly unaffected. He 'explained' this in terms of subjective utility calculus – the peasant farmer could push his labour input much further than the wage-paid labour that was employed on the capitalist farm, lowering the return to his labour below the wage rate (because it was 'advantageous' for him to do so given his objective of feeding the family). The modern reader will find the same positions being articulated in present-day neoclassical models which similarly assume a homogeneous peasantry and talk of the economy of 'the peasant', whether he is small owner or tenant farmer, being more 'efficient' than the capitalist farmer, because the peasant did not subjectively 'cost' or 'count' his family labour at the market wage rate.

Lenin rejected the Narodnik argument on the grounds that, firstly, small peasant farms actually had lower yields (1908b: 89) and, secondly, the peasants could only compete with the capitalists by taking cuts in reward to labour and in consumption, by lowering their consumption standard:

> Under capitalist social conditions 'not to count' one's labour means to work for nothing (for the merchant or another capitalist); it means to work for incomplete remuneration for the labour-power expended; it means to lower the level of consumption below the standard . . . economists have deafened us with their praises of the 'viability' of the small peasant, who, they say, *need not count his own labour,* or chase after profit and rent, etc. These good people merely forget that such arguments confuse the social–economic conditions of natural economy, simple commodity production, and capitalism. (Lenin 1960: 124)

Kautsky had similarly pointed out that the ability of small farmers to survive competition from capitalist farms did not arise from their higher productivity but from 'overwork and underconsumption', providing detailed evidence from German farm data.

The crucial assumption made, without any discussion of it, by all the populists including Chayanov, as well as in all modern neoclassical models, is that *peasants and capitalists operate with the same production possibilities, that is, they have identical production functions.* Without this assumption their conclusions do not follow. It is this assumption of identical production possibilities that was correctly rejected by both Kautsky and Lenin. Indeed, the very assumption of identical production functions for peasants and capitalists contains a logical contradiction, as has been demonstrated: the capitalist necessarily gets a 'profit' income that is only a fraction of the bare subsistence level income of the peasant, and cannot be a 'capitalist' at all by any sensible definition.[7]

With regard to the questions of what determined whether a farm was to be considered 'small' or 'large' and whether 'small' farms were being displaced by 'large' farms, Lenin made a very important distinction between the size of farms as measured only by physical area, and the size of farms *as economic enterprises*. This distinction, which had been made earlier by Karl Kautsky as well, remains of great importance for analysing the dynamics of contemporary agrarian relations, and is too often forgotten, leading to fallacious arguments to this day. Lenin argued that when a process of capitalist differentiation was taking place, it could take the form of more investment by the emerging capitalists on a given land area, rather than simply a lateral addition to land area (which, in any case, would be difficult, since land, unlike other assets like machinery, could not be bought in one place and shifted elsewhere to add to an existing estate, while contiguous areas would not be available for purchase as and when required).

Owing to what Lenin termed 'capital intensification', over time, the share of total non-land assets and of total output in the hands of emerging capitalists would rise. Increasing economic concentration could take place, without necessarily increasing concentration of land – in fact, land concentration could even decrease in principle. Lenin supported and developed Kautsky's proposition that an intensively cultivated small estate could be larger in economic terms than an extensively cultivated large estate – '*Une petite propriété cultivée d'une manière intensive peut constituer un exploitation plus grande qu'une propriété plus entendue cultivée d'une manière extensive*' (Kautsky 1900: 221).[8] Both Kautsky and Lenin strongly refuted the populist argument, based on changing acreage distribution, that small farms were growing at the expense of large farms, by pointing out that 'small' and 'large' were being inadequately defined, only with respect to physical area and not with respect to other important economic indices like value of output, value of assets, use of hired labour and so on. There was an increase in the numbers of small 'farms' in Germany, which were actually small allotments given to farm labourers to tie them effectively to the capitalist estate in order to provide labour at the beck and call of the employer.

The proposition on the difference between the physical and the economic measure of the size of farms was illustrated further by Lenin in analysing the 1910 Census of the USA, which contained detailed economic data on farms, in a very interesting and little quoted paper entitled 'New Data on the Laws Governing the Development of Capitalism in Agriculture' (Lenin 1915). These data, which were already grouped according to the area of farms, showed that the smaller farms tended to more intensively use material inputs and labour, and thereby had higher output value per unit of area (the same findings on the 'inverse relation between farm size and yield' are found in the post-independence period in India and in many other countries including pre-1917 Russia). Lenin disputed the logic of grouping farms by their physical size measured by area alone since this did not give any idea of the actual scale of operations of farms. He showed that while the extensively cultivated grain farms of north-central USA were large in area, the much more intensively cultivated farms with smaller areas were larger on every other economic index.

> The grouping of farms by acreage . . . is obviously inadequate for it completely fails to take account of the intensification of agriculture, the increasing expenditure of capital per unit of area in the forms of livestock, machinery, improved seeds, better methods of crop cultivation, etc. Meanwhile, with the exception of very few areas and countries with a primitive or purely extensive agriculture, it is this very process that is most typical for capitalist countries everywhere. For this reason the grouping of farms by acreage in the vast majority of cases gives an over-simplified and entirely inadequate picture of agricultural development in general, and of capitalist development in agriculture in particular. (Ibid.: 58)

Thus, Lenin had moved ahead of his analysis in *The Development of Capitalism in Russia*, which had perforce relied on size-grouping as available in the published *zemstvo* statistical returns. (Access to the original schedules – which he did not have – would have been necessary for any other method of analysis.) He now proposed, in a section headed 'A More Exact Comparison of Small and Large Enterprises', an additional and alternative method of grouping farm data, namely, by the annual output value per farm. He regrouped the farms in the US Census by their annual output value. With acreage as the measure of the 'size' of farms, small farms were more intensively cultivated than large farms. With output as the measure of the size of farms, the converse was true. Lenin showed that US farms with larger output value, irrespective of their area, used more material inputs, more hired labour as well as more machinery per unit of area, and produced higher yields than farms with smaller output value, regardless of their varying area. He concluded that, 'of the theoretical sources of the erroneous notion of the "superiority" of small scale production . . . the most important one is the uncritical, routine attitude to the hackneyed methods of comparing enterprises only by their total acreage' (Lenin 1915).

Applying Lenin's suggestion of re-analysing farm data by the alternative index of output value to measure the scale of production, we find for India too that the inverse relation between farm size and yield vanishes: we get exactly the same results as Lenin did, that the larger the farm in economic terms, the more intensive the application of inputs and use of labour per unit area, and the higher the yield.[9] Further exercises of directly separating out the hired labour-based farms from the family labour-based ones also show that the former have significantly higher intensity and yields.

The core ideas of the neo-Narodnik or neo-populist school of thought, against which Lenin fought his intellectual and political battles, still exist today in all societies with a substantial peasantry. The idea that small family labour-based farms are more 'efficient' than capitalist farms in producing higher yields put forward today in mathematical models are based on the same untenable assumption of identical production functions and using the same logically falla-cious arguments that had been advanced by the Narodniks. Russia had its revolu-tion, but in developing countries like India, we find continued idealization of the miserable condition of small peasants and a related callousness with regard to ameliorating their condition.

Concluding Remarks

It is impossible to do justice, in this brief chapter, to the many-faceted contributions on the agrarian question by Lenin, who I consider to be the most outstanding intellect of the twentieth century. Intellect is not merely a matter of intelligence; it is ultimately also a question of uncompromising intellectual in-tegrity and commitment. Those who compromise their intellectual integrity for any reason whatsoever – and, unfortunately, we see too many such cases – do not deserve our respect, no matter what worldly and academic honours may be showered on them.

Lenin's writings emanate an intellectual integrity that has a blazing qual-ity, which cauterizes, as it were, all humbug based on incorrect, class-biased and fallacious reasoning. Lenin applied the Marxist method of analysis consistently to the question of the development of capitalist relations of production, not only to Russia before the Revolution and to the Soviet Union after the Revolution, but also to other countries, including developed industrial nations like the USA. He thereby produced a rich corpus of work that spans the disciplines of history, sociology and economics, which helps us to critique present-day fallacious reas-oning relating to agrarian relations and guides us in the direction of logically correct analysis.

Notes

1 *Zemstvo* house-to-house censuses were investigations of peasant farms undertaken by statistical agencies of the *zemstvo* or rural government bodies, mainly for taxation purposes. The wealth of factual materials was published in statistical abstracts cover-ing the different *gubernias* or districts, and their *uyezds* or sub-divisions.

2 1 *desyatina* = 2.7 acres.

3 A similar system was to be found up to the early eighteenth century in south India where the original settlers of villages undertook periodic redistributions, but with the introduction of private property under colonial land settlements, the system dis-appeared.

4 A census of the number of horses fit for army service was taken in Czarist Russia every six years. Censuses were carried out in 1876 (in 33 *gubernias*), 1882 (all of European Russia), 1888 (in 41 *gubernias*) and 1891 (in the remaining *gubernias*). The data abstracts were published by the Central Statistical Committee.

5 Examples are Sen (1966) and Easwaran and Kotwal (1989).

6 Stolypin's 1906 Decree sought to break up the *mir* from above, by legally allowing peasants to take their allotted land as private property in a consolidated block. Poorer peasants came under pressure to sell their share. Hence, the reference is to 'the police and bureaucratic manner' of breaking up the commune.

7 Coexistence of peasants and capitalists with identical production functions means that the same marginal value productivity of labour curve is applied to both. The peasant struggling for subsistence will then always have an income higher than the profit of the capitalist – which is impossible. The fallacy is a verbal fallacy, which ignores the definition of the term 'capitalist' compared to the term 'peasant'. Every fallacy in discourse, in *logos,* is a logical fallacy. For the routine use of this fallacious assumption of identical production functions, see Sen (1966), Caballero (1983), Cheung (1969), Martinez–Alier (1983), Stiglitz (1989), and every model in this tradition. For a critique, see Patnaik (1979), (1994). In theory and in reality, capitalists necessarily operate more productive techniques.

8 The 1900 French translation is quoted here because the 1988 English translation – 'An intensively farmed small estate represents a larger enterprise than a large, extensively cultivated area' – of this sentence is inaccurate (Kautsky 1988 [English translation]: 149). It is too categorical, suggesting that intensively cultivated estates are always larger, but the matter depends on the degree of intensity and how extensive the large estates are.

9 Those interested may see Patnaik (1987), which applies an index of scale, and also a labour exploitation index, to capture class status based on Lenin's *Preliminary Draft Theses on the Agrarian Question*, to re-analyse Indian farm economics data.

References

Note: All references to Lenin's writings are from V.I. Lenin, *Collected Works*, 45 volumes (Moscow: Foreign Languages Publishing House), first printing, 1961. The date after each specific reference indicates the year it was published, except for Lenin (1908b), which was written for an Encyclopaedia, but was censored and published only in 1918.

Caballero, J.M. (1983), 'Sharecropping as an Efficient System: Further Answers to an Old Puzzle', in T.J. Byres, ed., *Sharecropping and Sharecroppers* (London: Cass).

Chayanov, A.V. [1915] (1966), 'Peasant Farm Organization', in *Theory of the Peasant Economy*, edited by Daniel Thorner, B. Kerblay and R.E.F. Smith (Homewood, Illinois: Irwin).

Cheung, S.N.S. (1969), *The Theory of Share Tenancy* (Chicago: University of Chicago Press).

Easwaran, M. and A. Kotwal (1989), 'Credit and Agrarian Structure', in Pranab Bardhan, ed., *The Economic Theory of Agrarian Institutions* (Oxford: Clarendon).

Kautsky, Karl (1900), *La Question Agraire*, translated from the original German, *Die Agrafrage*, by E. Milhaud and C. Polack, Paris, translated into English by P. Burgess as *The Agrarian Question*, 2 volumes (London: Haper Collins, New York: Pluto Press), 1988.

Lenin, V.I. (1899a), *The Development of Capitalism in Russia*, in *Collected Works*, Vol. 3 (Moscow: Foreign Languages Publishing House): 9–658.

——— (1899b), 'Review of Karl Kautsky, *Die Agrarfrage*', in *Collected Works*, Vol. 4 (Moscow: Foreign Languages Publishing House): 94–99.

——— (1899c), 'Capitalism in Agriculture: in Kautsky's book and Mr Bulgakov's Attack', *Collected Works*, Vol. 4 (Moscow: Foreign Languages Publishing House): 105–59.

——— (1908a), 'The Agrarian Programme of Social Democracy in the First Russian Revolution', in *Collected Works*, Vol. 13 (Moscow: Foreign Languages Publishing House): 217–431.

——— (1908b), 'The Agrarian Question in Russia towards the Close of the Nineteenth Century', in *Collected Works*, Vol. 15 (Moscow: Foreign Languages Publishing House): 71–147.

——— (1915), 'New Data on the Laws Governing the Development of Capitalism in Agriculture', *Collected Works*, Vol. 22 (Moscow: Foreign Languages Publishing House).

——— (1920), 'Preliminary Draft Theses on the Agrarian Question', presented to the Second Congress of the Comintern, in *Collected Works*, Vol. 31 (Moscow: Foreign Languages Publishing House): 152–64.

Lorenz, M.O. (1905), 'Methods of Measuring the Concentration of Wealth', *Journal of the American Statistical Association*, New Series, 70, June: 209–19.

Martinez-Alier, M. (1983), 'Sharecropping: Some Illustrations', in T.J. Byres, ed., *Sharecropping and Sharecroppers* (London: Cass).

Marx, Karl ([1881] 1964), *Pre-Capitalist Economic Formations*, edited by E.J. Hobsbawm (London: Lawrence and Wishart).

Owen, L.A. (1937), *The Russian Peasant Movement, 1905–1917* (London: P.S. King and Son).

Patnaik, Utsa (1979), 'Neo-Populism and Marxism: The Fundamental Fallacy of Chayanovian Theory', *Journal of Peasant Studies*, 6 (4); reprinted as 'Neo-Populism and Marxism: The Chayanovian View of the Agrarian Question and its Fundamental Fallacy', in Utsa Patnaik (1999), *The Long Transition* (New Delhi: Tulika Books): 1–62.

——— (1987), *Peasant Class Differentiation: A Study in Method with Reference to Haryana* (New Delhi: Oxford University Press).

——— (1994), 'Tenancy and Accumulation', in Kaushik Basu, ed., *Agrarian Questions* (New Delhi: Oxford University Press).

Sen, A.K. (1966), 'Peasants and Dualism With and Without Surplus Labour', *Journal of Political Economy*, 74, October: 425–50.

Stiglitz, J.E. (1989), 'A Theory of Rural Organization', in Pranab Bardhan, ed., *The Economic Theory of Agrarian Institutions* (Oxford: Clarendon Press).

Watters, Francis M. (1968), 'The Peasant and the Village Commune', in W.S. Vucinich, ed., *The Peasant in 19th Century Russia* (Stanford: Stanford University Press).

Marshall as a Development Economist

Renee Prendergast

Marshall's *Principles of Economics* was first published in 1890. It was a product of more than twenty years of work on economic problems, and was further revised over the next thirty years, during which a total of eight editions were published. *Principles* is not much read nowadays and, in the main, Marshallian economics is identified with the neoclassical partial equilibrium approach. This is not surprising. By Marshall's own account, the form of his work was influenced by the mathematical conceptions of continuity derived from Cournot and, to a lesser extent, von Thunen (Marshall 1961: ix–x). In adopting Cournot's marginal approach, Marshall utilized diagrams rather than mathematical symbols, and even these, he relegated to footnotes in *Principles*. These diagrams showing price on the *y* axis and quantity on the *x* axis are familiar to every beginner student of economics. They are part of the apparatus through which the student learns how the market system allocates scarce resources efficiently. Yet, Marshall's ambitions for his system were quite different. In the preface to the first edition of *Principles*, he announced to the world that the views expressed in his work had two kinds of influences more than any other. These were biology, as represented in the work of Herbert Spencer, and history and philosophy, as represented in Hegel's *Philosophy of World History*.

Despite Marshall's apparent optimism in the preface to the *Principles* about the potential of the Cournot method as a means of analysing development issues, in the body of the work itself, he expressed deep reservations.

> It has already been indicated that the theory of stable equilibrium of normal demand and supply in its most abstract form assumes a certain rigidity in the conditions of demand and supply, which does not really exist. This theory, however, especially when aided by diagrams, helps to give definiteness to our ideas; and in its elementary stages it does not diverge from the actual facts of life so far as to prevent its giving a trustworthy picture. . . . It is only when pushed to its more remote and intricate logical consequences, especially those connected with multiple positions of equilibrium, that it slips away from the conditions of real life, and soon ceases to be of much service in dealing with practical problems. (Marshall 1961, II: 522)

There can be little doubt that Marshall employed a wide variety of developmental metaphors in *Principles*, which were later purged by his main successors to produce the neoclassical partial equilibrium apparatus with which we are now familiar. Does this mean that Marshall's concern with development was mere rhetoric and insufficiently embedded in his thought? There is little agreement on this among students of Marshall. On the one hand, G.L.S. Shackle (1965: 36) has argued that Marshall achieved 'a peculiar triumph in his creation of a unity out of the conceptions of equilibrium and evolution'. On the other hand, writers such as Levine (1980), Thomas (1991) and Hodgson (1993) have argued that Marshall merely paid lip service to biological analogies. A third view suggests that Marshall's interest in development was deep and profound, but ultimately proved incapable of incorporation within the theoretical apparatus he developed.

This chapter assesses the case for seeing Marshall as a development economist. It seeks to establish the nature of Marshall's views on development and to show that a belief in progress was fundamental to his vision as an economist. It also examines the ways in which Marshall sought to incorporate his vision of progress within the partial equilibrium framework, and why he eventually failed in this endeavour.

Vision of Progress

When Marshall's developing interest in social and philosophical issues, especially the problem of poverty, led him to forsake mathematics for political economy in the late 1860s, John Stuart Mill was the leading authority in the field. In his *Principles of Political Economy*, Mill had attempted to move away from crude *laissez-faire* positions and to place political economy in a wider setting. As Marx put it, Mill sought 'to harmonize the political economy of capital with the claims, no longer to be ignored, of the proletariat' (Marx 1977: 25).

In this respect, Mill's major innovation was his distinction between the laws of production and the laws of distribution. According to Mill, the laws of production were real laws of nature, dependent on the properties of objects and not alterable by human will, while the laws of distribution were matters of human institution. As such, the laws of distribution were subject to human control and had a provisional character likely to be much altered by the progress of social improvement (Mill 1909: 199–201). Following a suggestion of Comte's, Mill also distinguished between the fundamental study of the condition of existence of society, or statics, and the laws of its continuous development, or dynamics. Book IV of Mill's *Principles* was conceived as adding a theory of motion to the theory of equilibrium – the dynamics of political economy to its statics (ibid.: 695). Despite the innovative language, there was little evidence of any deviation from the Ricardian heritage, with the main content of the book being an abstract argument as to the effects on prices, rents, profits and wages of the progress of population, capital and the arts of production in various combinations (ibid.:

xx). Like Ricardo, Mill saw the economy as tending to a stationary state. Mill did not regard this as a problem because he thought that it was only in backward countries that increased production was still an important object. In the most advanced countries, what was needed was better distribution. The indispensable means of achieving this was 'a stricter restraint on population' (ibid.: 749–50). Other measures (for example, inheritance taxes) aimed at the equalization of fortunes would also be helpful, as would schemes for sharing profits, either directly or through cooperative societies.

While Mill provided Marshall with the starting point for his own economic studies, Marshall soon departed from Mill in a number of significant ways. First, and most important, Marshall formed the view that, rather than tending to a stationary state, advanced economies, such as Britain's, were in a process of continuing evolutionary progress. Given that he was also of the opinion that existing output, however distributed, was not adequate to meet the needs of society, he focused on growth, rather than redistribution, as a means of alleviating poverty. Second, Marshall's comments on Mill's statements about the provisional character of the laws of distribution indicate that he was not convinced by Mill's views (Pigou 1925: 119–33). Mill's arguments, he wrote, had to be considered in the context of the overall structure of his political economy, and, if this was done, it would be clear that Mill envisaged distribution as being 'effected by the instrumentality of a "machinery of exchange", the greater part of which would be put in requisition under almost any social arrangements that are likely to exist in the civilized world' (ibid.: 125).

In line with this view, Marshall's own recipe for improving the lot of the poor was: (i) to increase real wages by increasing productivity; (ii) to raise both average income and the share of it accruing to unskilled labour by diminishing the supply of labour incapable of any but unskilled work. The latter would require improvements in education for which the state 'seems to be required to contribute generously and even lavishly' (Marshall 1961, I: 717–18). This proposal is consistent with the view Marshall expressed in *Principles*, that changes which brought only small increases to the efficiency of production would be worth having if they made mankind ready and fit for an organization 'which will be more effective in the production of wealth and more equal in its distribution' (ibid.: 249).

Marshall's scepticism with regard to the extent to which the laws of production and distribution could be separated in a system of commodity production, should not be taken to mean that he was opposed to all non-market schemes for redistribution. In general, he favoured forms of redistribution that tended to promote growth and opposed forms of redistribution likely to slow it. Thus, supporting the right of rural workers to unionize in the early 1870s, Marshall argued that increased wages would be beneficial to both farmers and labourers because, if wisely spent, they would lead to an increase in the efficiency of labour (Groenewegen 1995: 574). On the other hand, he opposed equalization by means of redistributive taxes on the grounds that, at best, it could only achieve limited results and, at worst, it might stifle initiative and enterprise; his position softened later in life, though. (ibid.: 597–98)

More than anything else, it was his belief that continuing economic progress would dominate any tendencies towards a stationary state that differentiated Marshall from his classical predecessors. This vision was sustained by the belief that continuing growth was possible, because of the scope for both continuing technological innovation and improvements in human beings themselves. Marshall's views on the scope for technological improvement, which are set out in the chapters on industrial organization in *Principles*, built on what he had inherited from Babbage, Mill and Marx, as well as his own observations of the factory system in Britain and America. As indicated above, he linked these views on technological development tendencies to the issue of improvements in human beings themselves. For Marshall, however, improvements in human beings were important not just for instrumental reasons but as ends in themselves. As he put it, 'The growth of mankind in numbers, in health and strength, in knowledge, ability and richness of character is the end of all our studies' (Marshall 1961: 139).

In the first of his chapters on industrial organization in *Principles*, Marshall referred to the many profound analogies between the action of the laws of nature in the physical and moral worlds. These related to 'the general rule . . . that the development of the organism, whether social or physical, involves an increasing division of functions between its separate parts on the one hand, and on the other a more intimate connection between them' (Marshall 1961: 241). This way of regarding evolution, which seems to have derived from Herbert Spencer, was basically a generalization of the economist's vision of progress as a product of the advancing division of labour. As such, it was a natural starting point for an economist interested in evolution. In Spencer's view, the process of evolution was essentially progressive in that it gradually pushed life towards higher states of organization and caused the evolution of new qualities (Bowler 1989: 239). While Marshall approved of the broad thrust of Spencer's evolutionary theory, he did not endorse Spencer's support for *laissez faire*, and was careful to point out that in the struggle for survival, those organisms best fitted to derive benefit from their environment did not necessarily benefit that environment (Marshall 1961: 242). Moreover, the struggle for survival might fail to bring into existence organisms that would be highly beneficial. In this context, Marshall pointed out that while Adam Smith had insisted on the advantages of a minute division of labour, he had also pointed to the 'many incidental evils which it involved', and suggested possible remedies (ibid.: 246). The view that each person, by pursuing his own interests, also promotes the general good was a doctrine of the highest importance, but its exaggeration had hindered the removal of the evil intertwined with the good. It also took no account of Spencer's doctrine that the organs are strengthened by being used (ibid.: 247).[1] What Marshall appears to have in mind is that progress could actually be speeded up by judicious intervention that would improve men's character and intellect. This was the case because, with the evolution of the division of labour, machinery was replacing purely manual skill and increasing the demand for complex skills and intelligence.

Marshall took the view that any manufacturing operation reduced to uniformity was certain, sooner or later, to be taken over by machinery. There might be delays and difficulties, but provided the work was on a sufficient scale, money and inventive power would be devoted to solving the problem of mechanization (Marshall 1961: 255). As a consequence, machinery was constantly supplanting purely manual skill. This influence, however, 'was more than countervailed by its tendency to increase the scale of manufactures and make them more complex; and therefore to increase the opportunities for division of labour of all kinds' (ibid.: 256). Machine-made machinery was allowing the system of interchangeable parts to develop rapidly. This system not only reduced the cost of producing complex machinery, but also greatly reduced the cost of repairs, both of which had the effect of greatly extending the use of machinery (ibid.: 256–57).

While the introduction of machinery displaced labour engaged in routine work, the use of machinery made by machinery tended to displace those forms of labour requiring high levels of manual skill but little by way of judgement. At the same time, greater judgement, intelligence and care were called for from the operatives who set up and maintained the modern automated machinery. Such operatives also enjoyed greater mobility because of the similarities between machines employed in different trades. On the whole, Marshall seems to have taken the view that the role of machinery was progressive. It reduced the strain associated with hard manual labour. In addition, since all standardized work was eventually taken over by machinery, it tended to reduce the monotony of work, and thus prevent the monotony of work involving monotony of life (Marshall 1961: 263).

It has to be said that the apparent optimism with regard to the effects of technological and organizational change on wider human development was somewhat more qualified in *Industry and Trade* than in *Principles*. This is particularly true of the chapters in which Marshall considers the scientific management movement that was highly influential in the early decades of the twentieth century, particularly in America (Whitaker 1999: 255–71). While Marshall allowed that the high productivity achieved through the application of scientific management techniques was often accompanied by higher wages for operatives, he was concerned that a great part of the work that used to be committed to operatives and foremen would now be absorbed by planning departments. In his opinion, this removal from the operatives of any duty other than that of carrying out his instructions carefully was 'not likely to be altogether good' (Marshall 1923: 388).

In the end, for Marshall, man was not merely an agent of production. The most economic use of man as an agent of production was wasteful if he was not himself developed by it.

It is needful then diligently to inquire whether the present industrial organization might not with advantage be so modified as to increase the opportunities which the lower grades of industry have for using latent mental faculties, for deriving pleasure from their use, and from strengthening them by use; since the argument that had such a change been beneficial, it would have already been brought about by the struggle for survival, must be rejected as invalid. Man's prerogative extends to a limited but effective control over natural development by forecasting the future and preparing the way for the next step. (Marshall 1961, I: 248)

Marshall's belief that men had limited but effective control over natural development, which would enable them to obtain the good without the evil and allow them to think out for themselves the solution to their own problems, reflects his rejection of *laissez faire* and the associated concept of freedom as absence of restraint. He was attracted to the Kantian view that true freedom consists in acting according to reason because, in this way, the individual finds liberation from mere natural impulse. This view was modified by Hegel so as to remove the apparent conflict between pursuit of freedom and the pursuit of goals such as happiness and wealth. Hegel's solution was to argue that true freedom could only be achieved in a rationally organized community in which the interests of the individual were harmonized with the interests of the wider society. Such a community had to have an institutional structure in which the capacity for freedom was nurtured through education and socialization, and in which freedom was sustained through practices and institutions that commanded universal support (Patten 1999: 102). These social practices and institutions, and individuals' duties in them, were to be viewed not as hindrances to freedom but as vehicles for its actualization.

Groenewegen (1990, 1995) has shown that Marshall was greatly impressed by Hegel's views on freedom and made them an important part of his own vision. This is reflected in his claim that the 'growth of knowledge and self-reliance' that came with it gave people 'that true self-controlling freedom which enables them to impose of their own free will restraints on their own actions' (Marshall 1961, I: 751). Marshall looked forward to an order of social life in which the common good over-ruled individual caprice, and in which individual freedom developed itself in collective freedom (ibid.: 752).

The Incorporation of Progress within the Partial Equilibrium Framework

It was noted above that Mill had followed Comte in distinguishing between the conditions of existence of society and the laws of its continuing development. A similar distinction between the circular flow of economic life and the development process was later made by Schumpeter in his *Theory of Economic Development*. Schumpeter suggested that Walras' theoretical apparatus was suitable for an analysis of the interdependence of economic quantities but not suitable for an analysis of economic change in time. Later, in 1928, he argued that his own use of the terms static and static equilibrium were 'perfectly in keeping with the fundamental drift of Marshallian analysis' (Schumpeter 1928: 368). Having noted Marshall's repeated protests about the limitations of the static apparatus, and his claim that reasoning by means of it is 'too far removed from life to be useful', Schumpeter argued that there was nothing 'unduly abstract in considering the phenomena incident to the running of economic life under given conditions'.

Whatever the plausibility of Schumpeter's views on this matter, it is clear that they were not shared by Marshall. Marshall acknowledged that a volume on foundations that used mechanical analogies and made frequent use of the term equilibrium, might suggest an approach that was static, rather than dynamic. In fact, he argued, this was not the case. His work was 'concerned throughout with forces that cause movement: and its keynote is that of dynamics rather than statics' (Marshall 1961: xiv). In the preface to the fifth edition of *Principles*, Marshall provided the following argument to support the view that statics and dynamics were not to be separated.

> He (Comte) thought that it was possible to divide 'the Study of Humanity' into two parts: the Statical, which deals with the Structure and the laws of Order; and the Dynamical, which deals with the laws of actual development and Progress. But such a division presents great difficulties. For, while a *description* of structure need not concern itself with causes or 'forces', an *explanation* of structure must deal the forces that brought that structure into existence: and therefore it must be in the physical sense of the term 'dynamical'. The existing structure and order are the outcome of progress in the past. (Marshall 1961, II: 48)

Marshall does not seem to have been entirely satisfied with the argument in this passage because he dropped it as early as the sixth edition. The passage is interesting, nonetheless, because it shows that he consciously rejected the strategy of separating statics from dynamics. Marshall's view that statics and dynamics could not be separated is part and parcel of his view that economics has to be concerned throughout with the tendencies of the economic system, and that the forward movement of the economy was continuous, rather than discontinuous.

> Economic evolution is gradual. Its progress is sometimes arrested or reversed by political catastrophes: but its forward movements are never sudden; for even in the Western world and in Japan, it is based on habit, partly conscious, partly unconscious. And though an inventor, or an organizer, or a financier of genius may seem to have modified the economic structure of a people almost at a stroke; yet that part of his influence which has not been superficial or transitory, is found on inquiry to have done little more than bring to a head a broad constructive movement which had long been in preparation. (Marshall 1961, I: xiii)

Here, Marshall explicitly rejects the view that the entrepreneur or great man is the source of change. The critique was not directed at any particular proponent of this view, nor was it, by any means, unique to Marshall. In arguing against Thomas Carlyle's glorification of the role of the great man, Herbert Spencer had argued that the great man was the result of 'a long series of complex influences which has produced the race in which he appears and the social state into which that race has slowly grown' (Hook 1945). Consequently, the real explanation for any decisive event was to be arrived at, not by attributing it to the great man who seemed to have been its immediate occasion, but by examining 'the aggregate of conditions out of which both he and they have arisen' (ibid.).

This sort of view of the role of leadership and human agency has points in common with Hegel, Engels, Lenin and, at least, the later Schumpeter, and can be directly contrasted with elitist theories that were current in the early twentieth century. Marshall's particular take on the issue involved not only a rejection of the elitist view, but also a rejection of the view that development was characterized by large discontinuities or revolutions. *Natura non facit saltum* – Nature does not make jumps – appears on the title page of *Principles*, and Marshall wrote in the preface to the first edition that in so far as his book had any special character of its own, it derived from the prominence it gave to 'applications of the Principle of Continuity'.

Having satisfied himself that development was essentially a continuous process, Marshall seems to have presumed it could be best analysed using the mathematical conceptions of continuity or differential calculus whose use in economic analysis had already been pioneered by Cournot. He soon realized that the use of Cournot's method in the context of development was fraught with difficulties. First, as Cournot himself realized, increasing returns appear to be incompatible with competition. In addition, there was the problem of irreversibility, which, although potentially a general problem, Marshall regarded as being particularly acute when the law of increasing returns was active.

Increasing Returns

In the opening chapters of the *Wealth of Nations*, Adam Smith advanced two important propositions. First, specialization and the division of labour were the sources of improvements in the productive power of labour. Second, the division of labour was limited by the extent of the market. Together, these two propositions allowed Smith and his classical successors to associate an increase in the size of the market with a fall in the cost of production. When Adam Smith referred to the size of the market, he did not necessarily mean the market for a particular product but, rather, the 'power of exchanging' or the market for goods in general. Even where the market in question was that for a particular good, the link between an increase in the size of the market and any reduction in the costs of production was seen as permissive, rather than compulsive.

If we move from this loose association and depict the fall in the cost of production as an exact functional relationship between quantity produced and

cost, it becomes necessary to ask why specialization is not everywhere pushed to
its limits, so that the economy is made up of highly specialized monopolies,
rather than competitive industries with large numbers of firms. This step was
taken by Cournot in 1838. Cournot concluded that if the marginal cost function
of an individual firm was decreasing, the operation of monopoly was not wholly
extinct (Cournot 1960). Despite his high regard for Cournot, Marshall took the
view that Cournot's position was mistaken, and attributed the mistake to inappro-
priate abstraction from the conditions of real life:

> The great Cournot himself misapplied mathematics here. He ignored the condi-
> tions which, in real life, prevent the speedy attainment of monopoly by a single
> manufacturing firm: and the general drift of his argument is practically mislead-
> ing. His failure contributed to make me hold back my diagrams as to value from
> formal publication for twenty years. (Marshall 1961, II: 69).

As indicated in the above comment, the problems associated with
increasing returns surfaced at an early stage in Marshall's work and were
already evident in *The Essay on Value* that he composed around 1870. In the
course of an investigation of questions relating to the uniqueness and stability of
equilibrium, Marshall realized that multiple equilibria were possible if an industry supply curve was downward-sloping. Then, while explaining how the transition between two points of stable equilibrium could be made, Marshall was
forced to confront the problem of whether plausible sources of increasing returns
were compatible with a downward-sloping supply curve. If the source of cost
reductions were the use of extra machinery and a more elaborate division of
labour by individual firms, there was no obvious reason why the same cost
reductions could not have been achieved by a displacement of other firms, rather
than an expansion of industry output.

Marshall's initial solution to this problem was to make the tacit assumption that 'an increase in the economy of labour which results from production on
a large scale depends on an increase in the total amount produced' (Whitaker
1975, I). Much of his subsequent work on the problem can be interpreted as an
attempt to justify this assumption. By the time the first edition of *Principles* was
published in 1890, the initial assumption had metamorphosed into 'external economies', which were defined as 'those economies, which do not directly depend on
the size of individual houses of business'. The most important of them, Marshall
suggested, result from the growth of correlated branches of industry that mutually assist one another, perhaps by being located in the same area (Marshall
1961, I: 317). Elsewhere, he described external economies as those that depend
on the general organization of the trade, the growth of knowledge and appliances common to the trade, and the development of subsidiary industries (Marshall
1898: 50).

The concept of external economies was regarded as the key element in
Marshall's attempt to reconcile increasing returns and competitive equilibrium
by such authorities as Edgeworth (1925), Pigou (1913, 1928), Sraffa (1925), Viner

(1931) and Chipman (1965). The view of this group may be summarized as depicting the representative firm in long-run equilibrium as operating at the minimum point on its long-run average cost curve with no un-exhausted internal economies. Since no internal economies were available to be exploited, any fall in average costs resulting from an increase in industry output has to be attributed to external economies. The main problem with this view is that it is difficult to conjure up plausible sources of external economies that meet its requirements.

The view that sees external economies as the source of declining average costs was contested by Robertson and others, who assigned the key role to the life cycle of the firm and to the associated concept of the representative firm (Robertson 1930, 1956; Shove 1930; Frisch 1950; Newman 1960; Whitaker 1987). Robertson argued that Marshall's concept of the life cycle of the firm[2] made it possible to conceive of an equilibrium in which the representative firm had un-exhausted internal economies. If this initial equilibrium was disturbed by an increase in demand, one factor in progress towards the new equilibrium would be the attempt by individual firms to reap the advantages of large-scale production. While Robertson's view is, in important respects, in line with Marshall's intentions, it suffers from the defect that the life cycle is given the task of preventing the firm from growing in one situation and of permitting it to become larger in another (Sraffa 1930).

While rival interpretations of Marshall's reconciliation exercise have focused *either* on external economies *or* the life cycle of the firm, there are grounds for regarding both elements as essential to any reconciliation exercise (Prendergast 1992). Both were further elaborated in *Principles*, where they were linked to the concept of the representative firm. Marshall argued that the concept of a representative firm was biological, rather than mechanical. Firms were seen as growing over time and reaching a maximum size when the forces making for further growth were exactly balanced by the forces of decay (Marshall 1961, I: 316). While some firms attained greater size than others, it was in general possible to identify a representative producer. Such a firm 'was the particular sort of average firm, at which we need to look in order to see how far the economies, *internal and external*, of production on a large scale have extended generally in the industry and country in question' (ibid.: 318).

> Now the growth of internal economies is generally more rapid than that of external. The rise and fall of individual firms may be frequent, while a great industry is going through one long oscillation, or even moving steadily forwards; as the leaves of a tree . . . grow to maturity, reach equilibrium and decay many times, while the tree itself is steadily growing upwards year by year. For very long periods the oscillation of internal economies may almost be neglected: except in so far as they are indirectly dependent on external; for a large industry offers a better field in most (not in all) ways for large individual firms than a small industry offers. (Marshall 1898: 50)

In general, the debates about the content of Marshall's reconciliation of increasing returns and competition have a great deal to do with the wider interpretation of Marshall's work. Those who see him as a partial equilibrium theorist in the neoclassical mould tend to emphasize the external economies argument, whereas those who see him as a theorist of economic evolution tend to emphasize the life cycle of the firm and, the related, representative firm approach. To some extent, this is a false dichotomy, because both elements are essential to Marshall's reconciliation exercise. It would be foolish not to recognize that Marshall constructed a framework which could accommodate more possibilities than the neoclassical model, but it would be equally foolish not to recognize that he sought to construct a framework which could, within the confines of the Cournot partial equilibrium approach.

It has been widely remarked that Marshall's concept of external economies is a somewhat elusive category which sometimes conceals, as much as it illuminates. Part of the reason for this is that Marshall used the distinction between internal and external economies to cover two different, albeit related, issues. The first concerns

> how far the full economies of division of labour can be obtained by the concentration of large numbers of small businesses of a similar kind in the same locality; and how far they are attainable only by the aggregation of a large part of the business of the country into the hands of a comparatively small number of rich and powerful firms. (Marshall 1961, I: 277).

The second relates to the classification of those economies arising from the expansion of an industry into 'those dependent on the general development of the industry, and those dependent on the individual houses of business engaged in it and the efficiency of their management' (ibid.: 314).

In the course of the controversies relating to the compatibility of increasing returns and competitive equilibrium, the focus has tended to be on the second of these issues; but, from the point of view of an understanding of industrial development, the first issue is more important. In one of his earliest discussions of this issue, Marshall noted that, with regard to many classes of commodity, it might be possible to divide the production process into several stages, in each of which the maximum efficiency of production might be attained by small firms. Where a sufficiently large number of small firms specialized in a particular stage of production, there would be the potential for the development of subsidiary industries adopted to meeting the special needs of those firms. Such subsidiary trades might be engaged in the production of special tools and machinery, the supply of parts, or the collection and distribution of output (Whitaker 1975: 196). Other advantages of agglomeration considered by Marshall included the development of a pool of specialized skills, and the development and dissemination of new ideas and new methods of production (ibid.: 87).

While Marshall was clear that economies of production on a large scale could be realized through networks of relatively small firms, he was aware that large firms possessed certain advantages, particularly with regard to innovation.

In mature industries where improvements in machinery were devised, mainly by machine-makers, small firms could have access to the best machinery available. However, this was unlikely to be the case in industries that were in an early stage of development or were rapidly changing in form, because these new machines and processes were mainly devised by manufacturers.

Marshall also noted that small firms were likely to lack the resources to conduct experiments and were consequently unable to create new wants by showing people something that they had never thought of having before (Marshall 1961, I: 279–82). Where the issue was one of improvement of processes and products, rather than the invention of new ones, the risks associated with experimentation might be less. But even here, the small firm was at a disadvantage because it would have difficulty in obtaining the full benefit of its innovation. Marshall did, however, note that trade associations and other forms of collective organization could go some way towards counteracting the difficulties of the small firm in matters of technical and business knowledge (ibid.: 284–85).

Before we leave the topic of increasing returns, it is worth noting that while Marshall's partial equilibrium framework made it necessary for him to devote a good deal of attention to increasing returns as they related to individual firms and industries, he was well aware that 'the economies of production on a large scale can seldom be allocated exactly to any one industry' (Marshall 1923: 188). As he wrote in the chapter on division of labour and the influence of machinery in *Principles*:

> Many of those economies in the use of specialized skill and machinery that are commonly regarded as within the reach of very large establishments, do not depend on the size of individual factories. Some depend on the aggregate volume of production of the kind in the neighbourhood; while others again, especially those connected with the growth of knowledge and the progress of the arts, depend chiefly on the aggregate volume of production in the whole civilized world. (Marshall 1961, I: 265–66)

Thus, increasing returns is more properly considered as a process of cumulative causation. Summarizing in the concluding chapter of Book IV of *Principles*, Marshall refers to man's power of productive work increasing with the volume of work that he does, and to every increase in wealth making a greater increase easier than before (ibid.: 314).

Irreversibility

Just as Marshall recognized at an early stage that it was difficult to accommodate increasing returns within his equilibrium framework, so also, the irreversible nature of economic events was discussed in the early 1870s in the *Pure Theory of Domestic Values* and the *Pure Theory of Foreign Trade*. In the former, Marshall wrote:

> It has been remarked that in economics every event causes permanent

alterations in the conditions under which future events can occur. This is to some extent the case in the physical world, but not to nearly so great an extent. The forces that act on a pendulum in any position are not to any appreciable extent dependent on the oscillations that the pendulum has already made. And there are many other classes of movement in the physical world, which are exact copies of movements that have gone before. But every movement that takes place in the moral world, alters the magnitude if not the character of the forces that govern succeeding movements. And economic forces belong to the mortal world insofar as they depend on human habits and affectations, upon man's knowledge and industrial skill. (Whitaker 1975, II: 163)

Given that economic forces encompassed human habits of all kinds, irreversibilities could be a feature of demand as well as of supply. If a temporary disturbance increased the demand for English wares in Germany, this would have the permanent effect of increased familiarity on the part of the German populace with the English produce and thus occasion a permanent alternation in the circumstances of demand (ibid.). Likewise, on the supply side, if a disturbance resulting in increased production of a commodity leads to the introduction of extensive economies, such economies are not readily lost when the disturbance is abated. This is because the development of mechanical appliances, of division of labour, of organization and of transport, once they have been obtained, are not readily abandoned (ibid.: 202).

Marshall revisited the issue of irreversibilities in Appendix H of *Principles*. Once again, he noted that habits that have once grown up around the use of a commodity when its price was low are not quickly abandoned when its price rises again. Consequently, 'the list of demand prices which holds for the forward movement of the production of a commodity will seldom hold for the return movement, but will in general require to be raised' (Marshall 1961, I: 807–08). Despite this acknowledgement, Marshall intimated in his marginal summary that no great violence was done by assuming that the list of demand prices is rigid. The same did not apply to the list of supply prices. The list that held for the forward movement would not hold for the backward movement, and would have to be replaced by a lower schedule in the case where costs decreased with output. This was true in all cases, but likely to be of special importance in the case of industries obeying the law of increasing returns.

Marshall was unable to offer any solution to the problem of irreversibilities except to express the hope that an improvement in analytical methods would allow them to be handled more satisfactorily.

Concluding Remarks

Marshall saw the economic system as evolving gradually over time. Each generation inherited resources, institutions and technology from its predecessors, and, on the basis of these, made its own contribution to development. Unlike his classical predecessors, Marshall was optimistic that progress would continue. He was confident that there was scope for continuing technological progress, but, above all, he was confident that there was scope for improvements in human beings themselves. These could be achieved by improvements in childhood care and in schooling, and by improvements in the nature of daily work.

For Marshall, improvements in human beings were not simply means to achieve higher levels of material output but, on the contrary, were themselves the end of economic activity. From this perspective, it was not just income that mattered for human welfare but the nature of the work by means of which that income was earned. Like Hegel, Marshall saw the growth of freedom in the form of self-reliance, independence, deliberate choice and forethought as the fundamental characteristics of modern life. While Marshall was convinced that the tendencies of economic evolution were, broadly speaking, progressive, he believed that the results of the free play of market forces were not uniformly good, especially when economic freedom degenerated into licence. This he contrasted with that true controlling freedom which enabled people 'to impose of their own free will restraints on their own actions' in pursuit of the common good (Marshall 1961, I: 751). The increased prosperity that had been achieved meant that many countries were 'now' strong enough to impose restraints on free enterprise which would lead to higher and, ultimately, greater gain, even if this resulted in some immediate material loss.

It is clear from all of this that, in Marshall's vision of progress, the excesses of nineteenth and early twentieth-century capitalism were to be removed by rational pursuit of the good and not forcibly by revolution. Marshall does not seem to have given any great consideration to the nature of the social forces that would take forward this reformist agenda – perhaps because much of it appeared to find ready acceptance in British government circles in the 1890s and 1900s. His own role was to set out the intellectual case for reform in terms that were economically sound and that might be expected to appeal to a broad spectrum of opinion.

Given the central role of development in Marshall's vision of the economic process, it is difficult to understand why he took the decision to incorporate his economic analysis within an analytical framework derived from Cournot. He was interested in the analysis of the tendencies of the system, and may have thought that the marginal method, with its emphasis on increments of quantities, offered an appropriate vehicle for this purpose. We saw above that the difficulties associated with the attempt to represent development within an equilibrium framework manifested themselves primarily as a conflict between increasing returns and competition, and, to a lesser extent, as problems relating to reversibility.

While acknowledging the importance of these issues, Loasby (1991: 16) has argued that the real source of Marshall's difficulty lay in his attempt to represent the incremental novelty of an open system within a framework that required a closed system. Loasby points out that perfect competition excludes all initiative and makes every agent a prisoner of circumstance. Consequently, it was singularly unsuitable for Marshall's purposes since it left no room for discretion or that 'true controlling freedom' in which he placed such great faith.

Much of Marshall's effort in the eight editions of his *Principles* and other writings involved creating a space for living force and movement within the optimization framework. As he wrote in the preface to the eighth edition, increasing stress has been laid on the fact that the notion of a margin is not uniform or absolute, that it varies with the conditions of the problem at hand and with the period of time to which reference is being made. Marshall's efforts in this direction were not always appreciated by his neoclassical successors. This is evidenced in Samuelson's accusation that Marshall attempted to achieve 'a spurious verisimilitude', and that he ended up being fuzzy and confusing (Samuelson 1967: 111–12). On the other hand, Schumpeter, in his later work, suggested that that Marshall's hybrid view of competition preserved the content of actual business behaviour that other theorists (including, presumably, his early self) had refined away (Schumpeter 1961: 975).

Notes

[1] This part of Marshall's argument was originally based on Lamark's theory of the inheritance of acquired characteristics, but, in his later work, it was based on the recognition that cultural and social forms provided evolutionary mechanisms of their own that did not depend on any direct analogy with biological evolution.

[2] The notion of the life cycle of the firm had already been introduced in *Economics of Industry*, which contains Marshall's most forthright admission of the economic advantages of large firms. But, in admitting these advantages, he argued that the sons and grandsons of a successful man of business seldom have 'that rare combination of ability and assidity which would enable them to carry on his work' (Marshall and Marshall 1879: 141–42). Consequently, vast inherited businesses tended to be unable to consolidate their advantages and were often destroyed.

References

Bowler, Peter (1989), *Evolution: The History of an Idea* (Berkeley: University of California Press).

Chipman, J.S. (1965), 'A Survey of the Theory of International Trade: Part II, The Neoclassical Theory', *Econometrica*, 33: 18–76.

Cournot, A.A. (1960), *Researches into the Mathematical Principles of the Theory of Wealth*, translated by N.T. Bacon (London: Hafner).

Edgeworth, F.Y. (1925), *Papers Relating to Political Economy*, 3 vols (London: Macmillan).

Frisch, R. (1950), 'Alfred Marshall's Theory of Value', *Quarterly Journal of Economics*, November, 64: 495–524.

Groenewegen, Peter (1990), 'Marshall and Hegel', *Economie Appliquee*, 63: 63–84.

—— (1995), *A Soaring Eagle: Alfred Marshall, 1842–1924* (Aldershot: Edward Elgar).

Hegel, G.W.F (1975), *Lectures on the Philosophy of World History, Introduction of Reason in History*, translated by H.B. Nisbet with introduction by D. Forbes (Cambridge: Cambridge University Press).

Hodgson, G.M. (1993), 'The Mecca of Alfred Marshall', *Economic Journal*, 103: 406–15.

Hook, Sidney (1945), *The Hero in History: A Study in Limitation and Possibility* (London: Secker and Warburg).

Levine, A.L. (1980), 'Increasing Returns, the Competitive Model and the Enigma that was Alfred Marshall', *Scottish Journal of Political Economy*, 27 (3): 260–75.

Loasby, B.J. (1991), *Equilibrium and Evolution* (Manchester: Manchester University Press).

Marshall, Alfred (1898), 'Distribution and Exchange', *Economic Journal*, 8: 37–59.

—— (1923), *Industry and Trade* (London: Macmillan).

—— (1961), *Principles of Economics*, 9th (variorum) edition, edited by C.W. Guillebaud, 2 vols (London: Macmillan for the Royal Economic Society).

Marshall, Alfred and Paley Marshall (1879), *The Economics of Industry* (London: Macmillan).

Marx, Karl (1977), *Capital*, Vol. I (London: Lawrence and Wishart).

Mill, J.S. (1909), *Principles of Political Economy*, edited with an introduction by W.J. Ashley, (London: Longmans Green and Co.).

Newman, Peter (1960), 'The Erosion of Marshall's Theory of Value', *Quarterly Journal of Economics*, November, 74: 587–601.

Patten, Alan (1999), *Hegel's Idea of Freedom* (Oxford: Oxford University Press).

Pigou, A.C. (1913), 'The Interdependence of Different Sources of Supply and Demand in a Market', *Economic Journal*, 23: 19–24.

—— (1925), *Memorials of Alfred Marshall* (London: Macmillan).

—— (1928), 'An Analysis of Supply'. *Economic Journal*, 40: 79–116.

Prendergast, Renee (1992), 'Increasing Returns and Competitive Equilibrium: The Content and Development of Marshall's Theory', *Cambridge Journal of Economics*, 16: 447–62.

—— (1993), 'Marshallian External Economies', *Economic Journal*, 103: 454–58.

Robertson, D. (1930), 'Reply to Sraffa's Criticism in "Increasing Returns and the Representative Firm: A Symposium"', *Economic Journal*, 40: 79–116.

—— (1956), *Economics Commentaries* (London: Staples Press).

Robertson, D.H, Piero Sraffa and G.F. Shove (1930), 'Increasing Returns and the Representative Firm: A Symposium', *Economic Journal*, 40: 79–116.

Samuelson, P.A. (1967), 'The Monopolistic Competition Revolution', in R.E. Kuenne, ed., *Monopolistic Competition Theory: Studies in Impact* (New York: John Wiley and Sons).

Schumpeter, Joseph A. (1928), 'The Instability of Capitalism', *Economic Journal*, 38 (151): 361–86.

—— (1961), *History of Economic Analysis* (London: George Allen and Unwin Ltd); first published in 1954 by Oxford University Press.

—— (1961), *The Theory of Economic Development*, translated by Opie Redvers (Oxford: Oxford University Press); first published in 1934 by Department of Economics, Harvard University.

Shackle, G.L.S. (1965), *A Scheme of Economic Theory* (Cambridge: Cambridge University Press).

Shove, G.F. (1930), 'The Representative Firm and Increasing Returns in "Increasing Returns and the Representative Firm: A Symposium"', *Economic Journal*, 40: 79–116.

Smith, Adam (1976), *An Enquiry into the Nature and Causes of the Wealth of Nations*, 2 vols, edited by R.H. Campbell, A.S. Skinner and W.B. Todd (Oxford: Clarendon Press).

Sraffa, Piero (1925), 'Sulla Relazioni fra Costa e Quantita Prodotta', *Annali di Economia*, 2.

—— (1930), 'A Criticism and Reply to Robertson's Reply in "Increasing Returns and the Representative Firm: A Symposium"', *Economic Journal*, 40: 79–116.

Thomas, Brinley (1991), 'Alfred Marshall on Economic Biology', *Review of Political Economy*, 3 (1): 1–14.

Viner, Jacob (1931), 'Cost Curves and Supply Curves', *Zeitschrift fur Nationalokonomie*, III: 23–46.

Whitaker, J.K. (1975), *The Early Economic Writings of Alfred Marshall, 1867–90*, 2 vols (London: Macmillan).

—— (1987), 'Alfred Marshall', in J. Eatwell, M. Milgate and P. Newman, eds, *The New Palgrave* (London: Macmillan).

—— (1999), 'Alfred Marshall and Scientific Management', in S.C. Dow and P.E. Earl, eds, *Economic Organization and Economic Knowledge: Essays in Honour of Brian J. Loasby*, Vol. 1 (Cheltenham: Edward Elgar).

Michal Kalecki and the Economics of Development

Jayati Ghosh

In the long and impressive catalogue of Michal Kalecki's contributions to economics, the proportion of writings devoted to what is now called 'development economics' is relatively small. And most of his work in this area is concise to the point of being terse, in short articles that simply state some crucial principles, typically without much elaboration. Nevertheless, these rather brief pieces are so full of insight and sharp analysis that they contain many of the basic principles that still constitute the theoretical armoury of the study of development issues. What is even more remarkable is that, although these pieces were generally written in the mid-twentieth century, in a period when many developing economies were experimenting with import-substituting industrialization, often in a planning or mixed economy framework, they remain very relevant. Indeed, almost all of Kalecki's work has strong contemporary resonance, and can be usefully applied to understanding economic policies and processes in the early years of the twenty-first century.

Michal Kalecki was born in 1899 into a poor Jewish family in Poland. One of the most productive economists of his generation, he was nonetheless largely self-taught in economics. While Kalecki's theoretical framework came essentially from Marx, his application and development of concepts were a result of observation of economic life around him, and consideration of data. Some of this must have been due to his early training. He studied civil engineering at Warsaw and Gdansk Polytechnic, but could not complete the course for financial reasons. His knowledge of economics was subsequently acquired 'on the job', so to speak, as a member of the Institute of Research on Business Cycles and Prices in Warsaw. This led to the publication of his first major work, *Essays on Business Cycle Theory*, in 1933. This work already described a developed capitalist economy as a demand-determined system in which involuntary unemployment is a likely outcome in the absence of government intervention. The various papers he published until 1935 reiterated this conclusion and indicated Kalecki's view of the short-run dynamics of such a system.

Throughout his life, Kalecki remained a non-conformist, providing recurring evidence of his strong intellectual and personal integrity. In 1936, for example, he resigned his job in Warsaw in protest against what he felt were politically motivated dismissals of two of his colleagues. He then went to Sweden and subsequently to England. He was in Cambridge for some time, where he interacted *inter alia* with Piero Sraffa and Joan Robinson, and also had to cope with the frustration of Keynes' failure to recognize Kalecki's independent elucidation of the principle of effective demand and the possibility of involuntary unemployment. In 1940 he moved to the Oxford Institute of Statistics, where his theoretical and applied contributions to economics continued, and he became the centre of a circle of émigré intellectuals.

At the end of World War II, Kalecki worked for some time at the International Labour Office in Montreal, and then in the United Nations Secretariat in New York, where he was responsible for presenting the *World Economic Reports*. This international exposure coloured some of his later interests and concerns, in particular the necessity of using different analyses to understand economic patterns in underdeveloped countries, whether socialist or non-socialist. In New York, his spirit rebelled against the growing intellectual intolerance of the McCarthyist period in the US, and he therefore returned to Poland in 1955.

Back in Warsaw, Kalecki very quickly became involved with the planning process through the Polish Planning Commission, as well as in wider economic research with the Polish Academy of Sciences. Much of his work on planning in socialist economies dates from that period. He was also invited for relatively long periods to several developing countries – notably India, Israel and Cuba – where he advised their governments on issues of development planning and honed his analysis of the problem of financing development. Frequent travel to Latin America, especially Mexico, gave him even wider experience of different developing economies.

In addition, some of his teaching and research activity at Warsaw brought him directly to the study of economic development. From the end of the 1950s onwards, he organized an Advanced Seminar for Experts on Planning Economic Development of Underdeveloped Countries. This eventually metamorphosed into the Centre of Research on Underdeveloped Economies in 1961, with Kalecki as chairman of the Research Board, which became a focal centre for such research. There was also involvement, in terms of policy advice, with nascent United Nations organizations such as UNCTAD and FAO.

Notwithstanding Kalecki's growing stature and recognition among all those involved with planning and development, there was sustained lack of appreciation of the originality and significance of his work in the mainstream English language academe. This was true especially of his seminal work on the macroeconomics of developed capitalism. Despite Joan Robinson emerging as his champion, there was almost no transatlantic recognition or even knowledge of Kalecki's contribution, and, even to this day, mainstream economists either assume that the major insights into unemployment equilibrium were all the fruits of Keynes' work, or restate many of Kalecki's propositions as if they are entirely original and new.

There are some features of Kalecki's approach to economics that are especially significant with respect to analysing development. There is no doubt that his approach to the problems of economic growth and change in the South was influenced to a significant extent both by his understanding of developed capitalist economies and his work on planning in socialist countries. However, he was always careful not to mechanically reproduce conclusions that were relevant in those contexts to other, rather different situations. He identified critical features of developing economies that made them fundamentally different from advanced capitalist economies, as discussed below. He was also extremely sensitive to the important roles played by particular social, political and economic configurations and historical processes, in affecting both macroeconomic processes and economic policy outcomes.

This does not mean that he therefore fell into the opposite trap of rejecting the applicability of economic theory for examining problems of development. Rather, his theories were always grounded in relevant stylized facts, and sought to examine issues with reference to the entire economy, indeed to the political process that underlay it. This highlights another essential feature of his analysis: his fundamental assessment that economics is ultimately about politics; that any analysis of an economy that seeks to abstract away from the socio-political determinants and implications of economic phenomena would not only be inadequate but plain wrong. In particular, the distributive implications of economic strategies were of great concern. This remains critically important, and serves as a useful antidote to the depoliticization of much recent work on the economics of development that tries to ignore such reality, or to subsume all political and distributive aspects under the misleading appellation 'governance'.

By the time Michal Kalecki died in 1970, his intellectual output was massive, diverse, and unfailingly penetrating and insightful. He was also largely unsung, having come under pressure even in Poland for his non-conformist positions on a range of issues. In 1968, as he had already done twice before, Kalecki resigned from his job, once again in protest at the unfair dismissal of some of his colleagues who were closely associated with him. However, he continued his intellectual activity until his death. Apparently, in his later years, he felt that his policy advice had been mostly unheeded, joking that he had been influential only in Israel, where the government had done exactly the opposite of what he had suggested. Yet, today, his assessments remain not only sharp and valid but eminently practicable, with the major constraints being only the political pressures of which he himself was so well aware.

The Macroeconomics of Developed Capitalist Economies

It is well known that Kalecki, working independently and coming from a very different theoretical tradition, worked out the essentials of what is now known as 'Keynesian' economics well before the publication of Keynes' *General Theory*. His early work on business cycles, dating from the early 1930s, had already established some of the basic principles – in particular, the importance of effective demand in driving the short-run dynamics of the system, the possibility of involuntary unemployment and the necessity for government intervention. Even these early contributions established the inherently cyclical character of change in a *laissez-faire* capitalist economy.

However, Kalecki's description of both the short-run and long-run dynamics of advanced capitalism had greater richness and complexity because he was not hampered by a reliance on standard equilibrium analysis, but was rather working with the inherently more dynamic notions of investment, oligopolistic behaviour, technical progress and the like. Unlike Keynes (whose theoretical framework remained essentially Marshallian), Kalecki based his analysis on the Marxian reproduction schemes, which made the crucial distinction between investment goods (Department I) and consumption goods (Department II). He distinguished between those variables that become active determinants of levels of income (such as investment, export surpluses, government deficits) and those that are passive outcomes of the process (such as workers' consumption).

Like Keynes, Kalecki emphasized that while *ex-post* savings and investment are equal, it is investment that is the active factor determining savings; further, the equality is brought about not by changes in the rate of interest (which he recognized to be a policy variable) but by changes in the level of economic activity. This was because Kalecki believed that, in general, there is unutilized capacity in capitalist economies. Within investment, he made the important distinction between investment decisions and actual investment outlays (which follow with a time lag). This is important because investment operates immediately to increase the level of output, but also raises capacity, and the increased capacity affects investment decisions in the next period. This, in turn, limits future output and creates over time a pattern of cyclical movement of output. This paradox, which is peculiar to capitalism, was summed up by Kalecki (1937: 77) as follows: 'The tragedy of investment is that it causes crisis because it is useful.'

Kalecki's theory of price formation was critical in relating aggregate income to its distribution in advanced capitalist economies. In his model, capitalists are assumed to spend on investment and luxury consumption; workers spend on wage goods and do not save. The prices of primary products (or raw materials) are determined by demand and supply; the prices of other products are cost-determined with oligopolistic mark-up. This mark-up, in turn, depends upon the 'degree of monopoly', which reflects forces such as the extent of concentration of production, the requirements and extent of sales promotion, and the bargaining power of workers. Therefore, the mark-up is not constant over time but reflects economic and political dynamics. The Kaleckian multiplier emerges from the wage share of national income, as well as the propensity to consume out of profits. The share of profits in income depends upon the degree of monopoly, while the amount of profit realized over a period depends upon capitalists' expenditure.

In this formulation, government intervention can prevent cyclical behaviour and allow for full employment. It is also not seen as necessary for the government to run continuous budget deficits to achieve this, since the expenditure can be met by taxing profits, which would simply reduce profits to the level that existed before the increase in government expenditure, while ensuring higher levels of production. But even loan-financed government expenditure can achieve the goal, so that, 'in this way, one of the basic contradictions of the capitalist system is solved by a sort of financial trick' (Kalecki 1966: 14). While this may appear to be strange, it reflects the tendency of unemployment of resources through inadequate effective demand which is inherent in the capitalist system. 'The artificiality of the underemployment of resources is overcome by the artificiality of the financial trick consisting of loan-financed *ad hoc* government expenditure' (ibid.).

The most rational course for a government wishing to increase public spending in a context of unemployment would be either to spend on investment and therefore contribute to future development, or to increase expenditure or reduce taxation in such a way as to improve the consumption of the masses. In general, in advanced capitalist countries, Kalecki felt that the means chosen is neither of these but, rather, government expenditure on armaments. This is wasteful and destructive but nonetheless preferred by workers in developed countries, because it provides levels of employment and wages that would otherwise not be possible in the absence of such spending.

However, Kalecki maintained that continuous full employment is unlikely under capitalism because of opposition from the domestic capitalist class. In his famous 1943 paper, 'The Political Aspects of Full Employment', he argued that capitalists would oppose such levels of government expenditure not only from a dislike of government interference in general and the direction of public spending in particular, but, even more crucially, because of the social and political changes (essentially, greater bargaining power of workers) resulting from the maintenance of full employment. His was therefore the first, and is still the most useful, model of a 'political business cycle'.

Kalecki (1954: 52) was also well aware of the significance of external markets in playing a role similar to government expenditure for a mature capitalist economy. He described the government deficit as 'internal exports' to be compared with the 'external profits' to be had from imperialist interaction with other less developed economies.

> The fight for the division of existing foreign markets and the expansion of colonial empires, which provide new opportunities for export of capital associated with export of goods, can be viewed as a drive for export surplus, the classic source of 'external' profits. Armaments and wars, usually financed by budget deficits, are also a source of this kind of profits.

According to Kalecki, there is nothing in the mechanics of advanced capitalism that makes long-run growth inevitable. However, two semi-exogenous factors interact to produce patterns of long-run economic change. The first is innovation, which Kalecki defined to include not only technological progress *per se*, but also the introduction of new goods, the opening up of new markets, organizational changes and so on. This obviously has a positive effect: the higher the intensity of innovation, the higher is the rate of growth of the economy. The other constraining factor is 'rentier savings', that is, savings outside firms, which depress investment and therefore inhibit growth. The relative strength of these two factors determines the long-run rate of growth. The contemporary relevance of this argument, in a world of rapid technological progress but also of financial liberalization and growth of rentier incomes, is worth noting.

Differences between Developed and Developing Economies

The essentials of the theoretical framework developed by Kalecki for developed capitalist economies were utilized by him for analysing capitalist or 'mixed' developing economies as well. Thus, the pattern of price formation remains the same, with the prices of primary commodities being determined by the interaction of demand and supply, while finished goods prices reflect oligopolistic mark-up. Political influences upon economic policies and processes also remain critical. However, in some major respects, the stylized facts that Kalecki observed were different for developing economies, and this meant that both economic mechanisms and the government policies that could be used to influence them, changed.

Kalecki saw the difference in the nature of unemployment as the most critical macroeconomic distinction to be made between developed and developing non-socialist economies. In developed capitalist economies, as described above, unemployment was seen to be related to the inadequacy of effective demand. This, in turn, meant that in a context of idle productive capacity, measures such as increasing government expenditure in order to raise the level of aggregate demand, through the 'financial trick' outlined above, would be effective in tackling the problem. In underdeveloped economies, however, Kalecki viewed the problem of unemployment (or underemployment) as structural, resulting from the basic and endemic shortage of capital equipment as well as bottlenecks in the supply of necessities. The solution to the problem was therefore also seen to be different and more difficult, since, in such a context, increased government expenditure could simply add to inflationary pressure.

This point became so central to all of Kalecki's subsequent analyses of development, that it deserves greater elaboration. Kalecki did not deny that in an underdeveloped economy there may be a deficiency of effective demand, or that even the meagre level of capital equipment that exists could be underutilized. However, he argued that the basic difference is that even if all the available capital equipment were to be utilized, it would still not absorb all the available labour force. This, in turn, means that the standard of living is typically low for the broad masses of the population. This makes the solution to the unemployment (or underemployment) problem more complicated and harder to do, since it must necessarily involve an expansion of productive capacity.

Therefore, the central macroeconomic issue in a developing economy becomes that of increasing investment. However, Kalecki envisaged three important obstacles to such a strategy. The first is that private investment may not be forthcoming at the desired rate. Of course, in such a case, government investment can fill the gap, although the crucial issue of financing such government investment remains significant. Second, there may be no physical resources to produce more investment goods. In this case, Kalecki mentioned the possibility of using foreign trade, that is, importing such investment goods, financed either through increasing exports or through reducing non-essential imports. Third, there is the problem of ensuring an adequate supply of necessities to cover the demand resulting from increased employment. Shortage of necessities (especially food) would create an inflationary problem that would not be overcome through taxation of profits and that would involve real wage declines, which Kalecki found to be unacceptable. This could be avoided if an increase in the supply of necessities matched the growing demand for them, in accordance with a planning process. However, Kalecki noted the considerable political and practical obstacles to introducing some sort of planned economy and extensive government control upon private economic activity.

Indeed, it was the political obstacles that Kalecki found to be the most critical, because of the adverse reaction of domestic and foreign capitalists, as well as other vested interests such as land-owning elites. There would inevitably be opposition to some of the requirements of balanced development, such as increasing public expenditure by taxing the rich and altering agrarian relations. This is why, according to Kalecki, rapid but balanced economic development is so rarely to be found in practice and, instead, two extreme patterns (or variations of them) are more commonly observed among underdeveloped economies: either non-inflationary but slow growth, or relatively rapid growth accompanied by violent inflationary pressures.

This meant that, for Kalecki, the basic condition for breaking out of the cycle of economic backwardness was a substantial increase in agricultural output (since food dominates in the basket of necessities). In this context, he recognized the basic constraint posed by land relations, and emphasized the need to change both ownership and land tenure regulations as a necessary precondition for non-inflationary redeployment of labour surpluses for industrialization. He even argued that the agrarian constraint could prevent industrial growth not just from the supply side, but also from the demand side. This point deserves to be emphasized, since his analysis helps in showing that a demand problem may coexist with the problem of inflation in developing countries. This insight became important in subsequent discussions of the development experience in India (see Chakravarty 1993) and elsewhere. The argument was briefly stated as follows:

> It may be shown that in some cases the rigidity of the supply of food may lead to the underutilization of productive facilities in non-food consumption goods. This will not be the case if the peasants profit from the increases in food prices, because then they buy more industrial consumption goods out of their higher

incomes. However, if the benefits of higher food prices accrue to landlords, merchants or moneylenders, then the reduction in real wages due to the increase in food prices will not have as a counterpart an increased demand for mass consumption goods on the part of the countryside; for increased profits will not be spent at all, or will be spent on luxuries. In this case, the high demand generated by a rapid development involving large-scale investment will not create a market for industrial mass consumption goods. (Kalecki 1955: 29)

This is why Kalecki emphasized that investment in infrastructure and industry must be accompanied by measures to expand agricultural production in the long and short term. Possible measures, according to him, ranged from land reform and cheap bank credit for the peasantry, to technological changes in cultivation practices, small-scale irrigation, and provision of cheap fertilizers and other inputs.

Such analysis was relatively unusual at the time, when most 'development economists' were focused singlemindedly on increasing industrial growth. But this idea, advocated in the mid-1950s, was vindicated by the food shortages that emerged across many developing countries a decade later. It was to prove extremely influential, making Kalecki an unwitting founder of the structuralist school in Latin America and elsewhere, which attached critical importance to structural factors in the development process.

The need to ensure non-inflationary (and therefore 'balanced') development was so important for Kalecki that the issue of financing development assumed centrality in his discussion of development. This is because he took the danger of inflation in developing countries extremely seriously. The fundamental reason for his abhorrence of inflation was its effect in reducing real wages, which he regarded as unacceptable.[1] The most obvious reason for such distaste was in terms of an ethical opposition, since, in both developed and developing capitalist economies (and, indeed, even in socialist economies), Kalecki resisted the possibility of financing growth at the expense of the working class. In poor countries with already low levels of workers' incomes, reduction in real wages was all the more impossible for him to accept. Therefore, the assumption that real wages must not fall was, for him, the starting point of any development strategy.

In addition, Kalecki was opposed to inflation because he believed that persistent inflationary pressures led to excessive and unproductive hoarding of stocks; to capital flight, currency speculation and consequent balance of payments difficulties; and to disturbances in the investment process itself. He felt that these consequences could make inflation permanent (in an early anticipation of what has become known as 'inflation inertia') and could even retard or stop the development process itself. He also recognized that intensifying inflationary pressures give rise to political tensions that the ruling classes in developing countries find dangerous, and which are therefore sought to be reduced by importing necessities financed through foreign capital inflows. Part of the problem is that the capitalist growth process itself generates inequalities and deflects resources into luxury consumption, which is why balanced development also requires measures to control growing inequality of incomes.

In the current mainstream dogma about inflation, monetary measures are given supremacy and, indeed, inflation control is typically viewed as the main function of central banks. However, Kalecki reiterated that the issue of avoiding inflationary pressures in the course of economic development is not a 'monetary' one at all but, rather, is solved by assuring a correct structure of national expenditure. This requires that the supply of necessities is in the desired relation to the level of national income; that expenditure on non-essential consumption is sufficiently restrained as to provide adequate savings for the financing of both public and private investment; and that private investment is sufficiently restrained as to allow for the financing of public investment.

Financing Development

In all of Kalecki's writings on development, the issue of financing of economic growth received probably the most attention. The problem was not seen in purely monetary terms but in terms of the more critical issue of the distributive implications of financing, that is, which groups in society (or outside) would bear the burden of increasing capital formation through reductions in consumption. For Kalecki, desirable economic development necessarily involved no inflationary price increases of necessities, especially staple foods; no taxes levied on lower-income groups or on necessities; and effective demand restrained only through raising direct taxes on higher-income groups or indirect taxes on non-essentials. This squarely puts the burden of financing investment on richer groups in the society, but it also entails larger domestic agricultural output.

As he argued, 'There are no financial limits, in the formal sense, to the volume of investment. The real problem is whether this financing of investment does, or does not, create inflationary pressures' (Kalecki 1955: 25). And this, of course, depends upon the possibility of expansion of the supply of mass consumer goods in response to increased demand. The associated need to increase food production and the methods through which this can be achieved have already been discussed; here, some further implications are considered.

As noted above, Kalecki argued that an increase in investment under conditions of inelastic food supply would cause a fall in real wages and would consequently generate an inflationary wage–price spiral. But this need not be associated with substantial increase in demand for mass consumption goods produced by industry. This is why expansion of the output of food is of central importance in the process of development, and why he stressed measures that would improve land productivity for agriculture.

It could be argued that increases in industrial productivity would have the same effect. However, Kalecki noted that, while an increase in food supply tends to raise real wages at a given level of non-agricultural employment, an increase in industrial productivity increases real wages through reducing employment at a given level of non-agricultural output. It is easy to see which alternative is preferable in a labour-surplus developing economy.

This approach also makes it clear why Kalecki emphasized the direct taxation of profits or the indirect taxation of luxury consumption items – not only to ensure resources for public investment, but also to prevent public investment from increasing profits and therefore capitalists' luxury consumption. In fact, this was seen to be an absolutely essential role of government in the industrialization process: to extract a part of private capitalist profit through taxes and use it for capital formation – which would also benefit the capitalists over time. However, such taxation would not neutralize the potentially inflationary impact of higher public investment.

It is noteworthy that Kalecki was quite sceptical of the use of foreign capital to finance this necessary investment for development. On the one hand, he recognized the importance of foreign capital inflow to enable essential imports including of capital goods for industrialization, and that such inflows could ease the domestic financing problem by allowing food imports. However, he felt that, in general, foreign capital presents problems of a very basic nature for a developing economy. Foreign direct investment tends to occur in areas (such as the production of raw materials for export) which may not be in line with the basic development plan of a country. In addition, profits transferred abroad can exceed the cost of servicing a foreign loan, while reinvested profits could simply add to the book value of foreign investment with no further inflow of capital. Foreign credits, or external commercial borrowings, involve interest repayment that can become a heavy burden in the future. Even foreign aid is problematic because of all the successive dislocations caused by additional imports financed through such aid.

In this context, Kalecki (1966: 66) proposed two criteria for evaluating foreign aid, which remain extremely relevant to assess all forms of foreign capital inflow. First, to what extent has this inflow improved the country's balance of payments position; and has this improvement been used to remove the bottlenecks in the supply of capital goods, necessities, luxuries or intermediate goods? Second, were the additional financial resources instrumental in raising the rate of growth by increasing investment over the level of domestic savings or releasing local savings for consumption; and, if they did so, did they finance an increase in the consumption of necessities, of luxuries, or materialize in a higher volume of social services?

Even the most cursory examination of the experience of the past two decades will suggest that, according to these basic criteria, most of the foreign capital inflow into developing country 'emerging markets' in the era of globalization did not achieve these most obvious goals of development. Thus, Kalecki's scepticism appears to be amply vindicated even by very recent international experience.

Indeed, Kalecki noted that, given the difficulty of securing desirable forms of foreign capital inflows into developing countries, it may be preferable for them to consider means of preventing capital export, which amounts to the same thing in terms of releasing foreign exchange resources. Here he noted that what must be regulated is not only visible capital flight, but also hidden transfers (such as through over-invoiced imports and under-invoiced exports), which are often of even greater quantitative significance. Another route could be to reduce the dividend repatriation by foreign enterprises. He also pointed out that an improvement in the terms of trade has an effect analogous to capital inflows without all the attendant difficulties of foreign capital. Conversely, of course, a deterioration in the terms of trade can take away the benefits of productivity growth in the export sector.

The Planning Process

A substantial proportion of Kalecki's work was devoted to the analysis of planning in socialist economies. Some of this continues to have substantial relevance for growth and planning even in mixed or capitalist developing economies, since the basic principles he elaborated still determine the possibilities for long-run growth. While Kalecki opposed some of the excesses of central planning, he was also wholeheartedly against the idea of 'market socialism', since this gave play to the capacity of the market to make wrong macroeconomic decisions. However, even under central planning certain contradictions persist, most significantly the trade-off between current and future consumption. He recognized that resolving this necessarily required political compromise, since it could not be reduced to purely economic considerations.

The other factor limiting freedom of choice in planning was the emergence of long-run development bottlenecks, such as limited natural resources, shortages of certain kinds of skilled labour and difficulties of adapting technological changes. Kalecki saw that all of these gaps could be bridged through foreign trade, but that would be at the expense of widening trade imbalances. This made him stress the need for moderate and realistic plans, rather than very ambitious growth targets.

A similar approach made him take a particular attitude with respect to the debate on choice of techniques in a developing country. The Dobb–Sen strategy (proposed by Maurice Dobb and Amartya Sen) relied on maximizing investible surpluses, maintaining constant real wages and using the entire increase in labour productivity to raise the rate of accumulation. Kalecki opposed the assumptions made in this argument, of unchanging technology (that is, no technological progress) and 'instant' recasting of the economy into a higher capital–output ratio. In addition, he felt that most capital-intensive techniques would have to be imported, making them even less attractive. He argued that 'the more capital-intensive technique is not *per se* either superior or inferior: the choice of "right" capital intensity depends upon the availability of labour (allowing for technological limitations and maintenance of real wages)' (Kalecki 1967: 94).

Kalecki's solution, therefore, preferred the technique that maximized output rather than surplus. Indeed, he considered labour-intensive techniques of production to be preferable in general for developing countries with large labour reserves, except in those sectors where the technology did not allow it. Even in agriculture, he was against mechanization, since he felt it usually did not increase output per acre but only output per worker, thereby creating rural unemployment. He emphasized, instead, ways of intensifying agricultural production in labour-intensive ways.

Chakravarty (1993) has noted that since Kalecki dealt with vertically integrated sectors in his formulation, this effectively short-circuited some of the inter-sectoral relationships in a growing economy. He also therefore missed out on the potential significance of the self-reproducing capital goods sector, which played such an important role in the planning models of Feldman and Mahalanobis, among others. While Kalecki did not address this range of questions, his insights into the planning process remain significant.

The Politics of Development

It is evident that Kalecki was acutely sensitive to the political pressures and constraints that informed the process of development, and was also well aware of the complex interaction between the power of different classes and groups, economic policies and their growth and distribution outcomes. Some of this consciousness, which permeated most of his work, was crystallized into a more specific formulation regarding 'intermediate regimes'. This is how he characterized some developing countries in which, according to him, the old feudal classes had been dispossessed and large capital had not developed, so that political power at independence had passed into the hands of the lower middle classes and peasantry. He characterized countries such as India, Egypt and Bolivia, for example, as 'intermediate regimes', and gave rise to a substantial, if controversial, literature on the subject.[2]

Kalecki argued that such a group, to keep in power, must gain a measure of independence from foreign capital, carry out land reform and assure continuous economic growth. This means that the government comes into conflict with 'comprador' elements, as well as with feudal landlords. Kalecki noted that it was possible that, over time, the lower middle class became subservient to big business, but that this is often prevented by the basic weakness of this class and its inability to undertake large-scale investment. This means that the basic investment for economic development must be carried out by the state, which is why lower middle class interests are amalgamated with those of state capitalism. Such state capitalism favours the lower middle classes (including small-scale businesses) and the peasantry, but continues to suppress the poor peasantry and rural proletariat, as well as urban workers.

Whatever one may think of the applicability of this analysis – and there have been numerous criticisms of it with reference to particular countries that Kalecki thought it applied to – there is no doubt that it represents an original and striking use of political economy concepts to understand both broad macroeconomic strategy and its effects in developing countries. The method of this analysis, rather than the analysis itself, serves as a useful inspiration to other assessments of development that look for explanation to political economy and class configurations to understand both economic policies and their effects. This is in sharp contrast to the seemingly 'technocratic' assessments that are currently so popular, which abstract completely from the basic politics of development or view it only in terms of rather limited 'interest groups'. This particular contribution of Kalecki remains of tremendous value in these times.

Conclusion

It is apparent that Kalecki's contributions to the economics of development covered a very wide range, and also provided insights that remain acute and immensely valuable several decades after he wrote. While many of his conclusions can still be usefully applied to understanding economic processes in developing countries, it may well be the case that the principal value of his contribution extends beyond the specific arguments he made. Rather, Kalecki's entire approach – which combined analytical rigour with a sense of historical specificity, awareness of political and social constraints, and acceptance of the complexity of the interaction between policies and socio-economic processes – is really what contemporary economists have to incorporate, if development economics itself is to be regenerated.

I am grateful to Abhijit Sen, C.P. Chandrasekhar, Jomo K.S. and Prabhat Patnaik for discussions and useful comments on an earlier draft.

Notes

1 It is interesting to note that as early as 1953, such a position had brought Kalecki (who was at that time working at the Economics Department of the United Nations) into conflict with economists at the World Bank and the International Monetary Fund who saw lowering wages as a means of improving external competitiveness and allowing for domestic stabilization.
2 In India, for example, K.N. Raj (1973) attempted an application of his theory to analysing the pattern of import-substituting mixed economy industrialization undertaken by the Indian state, although this was severely criticized by many, *inter alia* Namboodiripad (1973).

References and Related Readings

Chakravarty, Sukhamoy (1993), 'M. Kalecki and Development Economics', in *Selected Economic Writings* (New Delhi: Oxford University Press): 234–46.

Dobrska, Zofia (1975), 'M. Kalecki on the Developing Economies of the Third World', reprinted in Kalecki, *Collected Works*, Vol. V, edited by Jerzy Osiatynski.

Feiwel, George (1975), *The Intellectual Capital of Michal Kalecki: A Study in Economic Theory and Policy* (Nashville: University of Tennessee Press).

Kalecki, Michal (1937), 'A Theory of the Business Cycle', *Review of Economic Studies*, 4 (2): 77–99; reprinted in *Collected Works*, Vol. I.

——— (1954), *Theory of Economic Dynamics: An Essay on Cyclical and Long-run Changes in the Capitalist Economy* (London: Allen and Unwin).

——— (1955), 'The Problem of Financing Economic Development', *Indian Economic Review*; reprinted in *Essays on Developing Economies* (Brighton: Harvester Press), 1972.

—— (1964), 'Observations on Social and Economic Aspects of "Intermediate Regimes"', reprinted in *Selected Essays on the Economic Growth of the Socialist and Mixed Economy* (Cambridge: Cambridge University Press), 1972, and in *Collected Works*, Vol. 5, edited by Jerzy Osiatynski, 1993.

—— (1967), 'Introduction to the Theory of Growth in a Socialist Economy'", in *Collected Works*, Vol. 4: *Socialism: Economic Growth and Efficiency of Investment*, edited by Jerzy Osiatynski (Oxford: Clarendon Press), 1993.

—— (1972), *Essays on Developing Economies* (Brighton: Harvester Press).

—— (1993), *Developing Economies*, Vol. 6 of *Collected Works*, edited by Jerzy Osiatynski (Oxford: Clarendon Press).

Kalecki, Michal, with Ignacy Sachs (1966), 'Forms of Foreign Aid: An Economic Analysis', *Social Science Information*, 5 (1): 21–44; reprinted in *Collected Works*, edited by Jerzy Osiatynski (Oxford: Clarendon Press, 1993).

Namboodiripad, E.M.S. (1973), 'On Intermediate Regimes', *Economic and Political Weekly*, 8 (48).

Raj, K.N. (1973), 'The Politics and Economics of Intermediate Regimes', *Economic and Political Weekly*, 8 (27).

Robinson, Joan (1972), 'Introduction', in Michal Kalecki, *Essays on Developing Economies* (Brighton: Harvester Press).

The Significance of Keynes for Development Economics

John Toye

Development economics in its modern form was struggling to be born just as John Maynard Keynes, ill and exhausted by immense public responsibilities, approached his premature death in April 1946. This fact alone meant that Keynes himself exercised no direct influence on modern development economics. His significance for the new sub-discipline was considerable, but it arose in ways other than by his direct influence.

The first of these other ways was Keynes' indirect influence, that is, the influence he exercised on the thinking of other economists who, after his death, participated in the creation of development economics. Economists who fit this description include Joan Robinson and Austin Robinson: they were Keynes' disciples and they contributed, in very contrasting styles, to the early construction of development economics (Harcourt 1998: 367–77). James Meade also falls into this category.

A second other way in which Keynes was significant was through his posthumous legend. The Keynes legend tended to affect especially younger economists who had not known Keynes personally, but nevertheless nurtured a view of him as a towering economist and role model of some sort – even when they rejected particular economic doctrines of his.

Finally, there is a sense in which what Keynes himself actually wrote about economic development remains significant, even though this failed to shape the sub-discipline at its birth, being either inaccessible or neglected. What Keynes had to say on various development issues could be significant for those today who are interested in rethinking the development economics that they have inherited. Let us take each of these different forms of significance in turn.

Keynes' Indirect Influence on Early Development Economics

Keynes's most notable economic doctrine was that the economy could be in equilibrium at less than full employment.[1] The implication of his new concept of involuntary unemployment was that resources were being wasted: what men and women did not produce today through enforced idleness would never be produced at all. To eliminate involuntary unemployment by government intervention, therefore, was to prevent the waste of resources and to allow their potential output to be made actual. In industrial societies, this waste was dramatically visible in the 1930s. It was there for all to see in the form of silent factories and mines, whose workers stood idly around outside locked gates. The political dangers of this economic waste were also obvious, and not only to Keynes. For him, they were the motive to advocate policies to eliminate unemployment, and to publicly explain how and why his policies would work.[2]

Joan Robinson, Keynes' junior collaborator in the making of *The General Theory of Employment* (1936), thought that the concept of full employment needed more careful definition, and she distinguished between open and disguised unemployment. Open unemployment affected wage workers who were laid off by their employers when demand fell. She believed that another type of unemployment was often present among own-account workers, though it was disguised by the fact that they kept themselves occupied in various ways. Disguised unemployment was particularly prevalent in the agricultural sector when there was excess population on the land. Perhaps as a result of her stay in India in 1926–28, she argued that in the agricultural sector and, by extension, in economies that are dominated by that sector, many people had occupations that contributed little to economic output, but this low productivity was not obvious because they appeared to be occupied.[3] Here, too, was a waste of resources, the same as with open unemployment.

In the early 1940s, Britain's Royal Institute for International Affairs began studies to assist the post-war reconstruction of Europe. In the course of these, it was calculated that at least 20 to 25 per cent of the agricultural population of Eastern Europe was surplus, in the sense that they could leave the land without reducing agricultural output (Royal Institute of International Affairs 1943). It was natural to believe that this surplus labour could be used for economic development if those in disguised unemployment could be absorbed into higher productivity occupations such as modern industries.

The Oxford Institute of Economics and Statistics undertook a similar project of reconstruction studies, using the talents of a number of scholars in exile from central Europe – including Michal Kalecki, E.F. Schumacher, Josef Steindl and Kurt Mandelbaum. As part of this project, Mandelbaum produced a pioneering projection model of an industrialization process, a process that he justified in the following terms.

> An expanding population adds continually to the number of people who are forced to work on fragmented or overcrowded holdings or on inferior soil where their productivity is nil or almost nil (disguised unemployment). If these surplus workers were withdrawn from agriculture and absorbed into other occupations, farm output would not suffer, while the whole new output would be a net addition to the community's income. The economic case for the industrialization of densely populated backward countries rests on this mass phenomenon of disguised rural unemployment. (Mandelbaum 1945: 2)

Mandelbaum's intellectual formation had been at the Frankfurt Institute for

Social Research, working on the agrarian question as formulated by Marx and Lenin. So it would be unwise to link the idea of disguised unemployment too exclusively with Keynesian macroeconomics (FitzGerald 1990: 3–25). Two different intellectual streams flowed into a single pool.

Nevertheless, when Paul Rosenstein–Rodan wrote in 1943 about the post-war development of south and southeastern Europe, he did so in Keynesian language. He referred to these regions as 'international depressed areas', owing to the problem of excess agrarian population and its disguised unemployment. Like Keynes, he believed that the price mechanism could not be relied on to generate the required adjustments, and that governments could, in such circumstances, play a positive role in raising national welfare. Yet, what the government would have to do was much more than what Keynes had advocated in industrial countries. Factories would have to be built and financed; labour would have to be trained to work in them; markets would have to be found for the new output without disrupting those of the foreigners who might be a source of external finance.

The chosen development strategy of Rosenstein–Rodan was 'the big push': substantial investment in a wide range of light industries that would create a demand for each other's output. This adaptation of Keynes' ideas indicated that, although demand was a problem in disturbed, war-time conditions, big problems of economic development also existed on the supply side of the economy, the flexibility of which Keynes was able to take for granted. Thus, right from the start, development economists had to consider how both demand and supply factors could be manipulated to realize the potential output of redundant agrarian labour.

Given the much more ambitious scope of the task, not to mention the disrupted war-time and post-war context, development economics at its birth was more dirigiste in spirit and practice than Keynesian macroeconomics ever was. While, in principle, private entrepreneurs could build and finance the missing factories, in practice, the uncertainties, shocks and coordination problems that affected private investment decisions meant that the government would have to lead, in the beginning at least, and the private sector would only be able to follow. Frank Burchardt, then deputy director of the Oxford Institute, expressed the contemporary view of the matter thus:

> For under-developed poor countries with surplus populations and a general shortage of social and private capital, different, and, in many respects, more formidable, problems arise. If a fairly rapid rate of industrialization is desired, a higher degree of direct controls and other methods, not unlike those employed in a war economy, will probably be needed (Burchardt 1944: iv)

Yet, given the government's leadership role in relation to development investment, only part of which could be financed from abroad, there was another lesson that could be learned from Keynes. His economics was not limited to devising policies for eliminating involuntary unemployment in a depression. The same underlying logic worked in reverse, bearing on the opposite problem of excess aggregate demand causing inflation in economies that were already operating at full capacity. His 1940 pamphlet, *How to Pay for the War*, had addressed this problem in Britain. It envisaged an economy soon to reach full capacity as a result of growing expenditure on war, and anticipated inflation unless methods of sufficiently limiting consumption could be found. As well as additional taxation, he recommended a form of forced savings called post-war credits, by which immediate compulsory reductions in income would be compensated by discretionary repayments later. If one thinks of development expenditure as similar to war expenditure – in that its benefits will accrue, if at all, in the future – Keynes' ideas on planned compulsory savings as an alternative to the inflation tax remain relevant.

However, Michal Kalecki was more influential than Keynes in shaping the theory of development finance. During the war, Kalecki had criticized Keynes' plans for war finance. He argued that compulsory savings could be offset by reductions in voluntary savings, and that those on low incomes would not be fully protected. Kalecki wanted a more extensive system of physical rationing of goods than the one Keynes advocated (Moggridge 1992: 630; Osiatynski 1997: 3–37). Kalecki was concerned not merely to reduce the pressure of aggregate demand, but also to apply controls such as rationing and price fixing to maximize the release of raw materials and labour for the war effort.

Other economists who debated on methods of managing the British war economy maintained this difference of philosophy between the two men. James Meade, who followed Keynes, was known as a 'thermostater' because he regarded control of the pressure of aggregate demand as a sufficient instrument of economic policy in itself. Austin Robinson, Richard Kahn, Brian Reddaway and others at the Board of Trade, who followed Kalecki in calling for additional controls, were known as 'Gosplanners', after the Soviet planning body Gosplan (Toye 2003: Chapter 8). The spirit of the Gosplanners, with its emphasis on directly attacking supply-side problems, was the one that inspired development economics, and not the exclusive post-Keynesian concern with aggregate demand.

This was due to the work of Kalecki himself, who played a major role in transferring his approach to British war finance, first of all into the economics of post-war reconstruction and then into the analysis of the financing of development (Arndt 1987: 124–26). He stressed that control of inflation during the course of economic development was not a purely financial matter to be achieved by fiscal and financial devices. It required the resolution of disproportions in the real economy and, in particular, overcoming the problem of an inelastic supply of food (Osiatynski 1993: 23–44). This was inextricably bound up with the intractable socio-political problem of land reform. More generally, rigidities and bottlenecks on the supply side became recognized as a defining characteristic of a developing economy, and as the major reason why orthodox policies of macroeconomic adjustment could not be expected to be effective. This 'structuralist' view dominated development economics up to and including the advent of structural adjustment policies in the early 1980s.

Although Kalecki was the dominant influence on the content of early development economics, Keynes was responsible for providing the statistical framework used by development planners. According to Donald Moggridge, 'finance ministers around the world still approach the problems of economic management in an analytical framework which, perhaps for want of a better word, commentators rightly call Keynesian' (Moggridge 1993: vii). Hans Singer has said that 'the national income framework of analysis first developed by Colin Clark on the basis of the Keynesian concepts . . . is surely the most striking preservation of the Keynesian heritage in current development planning' (Singer 1987: 67–68). After Clark, James Meade and Richard Stone extended the estimation of national income into an interlocking set of national income, expenditure and production accounts. This tripartite system was then applied, on the initiative of Austin Robinson, to selected British colonies. Examples were the work of Phyllis Deane on national accounts for northern Rhodesia (now Zambia) and of Arthur Lewis for Jamaica (Thirlwall 1987: 144–45). These exercises and others like them provided the statistical infrastructure within which post-independence development planning took place.

The development planning of the 1950s and 1960s, which was heavily macroeconomic in emphasis, thus combined a Kaleckian view of how the economy worked with a Keynesian statistical apparatus. This combination proved less incompatible than it appears *prima facie*. Its objective was to identify the highest feasible rate of investment – assumed to generate additional income through a simple linear relation, the incremental capital–output ratio. The national accounts framework (plus an input–output table) ensured that, for any particular rate of income growth, all the components of income, expenditure and production could be projected consistently. The choice of target rate of growth then depended on judgements of feasibility, judgements that were informed by Kaleckian considerations. Thus, practical development planners like Arthur Lewis emphasized the difficulty of rapidly expanding the supply of food, and warned of the inflationary consequences of attempting to expand investment faster than was consistent with the realistically likely growth rate of the economy's food supply (Lewis, 1966: 43–44, 53–54 and 154–55). Given a set of feasibility constraints, the maximum rate of growth could be calculated and its components planned consistently. Thus, the Keynesian accounting structure was flexible enough to be used for the macroeconomic planning of an economy with Kaleckian features.

Nevertheless, it had plenty of critics among development economists. Gunnar Myrdal, for example, objected that it classified expenditure on education as consumption, rather than as an investment, which is how he believed it should be treated in the context of development (Myrdal 1968: 1916–17). Dudley Seers, an economic statistician who had worked for Kalecki at the United Nations, launched a more thorough attack, denying that achieving development as equivalent to maximizing the rate of growth of the gross national product

(Seers 1969: 2–6; Seers 1976). He criticized the omission of economic activity in the informal sector, which he saw as a positive force for development; he also objected to the neglect of income distribution, environmental costs and unpaid labour normally undertaken by women (Toye 1989: 53–58). This critique gave considerable impetus to the search for alternative measures of development, such as the UNDP's Human Development Index, which appeared in 1990. None of the alternatives has yet ousted the Keynesian framework from economic management in developing countries, and it still survives in ghostly form in the World Bank's RMSM programming model.

From the mid-1970s, the Keynesian consensus in developed countries began to disintegrate. The experience of 'stagflation' – slower growth with accelerating inflation – could not be easily explained in terms of the Phillips curve, according to which there was a growth–inflation trade-off. The division of economics into 'macro' and 'micro', for which Keynes was responsible, now began to appear problematic. Keynes had persisted with the microeconomic assumption of competitive markets, although it was not consistent with his aggregate theories. The inconsistency raised the question of how to work out logically adequate micro-foundations for macroeconomics, leading to the sprouting of new, less-than-Keynesian macro-theories in the 1980s and 1990s. The search for the missing micro-foundations affected development economics adversely. Neither Kalecki nor Lewis had developed the economic theory of surplus labour and the agricultural marketed surplus rigorously at the micro level. Development economics was thus increasingly criticized as the star of Keynesian macroeconomics waned in the developed countries.

The Legend of Keynes

In addition to the indirect influence that Keynes exerted on specific elements of development economics through his disciples, he also influenced development economists through his powerful posthumous legend. Indeed, he was already a legend in his own lifetime. It was a legend he cultivated, because he thought that it enhanced his power of persuasion in matters of public policy. After his death, Roy Harrod, who published Keynes' official biography in 1951, further burnished this legend, again for the purpose of preserving the persuasive influence of Keynesian ideas (Harrod 1951). Harrod's *Life* portrayed Keynes as 'a brilliant thinker, an entrancing personality and a great world benefactor'. Reviewers who did not know Keynes, or knew him only in his final heroic years, found Harrod's portrait moving and convincing (Skidelsky 2000: 494). Many younger development economists must also have been affected in this way. For them, Keynes became an icon and a role model.

What image of Keynes did the legend project? Keynes had shot to international fame at one stroke when he published *The Economic Consequences of the Peace* (1919), his great polemic against the economic terms of the Treaty of Versailles. After that he was never out of the public limelight for long, as he published his policy analyses and advice in the press and corresponded with world leaders on economic issues. It was unprecedented for an economist to operate with this degree of publicity, even if policy-makers frequently ignored his advice. During the inter-war years, Keynes was as much a political figure in Britain as any of the elected politicians of the day. Originally regarded as rather unsound, he was later fully accepted by the political establishment, becoming the country's leading economic statesman. For a while, he seemed to hold Britain's post-war future in his hands. No economist had been in such a powerful position before.

The other aspect of the legend was Keynes' intellectual stature, exhibited in his *General Theory of Employment, Interest and Money* (1936). In this work, he had provided a theoretical explanation for the persistence of mass unemployment and a theoretical justification for the policy of increased government expenditure in a depression – a policy that many other economists decried. He had shown the importance of analysing the aggregate demand and supply of the economy, the interdependence of monetary and real factors in inducing economic fluctuations, and the inadequacy of looking only to price adjustment in the labour market to reduce unemployment. He created a new 'macro-economics', very different from what had existed before – which might be described in summary terms as Alfred Marshall's microeconomics plus the Cambridge version of the quantity theory of money. He saw himself, and others saw him, as creating a revolution in the discipline of economics.[4] The fact that the Keynesian revolution retained an unexplained separation of macro and micro economics did not inhibit its initial success.

This extraordinary combination of political prominence and successful academic innovation gave Keynes a unique place in British economics, as well as great respect among economists in the rest of the world. After his death, his legend became an ideal for economists to emulate, including many of those drawn into the professional world of development economics. To them, it seemed obvious to make a parallel between the scourge of mass unemployment in the 1930s and that of the persistence of global poverty (despite western affluence) in the 1950s. The latter problem, like the former, seemed to require the economists who succeeded Keynes also to undertake a theoretical revolution, on the grounds that the economics of the day lacked the tools to provide an effective remedy.

The effect of the Keynes legend, then, was to encourage development economists to seek for theoretical revolutions. As the title of his masterpiece suggested, Keynes claimed to have created a more general theory of employment than the classical economists had. Neoclassical economists subsequently reversed this claim, however, arguing that Keynes had invented only a special case of neoclassical theory – a case where the wage level is fixed. Anti-Keynesian development economists on the political left, like Dudley Seers, then adapted this argument as follows: all neoclassical economics, including the Keynesian variant, is a special case – a case of smoothly functioning markets in capitalist economies.

Thus, a new theory was sought in order to embrace the more general case, the case of the developing countries, whose economies are beset with bottlenecks and rigidities, and where well-functioning markets are absent (Seers 1963: 77–98). Albert Hirschman later changed the general/special distinction into a simple dualism. He argued that Keynes in his 1936 book had defeated 'monoeconomics'. His invention of another, radically different economics opened the way for the birth of development economics; 'the idea that there might be yet another economics had instant credibility'. In that sense, the step that Keynes had taken was 'crucial' for the new development economics (Hirschman 1981: 6–9).

One thing that unites Seers and Hirschman is that they argue – not without some paradox – from the irrelevance of Keynes' economics in developing countries to his significance for development economics. They also share a tendency to emphasize the absoluteness of the distinction between development economics and other branches of the discipline. In this they were following the Keynes legend that deliberately played up the fundamental nature of his quarrel with 'the classics'. However, just as Keynes exaggerated the depth of his quarrel, so Seers and Hirschman are in danger of exaggerating the theoretical gulf between development economics and other sub-disciplines of economics. Their point about missing markets in developing countries is well taken. The more interesting question, however, was not followed up at that time. Which markets are missing, and what exactly are the economic consequences when certain markets are present but others are absent? (de Janvry, Fafchamps and Sadoulet 1991: 1400–17.) It is hard to answer these questions without reverting to a less dualistic conception of economics that the one that Seers and Hirschman seem to embrace.

Anti-Keynesian economists on the political right did not seek a further theoretical revolution but, rather, a counter-revolution in theory. The main impact of this was felt in macroeconomics for the developed countries from the late 1970s onwards, specifically with widespread conversions to what was known as 'monetarism'. However, this counter-revolution also affected development economics, as Harry G. Johnson indicted the influence of Keynes in this field too (Johnson 1978: 227–33). The burden of Johnson's complaint was that Keynes was responsible for persuading the elite in the developing countries to be obsessed with capital accumulation and enthused by 'collectivism', when neither was appropriate and both were positively harmful to their prospects of economic development. As we shall see, this critique lacked a historical basis. Rather, it seems to illustrate the precept that, to beat a legend, you need an anti-legend.

The practical inheritance of the Keynes legend derived from the aftermath of his final efforts at designing world economic institutions that would provide for stability, growth and welfare. This was subsequently regarded in many quarters as unfinished business. Keynes' design for an international clearing union, and his disciple James Meade's design for an international commercial union, continued to command support after they had lost out to US blueprints for new international institutions for finance and trade. Keynes' vision for the international economy was based on his long-standing opposition to deflation as a method of economic adjustment. He believed that disappointing the expectations of the rentier via inflation was preferable to disappointing the expectations of the worker via unemployment. He therefore wanted an International Monetary Fund that was better resourced than the one that came about, and he wanted the burden of balance of payments adjustment to be shared by deficit and surplus countries, rather than borne by only the former. The issue of whether the working of the International Monetary Fund could be adjusted in order to have a less deflationary impact on developing countries continued to be agitated through the 1950s and 1960s. So did the question of whether an International Trade Organization (including provisions for international commodity agreements) could ever supersede the purely interim GATT (General Agreement on Trade and Tariffs) arrangements.

The claim – made by Gottfried Haberler and Raul Prebisch among many others – that the Bretton Woods system was incomplete, and, moreover, unhelpful to developing countries in relation to trade and finance, eventually prompted the birth of the United Nations Conference on Trade and Development (UNCTAD) in 1964. Keynes had worked on a war-time proposal for a series of commodity buffer stocks (Keynes 1980: 105–99). The policy of commodity buffer stocks remained popular with the developing countries, and Gamani Corea made a demand for an integrated programme of buffer stock finance the central feature of the minimally successful UNCTAD campaign for a new international economic order from 1974 to 1980 (Toye and Toye 2004: Chapter 10). The Report of the Independent Commission on International Development Issues (1980), chaired by Willi Brandt, was perhaps the last major incarnation of this particular Keynesian inheritance in the realm of international economic policy.

The attitudes created among development economists by the Keynes legend are not to be taken wholly at face value. There was surely some element of disingenuousness in these claims, based on a Keynes-like appreciation of the value of hyperbole in getting oneself heard and understood. Even if Keynes did argue for a more generous design of the Bretton Woods institutions, for example, it would be an act of faith to believe that, had his view prevailed, his institutional design would necessarily have lasted long without subsequent adjustments (Williamson 1987). We are here in the world of historical might-have-been.

Certainly, Keynes' enthusiasm for commodity buffer stocks has been exaggerated. His proposal was made to counter what he regarded as a much more damaging US plan for an international wheat cartel in 1942. When his scheme for 'commodity control' was rapidly and generally dismissed as impractical because of the opportunities that it would have created for speculators, he did not return to the theme (Skidelsky 2000: 234–36).

The legend of Keynes was significant for development economics because it constituted a standing temptation to its practitioners to indulge in the grandiose, both in the sphere of theory and practice. The search for the next revolution in economic theory, or the next new paradigm, could easily degenerate into mere shifts of conceptual fashion, which alienated more than they excited. In the end, the search for a new international economic order became an attempt to defy the laws of gravity in international political negotiation. If this was what Johnson had meant by 'the shadow of Keynes', there would have been some truth in it. The towering figure of Keynes inspired people of lesser genius to try to imitate his successes in circumstances that had inevitably and irrevocably changed.

The legend of Keynes thrived in a period when personal memories of him faded or grew dim, and before a more authoritative historiography of his life and work produced its fruit. The sorting of his papers, ensuring their availability in the archive, the publication of a substantial scholarly edition of his collected writings, and the writing of two excellent biographies by Robert Skidelsky and Donald Moggridge occupied several decades after Keynes' death. This necessary hiatus delayed a more refined understanding of the man and his work, and it coincided with the early constructive phase of development economics. In these circumstances, the views of the historical Keynes on the economics of development remained neglected or unknown. The irony of it is that some of his views were produced again, as if new, by later commentators, including those that carried an anti-Keynesian banner. We now turn to two topics relevant to economic development where Keynes' views have so far been imperfectly understood.

The Historical Keynes: On Population and the Terms of Trade

The first is the question of the role of population in the process of economic development. Population was one of Keynes' many intellectual interests, although, in comparison with monetary economics, population questions always remained secondary, and he never wrote a treatise on demography. Nevertheless, he continually discussed population issues in his books and academic papers, as well as in his journalism, until 1937, when illness and then war-time duties supervened.

Keynes lectured to Cambridge undergraduates on the 'Principles of Economics' from 1910/11 to 1913/14 (Moggridge 1992: 188). For him, population issues fell squarely within the rubric of economics, and he followed Marshall's *Principles of Economics* in discussing population in relation to the supply of labour as part of the treatment of factors of production. Departing from Malthus' conclusion that population will always press on the limits of available means of subsistence, Keynes found in statistics of declines in the marriage rate and in the number of children per marriage, evidence that, contrary to Malthus, fertility did diminish as prosperity increased. However, fertility decline was limited to what Keynes called 'civilized countries'. Suspension of the Malthusian threat in such countries had created, in his view, a variety of new dilemmas, which he placed in a post-Darwinian framework. Suspension of the Malthusian law of population for certain classes of society, or portions of the world, implied – for Keynes – that natural selection in humans would work perversely, in the sense that the average quality of the population would tend to fall. Here, he related to some of the concerns of the eugenics movement.

Keynes also thought that the suspension of the Malthusian threat to industrial countries was only temporary. Following J.S. Mill, Keynes believed that proof of overpopulation could be found in statistics of the unit values of manufactured exports, relative to the unit values of food imports. Moreover, he thought that he had found proof, in that the trend in the exchange ratios of manufactures against raw produce had begun to decline. He published a two-page review of the Board of Trade's annual return of UK import and export statistics (1900–11) in the *Economic Journal* of December 1912 (Keynes 1983: 219–22). From these, he concluded that 'the comparative advantage in trade is moving sharply against industrial countries'. After a 'turning point' in 1900, he thought that the Malthusian threat had begun to revive.

In a 1914 lecture on *Population*, Keynes advanced the thesis that the world of his day was overpopulated. His analysis was in two parts – of the west and of the east. The situation of the west has become bleaker because of the alleged 1900 turning point in the terms of trade, indicating that the period of reprieve from Malthusian mechanisms was coming to an end. His account of the east was that these mechanisms had never been in abeyance. He used the cases of India, Egypt and China to illustrate this, and to suggest that colonial governments' measures to raise the standard of living were doomed to fail because of relentless population increase under the sanction of popular religion. In these circumstances, and given the existence of a world market for food, Keynes argued that there was a collective action problem of insufficient incentive for any single country in the world to try to curb its population growth.

In the period of temporary abeyance of Malthusian mechanisms in the west, he saw the falling birth rate as a result of favourable developments: the reduced desire and reduced opportunity (within marriage) for procreation, and the increased ability, by means of artificial checks, to avoid undesired children. He saw the need, in the worsening (as he thought) of economic conditions in the west, to spread the use of artificial checks from the upper and middle classes to the working classes. He therefore vigorously denounced the superstition and obscurantism of those who opposed the diffusion of contraception and even open public discussion of the issue.

In his 1912 lecture notes, Keynes observed that perverse natural selection operated between countries as well as between classes. 'It is in the most civilized countries that the birth rate is falling off fastest.'[5] Yet, in other countries, he thought that the diffusion of artificial checks would be impossible. 'I do not see what hope there is for much improvement, moral or material, for the races of India and China, so long as the popular religions of these countries attach so great an importance to early marriage and numerous offspring.'[6] For Keynes, then, the policy problem was to find appropriate defences against 'the fecundity of the East' (Toye 2000: 71). Without them, he thought it would be harder to press the argument for more widespread contraception in Britain. He was sensitive to the charge that he was advocating 'race suicide', but he put his trust in draconian measures of immigration control and restrictive intervention in the international food trade to turn the trick for 'the most civilized nations'.

The major dilemma that he saw was that policies that encouraged the British rate of population growth to decline further would have only a slight impact on protection of the British standard of living. The significance of the development of an international market in foodstuffs, on which Britain had become dependent, was that food prices were set in a global market, in which Britain's demand was but one element of total demand. If world food supplies had reached a plateau while world demand was expanding because the over-populated countries were failing to restrict their population growth, a moderation of British demand would hardly arrest the rise in food prices and the consequent loss of welfare. As Keynes put it, 'the advantage of a fall in the birth rate in any country is shared by the whole world' (Toye 2000: 65–66). By the same token, a rise in the birth rate in any country will, *ceteris paribus*, cause a welfare loss to the whole world. Small countries that attempt to restrain their own population growth will not offset this loss. Keynes thus put a new and different twist on Marshall's argument that England's population growth was not significant enough to push up the price of cheap imported food. If that were so, a slackening of English population growth would not be significant in pushing down the price of imported food, if other factors were making it dearer.

From an analytical viewpoint, this sketch of a model of the welfare implications of differential population growth in what would be known today as the North and the South is the most interesting thing to be found in *Population*. It is not fully worked out. It plainly abstracts from some crucial aspects of the problem that it addresses. It assumes that the extra food demand of the South's as well as the North's additional population will all be met by the international market. It ignores the fact that the strength of the South's additional food demand will be mediated by income, of which, by definition, the South has less per head. Keynes did not try, even on the back of the proverbial envelope, to calculate the welfare effects of plausible population growth rate differentials. Like Marshall before him, he underplayed British dominance in the world food market: at that time, Britain was much the largest food importer in the world.

Keynes presented an early example of an 'isolation paradox', a paradox of population growth that prefigured his later famous paradox of thrift in *General Theory*. As he put it, 'every patriot urges his country forward on a course of action (that is) in the widest sense anti-social', just as he was to argue, much later, that the more virtuous people are in being thrifty, the further the national income will fall (Toye 2000: 66). Such paradoxes, based on the insight that the structure of individual incentives is inconsistent with the achievement of social good, have characterized political economy and economics from Mandeville to the modern environmentalist concern for the 'tragedy of the commons'. They provide one link between the intellectual approaches of Malthus and Keynes, and of Keynes and modern development economists.

When Keynes repeated these views on population in the second chapter of *The Economic Consequences of the Peace* (1919), Sir William Beveridge challenged him. Keynes tried to defend his views, but Beveridge (1924: 1–20) demolished his defence. He showed that Keynes' statistics on the '1900 turning point' followed from his splicing of two indices that were not equivalent, which neglected the change in the composition of manufactured exports, and which covered only between 65 and 50 per cent of all of UK's manufactured exports. The '1900 turning point' was a statistical artefact. More important, Keynes' argument confused the falling food purchasing power of a manufactured item with the falling food purchasing power of a unit of labour applied to manufacture. A downward drift in the former was compatible with an upward drift in the latter when technical progress was achieving increasing returns to labour in manufacturing (ibid.: 14–16). As Moggridge concluded:

> Keynes' long-standing worry about the secular tendency for the terms of trade between primary products (especially foodstuffs) and manufactures to turn automatically against the latter to the detriment of European standards of life was certainly misplaced, as well as theoretically incorrect. . . . What should really concern one in such cases are not the gross barter terms of trade considered in *Economic Consequences* and elsewhere but rather the single or double factoral terms of trade which relate to the actual resource costs involved. (Moggridge 1992: 345 and note o)

Keynes' defeat in debate on these issues provides the necessary background for understanding his short and rather enigmatic essay of 1930, 'Economic Possibilities for Our Grandchildren'. In this, he deserts his characteristic preoccupation with the short run and, for once, looks far into the future. He conjectures that within a hundred years, the economic problem will be solved, and that the pressing problem will be the psychological one of how to adapt to the abundance of leisure. He celebrates the idea that, by then, capitalism will have fulfilled its historic mission, liberating people to put aside the dubious arts of money-making, to attend to the more morally uplifting arts of life. Some have seen this as his acceptance of the stationary state of the classical political economists. Others have suggested that it represents his personal theory of development. The latter surmise is far-fetched, given that the only stated mechanism by which the economic problem will be solved is technical progress. A more likely explanation for this unusual piece is that he was trying to induce some public optimism amid the gloom of the great crash, and that, while doing so, he took the opportunity to make an unacknowledged recantation of his neo-Malthusian error, cruelly exposed by Beveridge.

In the 1930s, Keynes was influenced by the population projections of Enid Charles and other British demographers. He understood them as a forecast that the British population was about to cease its long period of growth and embark on a precipitous decline. His Galton lecture of 1937 focused on the implications of population decline for effective demand, savings and the rate of interest. He concluded that excessive population decline would threaten to increase unemployment, just as excessive population growth would threaten to reduce average living standards. Keynes' final view of the need for a balanced relation between the growth of population and capital paved the way for the balanced growth theories of Roy Harrod and Evsey Domar in the 1940s.

The Harrod–Domar equation was useful in concentrating attention on the fundamentals of the development problem under capitalism. This was the relation of the rate of economic growth at which the growth of fixed capital would sustain itself (the 'warranted rate'), and the rate of growth of population and technical progress (the 'natural rate'). Depending on the relation of these two rates, the economy would face either a growing pool of unemployed labour, when the natural exceeded the warranted rate, or a labour shortage and over-heating, when the warranted exceeded the natural rate. This insight reinforced the perception that consistency was an essential requirement of the development planning process. The Harrod–Domar model has had a long life in the practice of development planning for a less creditable reason, however. Its doubtful assumptions of fixed coefficients between investment and growth, and foreign aid and investment and growth, make it a simple, apparently objective yet misleading basis on which the international economic institutions can produce another set of investment and aid targets for their developing country clients (Easterly 1999: 423–38).

The Malthusian threat certainly remained in the minds of Keynes' disciples who wrote on the economic development of Asia. Austin Robinson reflected on the possibility of a Malthusian crisis in Bangladesh as late as 1974 (Austin Robinson 1974: 521–24). Joan Robinson courageously pointed out the dangers of population growth in the Peoples' Republic of China despite the Marxist doctrine that such statements were capitalist scaremongering (Harcourt 1998: 374). 'Of all economic doctrines,' she asserted, 'the one most relevant to the underdeveloped countries is that associated with Malthus' (Robinson 1962: 107). It should be noted, however, that the neo-Malthusianism of Keynes differed from Malthus' own doctrine in three ways. It abandoned the precision of the geometric and arithmetic growth ratios; it advocated, rather than condemned, artificial contraception; and it did not regard, as Malthus did, the existence of checks to population growth as manifestations of divine providence.

Were Keynes' views on population 'imperialist'? They did reflect one strand of 'imperial' discourse that was characteristic of certain late nineteenth-century Indian civil servants. Some in the ICS favoured rural development projects, like canal building in Punjab and the implementation of famine alleviation schemes. Others did not, believing that they were self-defeating in the face of steady population growth. Keynes belonged to the latter group (Toye 2000: 104–05). Keynes also tended to think in terms of race stereotypes, which combined biology and culture. It would be anachronistic to brand him as a racist, but he did hold caricatured views of the national character of foreigners. These were widely shared in Bloomsbury and elsewhere, although others at the time, like H.G. Wells, were perfectly aware that they were false and unscientific.

The Historical Keynes: The Critique of Russian Economic Development

It is often said that Keynes never visited a developing country, except to go on holiday. It is certainly true, as suggested above, that he was not very interested in studying foreign places and their peoples impartially. However, after his marriage to the Russian ballerina Lydia Lopokova, he did visit Soviet Russia three times – in 1925, 1928 and 1936 – and then wrote up what he saw. In his commentaries on the management of the Soviet economy, Keynes raised important issues that were to surface again in the neoliberal critiques of development economics of the 1970s and 1980s.[7] It is important to realize that his comments were not made initially from a position of outright opposition to the Bolshevik revolution. While acknowledging the 'cruelty and stupidity of New Russia' at first, he hoped that it might also embody 'some speck of the ideal'. He also advocated agricultural loans to the new regime, to prevent famine and promote the resumption of grain exports (Keynes 1978: 394). It was only at the end of the 1920s that he abandoned these hopes.

Keynes' information about the management of the Soviet economy came from an impeccable source: E.A. Preobrazhensky, whom he met in Geneva in 1922. At that time, Preobrazhensky was chairman of the financial commission of the Central Committee, charged with implementing the New Economic Policy. He had also prepared a report on the means of extending Soviet power into the countryside. Since the Soviet objective was to subordinate the peasantry to large-scale industrial production, he advocated government monopoly of the banking system and of foreign trade, which would oblige the peasants to exchange their surplus at prices that the government could control. This would also permit the use of an inflation tax without thereby weakening the external value of the currency.

Keynes analysed these key features of the Soviet economy in his 'A Short View of Russia' (1925). There, he described 'the official method of exploiting the peasants'. It was done not by taxation but by the official manipulation of domestic prices that the foreign trade monopoly made possible (Keynes 1978: 264). The peasants' wheat could be bought at a price in domestic currency below the world price at the official exchange rate, while textiles and manufactured goods would be priced in domestic currency above the world price at the official exchange rate. This price policy created the protection necessary for an internationally uncompetitive industrial sector. Keynes saw the ill consequences clearly enough: given the incentives he faced, the peasant would underproduce, and given the inflated industrial wage, there would be excess migration to the towns. Keynes summarized his analysis in the following terms: 'This state of affairs serves but to enforce a lesson of bourgeois economics as being equally applicable in a Communist state, namely that it impairs wealth to interfere with the normal levels of relative prices or with the normal levels of relative wages' (ibid.: 265).

The question must be asked whether Keynes' appeal to bourgeois economics was his last word on the matter. Surely, he later changed his mind and showed there was 'another economics', apart from the orthodoxy in which he had been schooled by Marshall? In the 1930s, did he not become an advocate of both protection and state planning? Indeed, he did, but it should be emphasized that these two shifts in his policy stance still left him at a considerable distance from the type of economic policies that he criticized in Russia in the 1920s. Even while making his cautious and limited case for protection in Britain, Keynes went out of his way to say: 'Russia exhibits the worst example which the world, perhaps, has ever seen of administrative incompetence and of the sacrifice of almost everything that makes life worth living to wooden heads.' He denied that by proposing a measure of protection for Britain, he was thereby endorsing 'all those things which are being done in the political world today in the name of economic nationalism' (Keynes 1982: 243–44). He contrasted the political context in which he was operating, one that allowed for experiment and free discussion of economic policy, with that of Stalin's Russia, where independent views were crushed.

Keynes also made his case for modest state planning by explicitly rejecting the relevance of what had been done by existing 'planned regimes to the south and the east' (Keynes 1982: 86). These regimes, he believed, had bought their limited industrial successes at a huge cost to welfare. By contrast, his support for state planning was limited to activities 'which in the nature of the case lie outside the scope of the individual' (ibid.: 88). They were to be complementary to, and not a substitute for, activities the individual could undertake, and they were certainly not an attempt to increase state power for its own sake. He was talking about measures of taxation, tariffs, foreign exchange control, the regulation of transport as well as town and country planning. He was not advocating a state-driven industrialization drive. When he conceded that the ideas of *General Theory* implied 'a large extension of the traditional functions of government', he also said that they gave no warrant for a 'system of State Socialism which would embrace most of the economic life of the community' (Keynes 1978: 378).

It should be clear that the historical Keynes, while advocating greater control of investment by the liberal state, maintained, to the end of his life, the objections that he had voiced in the 1920s to the 'official method of exploiting the peasants'. If anything, his comments on the political economy of the Soviet Union became sharper and more hostile as he became more aware of the enormity of the economic mistakes possible in authoritarian regimes.[8] As Joan Robinson said of him much later: 'Capitalism in some was repugnant to him but Stalinism was much worse' (Robinson 1975).

Conclusion

The significance of Keynes for development economics is traditionally said to rest on two parts of his work. The first was his invention of the macroeconomics of employment, modulated by Joan Robinson into the concept of 'disguised unemployment'. The second was his contribution to the construction of the Bretton Woods international economic institutions, including his proposal for commodity price stabilization. Both these components of his work were indeed influential in the early years of development economics for two main reasons. Either they influenced his disciples, who then wrote on economic development, or development economists who had not known him personally perceived them as key elements in the legend of Keynes.

In addition to these two sources of Keynesian influence, the beliefs of the historical Keynes on the subject of economic development are also of significance to contemporary development economics, even though they had very little influence on its early formation. One such theme is population growth and movements in the terms of trade. Here (until 1930), Keynes maintained that industry's terms of trade faced a secular decline – the exact opposite of the Singer–Prebisch view that came to dominate development economics after 1950. In expositions of his neo-Malthusian approach, however, Keynes anticipated two modes of thinking that have subsequently become familiar in development economics: the isolation paradox and the North–South model. His later concerns about the balance of investment and population growth led to the influential Harrod–Domar model.

The other significant theme to be found in the historical Keynes is his analysis of the use of economic controls in Soviet Russia in the 1920s and 1930s, when it was the contemporary equivalent of today's 'developing country'. In several ways, Keynes' perceptive critique of Soviet economic policy anticipated neoliberal criticisms of the industrial policies of many post-war developing countries. Ironically, some development economists of the 1970s, who proclaimed themselves anti-Keynesian because they were reacting against the legend of Keynes, were in fact elaborating on ideas that Keynes had sketched out fifty years previously, and of which they were blissfully ignorant. So easy it is, if the history of economics is disregarded or disparaged, to become 'the slave of some defunct economist'.

Notes

1 By 'most notable', I mean the one that made the widest impact on the public consciousness, and not necessarily the one that the academics of the day found the most original or controversial.
2 Keynes' political motivation is well captured in Harrod (1936).
3 The first reference to disguised unemployment dates from 1936 (Robinson 1936: 225–33), and recurs in her 'Planning Full Employment' (Robinson 1951: 84). See also her later 'Notes on Economic Development' (Robinson 1960: 96–98).
4 'I believe myself to be writing a book on economic theory, which will largely revolutionize – not, I suppose at once but in the course of the next ten years – the way the world thinks about economic problems', said Keynes in a letter to George Bernard Shaw of 1 January 1935 (Keynes 1982, Vol. XXVIII: 42).
5 See the transcript of the 1912 lecture notes in Toye (2000: 41).
6 See the transcript of the 1914 lecture notes in Toye (2000: 69).
7 I have treated this theme in greater depth in Toye (1993: 239–65).
8 Keynes' views thus contrasted with the distinctly more positive comments Austin Robinson, one of the 'Gosplanners', made after visiting Soviet Russia in July 1945. I am grateful to Richard Toye for pointing this out to me. See Cairncross (1993: 94) for more detail.

References

Arndt, H.W. (1987), *Economic Development: The History of an Idea* (Chicago: University of Chicago Press).

Beveridge, William (1924), 'Mr Keynes' Evidence for Over-population', *Economica*, 4: 1–20.

Burchardt, Fritz A. (1944), 'Foreword', in F.A. Burchardt *et al.*, eds, *The Economics of Full Employment* (Oxford: Basil Blackwell).

Cairncross, Alec (1993), *Austin Robinson: The Life of an Economic Adviser* (London: St Martin's Press).

De Janvry, Alain, Marcel Fafchamps and Elisabeth Sadoulet (1991), 'Peasant Household Behaviour with Missing Markets: Some Paradoxes Explained', *Economic Journal*, 101, November.

Easterly, William (1999), 'The Ghost of Financing Gap: Testing the Growth Model Used in the International Financial Institutions', *Journal of Development Economics*, 60: 423–38.

FitzGerald, E.V.K. (1990), 'Kurt Mandelbaum and the Classical Tradition in Development Theory', in Kurt Martin, ed., *Strategies of Economic Development: Readings in the Political Economy of Industrialization* (Basingstoke: Macmillan).

Harcourt, G.C. (1998), 'Two Views on Development: Austin and Joan Robinson', *Cambridge Journal of Economics*, 22: 367–77.

Harrod, Roy (1936), 'Review of *The General Theory of Employment, Interest and Money*', *Political Quarterly*, 7, April–June: 293–98.

—— (1951), *The Life of John Maynard Keynes* (London: Macmillan).

Hirschman, Albert (1981), *Essays in Trespassing: Economics to Politics and Beyond* (Cambridge: Cambridge University Press).

Independent Commission on International Development Issues (1980), *North–South: A Program for Survival* (Cambridge, Massachusetts: MIT Press).

Johnson, Harry G. (1978), 'Keynes and Development', in Elizabeth S. Johnson and Harry G. Johnson, eds, *The Shadow of Keynes: Understanding Keynes, Cambridge and Keynesian Economics* (Oxford: Basil Blackwell).

Keynes, John M. (1978), *The Collected Writings of John Maynard Keynes*, Vol. XVIII (London: Macmillan).

—— (1978), *The Collected Writings of John Maynard Keynes*, Vol. IX (London: Macmillan).

—— (1978), *The Collected Writings of John Maynard Keynes*, Vol. VII (London: Macmillan).

—— (1980), *The Collected Writings of John Maynard Keynes*, Vol. XXVII (London: Macmillan).

—— (1982), *The Collected Writings of John Maynard Keynes*, Vol. XXVIII (London: Macmillan).

—— (1982), *The Collected Writings of John Maynard Keynes*, Vol. XXI (London: Macmillan).

—— (1983), *The Collected Writings of John Maynard Keynes*, Vol. XI (London: Macmillan).

Lewis, Arthur W. (1966), *Development Planning* (London: George Allen and Unwin).

Mandelbaum, Kurt (1945), *The Industrialization of Backward Areas* (Oxford: Basil Blackwell).

Moggridge, Donald (1992), *Maynard Keynes: An Economist's Biography* (New York: Routledge).

—— (1993), *Keynes* (Toronto: University of Toronto Press).

Myrdal, Gunnar (1968), *Asian Drama: An Enquiry into the Poverty of Nations* (London: Pelican).

Osiatynski, Jerzy, ed. (1993), *Collected Works of Michal Kalecki*, Vol. V (Oxford: Clarendon Press).

——, ed. (1997), *Collected Works of Michal Kalecki*, Vol. VII (Oxford: Clarendon Press).

Robinson, Austin (1974), 'The Economic Development of Malthusia', *Modern Asian Studies*, 8: 521–24.

Robinson, Joan (1936), 'Disguised Unemployment', *Economic Journal*, XLVI (182): 225–33.

—— (1951), 'Planning Full Employment', in Joan Robinson, *Collected Economic Papers*, Volume I (Oxford: Basil Blackwell).

—— (1960), 'Notes on Economic Development', in Joan Robinson, *Collected Economic Papers*, Volume II (Oxford: Basil Blackwell).

—— (1962), *Economic Philosophy* (Harmondsworth: Penguin).

—— (1975), 'What Has Become of the Keynesian Revolution?', in Milo Keynes, ed., *Essays on John Maynard Keynes* (Cambridge: Cambridge University Press).

Royal Institute of International Affairs (1943), Committee on Reconstruction, 'Memorandum on Surplus Agricultural Population' (London: Royal Institute of International Affairs).

Seers, Dudley (1963), 'The Limitations of the Special Case', *Bulletin of the Oxford Institute of Economics and Statistics*, 25 (2): 77–98.

—— (1969), 'The Meaning of Development', *International Development Review*, 11 (4): 2–6.

—— (1976), 'The Political Economy of National Accounting', in Alec Cairncross and Mohinder Puri, eds, *Employment, Income Distribution and Development Strategy: Essays in Honour of Hans W. Singer* (London: Macmillan).

Singer, Hans (1987), 'What Keynes and Keynesianism Can Teach Us about Less Developed Countries', in A.P. Thirlwall, ed., *Keynes and Economic Development* (London: Macmillan).

Skidelsky, Robert (2000), *John Maynard Keynes. Volume 3: Fighting for Britain, 1937–46* (London: Macmillan).

Thirlwall, A.P., ed. (1987), *Keynes and Economic Development* (London: Macmillan).

Toye, John (1989), 'Nationalism and Structuralism: Two Themes in the Work of Dudley Seers', *IDS Bulletin*, 20 (3), July: 53–58.

—— (1993), 'Keynes, Russia and the State in Developing Countries', in Derek Crabtree and A.P. Thirlwall, eds, *Keynes and the Role of the State* (Basingstoke: Macmillan): 239–65.

—— (2000), *Keynes on Population* (Oxford: Oxford University Press).

Toye, John and Richard Toye (2004), *The UN and Global Political Economy: Trade, Finance and Development* (Bloomington: Indiana University Press).

Toye, Richard (2003), *The Labour Party and the Planned Economy, 1931–1951* (London: Royal Historical Society).

Williamson, John (1987), 'Bancor and the Developing Countries: How Much Difference Would It Have Made?', in A.P. Thirlwall, ed., *Keynes and Economic Development* (London: Macmillan).

Keynes, Kaldor and Economic Development

Amiya Kumar Bagchi

Both John Maynard Keynes and Nicholas Kaldor believed in capitalism, seeing it as a system that delivers growth by encouraging enterprise. However, both of them also held that capitalism is inherently unstable and, consequently, needs to be regulated. The development of development economics after World War II has drawn on many sources. The direct and indirect theoretical and methodological contributions of Keynes and Kaldor included analysis of the macroeconomics of growth, the nature and implications of financial arrangements, the problems of stabilizing the prices of primary commodities, and many other concerns. Furthermore, the counter-revolution against development economics in recent decades has proceeded almost in tandem with the trashing of Keynesianism.

Keynes' analysis of stockmarkets has come to be acknowledged as more relevant than ever in today's world of financial liberalization, which has caused havoc to the global economy, with the developing countries being the most victimized. Kaldor too left a distinctive imprint on development economics, creatively elaborating the Keynesian macroeconomic approach in such crucial fields as tax reform and commodity price stabilization, with the aim of constructing a macroeconomic framework that could stimulate investment and growth, raise income and effective demand in developing economies, and thereby stabilize and stimulate the global economy as a whole.

The Three Lives of Keynes, Development Economics and Macroeconomics

As an economist, Keynes led at least three different lives in three phases of his career. The first phase lasted from his entry into the India Office until the time he was defending his *Economic Consequences of the Peace*, that is, say, up to the end of 1921. His view of the world remained centred on the place of the British empire in the world, and on the place of Europe as the fountainhead of world civilization and the anchor of global prosperity, and a world that could be recreated if only European prosperity could be restored by restraining the madmen who had crafted the Versailles Treaty and the bankers who hankered after the pre-war (gold) parities of the major currencies, especially sterling (Keynes 1919). Elsewhere, I have argued that up to the outbreak of World War I, Keynes not only viewed the world through the lens of an instinctive defender of the empire, but also, in many ways, including through his monetary theory and his view of the evolution of the terms of trade between industrial and primary products, he remained rooted in the tradition handed down from Ricardo (Bagchi 1991; see also Moggridge 1992: Chapter 8; Toye 1997).

The second life of Keynes began from his editing of the *Manchester Guardian Supplements* on Europe, and stretched to his writing and defence of the *General Theory*. This was the phase in which he alerted the world and the British public about the dangers of deflationary policies, competitive devaluation, free mobility of capital, and lack of coordination among central bankers regarding the acceptable levels and necessary changes in exchange rates.

In the third phase of his life, Keynes began drawing up and ceaselessly defending his plans for an international clearing union and for stabilization of prices of primary products. Along with Harry Dexter White, he can be seen as the intellectual parent of the Bretton Woods institutions.

In none of these phases did Keynes cease to be a defender of the empire; nor did he display much sensitivity about the needs of the poor countries, the vast majority of whom lived in colonial or semi-colonial dependencies. On at least two occasions, for example, the policies advocated by Keynes would have done further harm to Indian interests. The first was when he defended a totally unrealistic exchange rate for the rupee at the end of World War I, of anywhere from 1s. 8d. to 2 s. (Keynes 1971: Chapter 5). His aim was both to deflate the Indian economy by forcing it to import more goods from abroad, and to prevent India from absorbing any substantial part of the gold reserves of the world. [It has to be said, to his credit, that in 1919–20, he put his money on the soundness of his advice, betted on the Indian currency along with dollars and lost all his money (Skidelsky 1992: 41–43).] In the post-World War II period, Keynes wanted to indefinitely block the balances accumulated by the members of the sterling area, including India and Egypt. (India and Egypt, in that order, were by far the largest creditors of Britain within the sterling area.) However, the Bank of England and Keynes' colleagues in the British Treasury objected to this, because they wanted to preserve the post-war convertibility of the British pound, at least within the sterling area (Keynes [1940–44] 1980: 305–07; Moggridge 1992: Chapter 29). At the Bretton Woods Conference, Keynes' speech on 10 July 1944 scuttled the proposal of the Indian delegation that a part of the sterling balances could be used for multilateral settlements (Keynes [1941–46] 1980: 85–87). This kept India firmly tied to the apron strings of the sterling area years after her independence.

Despite all this relative indifference to the welfare of the world outside England, Europe and, by extension, the North Atlantic seaboard, Keynes made seminal contributions to the evolution of development economics in at least three directions. First, he forged the tools of macroeconomics and they began to be applied to issues of development from the 1950s. Second, his signposting of the dangers of unlimited capital mobility has acquired special significance since the onset of financial liberalization in the late 1970s. Third, the extended analysis of the necessity for paying attention to all aspects of growth and stabilization in the world economy – including the curing of unemployment, the stabilization of primary product prices and regulation of financial markets, including stockmarkets – remains as contemporary as ever. He also played a major role in the designing of the two Bretton Woods institutions, namely, the International Monetary Fund (IMF) and the International Bank for Reconstruction and Development (IBRD), also known as the World Bank. It has been argued that it was Harry Dexter White, who led the US team at Bretton Woods, rather than Keynes, who had the final say in the shaping of the two institutions, and that there were some important differences in their perspective on post-war economic policy (Boughton 2002). White's dominance is explained to a large extent by the emergence of the USA as the hegemonic capitalist economy of the world. The subsequent evolution of the two institutions and their pursuit of goals that were antithetical to those of either Keynes or White is largely to be attributed to the start of the cold war soon after the end of World War II, and the assault mounted against the working class and the developing economies from the 1970s.

Development Economics and Its Enemies

Development economics arose long before Keynesian macroeconomics was applied to problems of growth and development. The impulse came from the Russian five-year plans and the lessons learned from Prussian policies that stimulated industrial growth in Germany. M. Visvesvarayya, an Indian engineer-turned-statesman, published a book in 1920 advocating policies for quickening economic growth in India. In 1934, he published a book explicitly advocating planning for stimulating Indian economic growth. By 1938, the Indian National Congress had established a national planning committee for India. In the meanwhile, the Russians had carried out two five-year plans, and the Turkish government had drawn up plans for accelerating industrialization and received Soviet aid for those plans.

During World War II, the British Indian government initiated moves to draw up plans for economic reconstruction after the war. Side by side, of course, central and Eastern European economists seeking refuge in England put forward the plans that John Toye has sketched. In 1952, Bhabatosh Datta published his book, *The Economics of Industrialization* (Datta 1952). Unlike in Britain and the crown colonies of that country, where the national accounting framework was hammered out by Keynes and his junior colleagues at the British Treasury, the statistical foundations of national income accounting and planning in India were laid mainly under the leadership of Simon Kuznets and P.C. Mahalanobis, a physicist-turned-statistician and planner. The theoretical framework for India's second five-year plan, drawn up by Mahalanobis, was inspired by the Soviet model, rather than by Keynesian macroeconomics. In fact, writings appeared that explicitly criticized the application of Keynesian economics to underdeveloped countries. However, almost simultaneously, other economists stressed the necessity of stimulating demand by expanding public expenditure when there was excess capacity, and of restraining it when there was a supply-side crunch as revealed by external deficits or inflationary pressures.

Already, in the 1950s, conservative economists such as Peter Bauer and Milton Friedman were arguing against the drawing up of deliberate development plans for poor countries or the use of fiscal instruments to control expenditure. Dependence on the working of free enterprise, rather than deliberate government action or social engineering, was their preferred route to economic development. Under successive attacks by Friedman and Robert Lucas, Keynesian economics in its different formulations (old Keynesian, structuralist or Kaleckian, IS–LM synthesis or post-Keynesian) lost its academic hegemony. The search for the micro-foundations of microeconomics led to a questioning of the very rationale for a separate branch of macroeconomics.

In the meanwhile, the Polak–Friedman monetarist doctrines were applied to draw up structural adjustment programmes (SAPs) and cause utter mayhem in the developing countries. While paying lip service to the necessity of putting microeconomic specificities above the generalizations of development economics and Keynesian economics, the SAPs were designed to work on the principle of 'one size fits all'. The latest poverty reduction strategy papers (PRSPs) are designed to ensure not only that all aid is directed towards the goals favoured by the Washington twins, but also that any residual autonomy enjoyed by the governments of poor countries is completely eroded.

But, in the current crisis of global political economy, Keynes' emphasis on preserving the policy autonomy of national governments, even while crafting institutions for international policy coordination, has become a matter, literally, of life and death for hundreds of millions of people all over the world. In assessing the roles of the different incarnations of development economics and Keynesian economics, it is essential to link them to strategies of hegemonic or imperialist powers from World War I to Iraq War II.

Kaldor: Pre-eminent Successor to Keynes

Nicholas Kaldor started out as a theorist of capitalism, rather than a theorist of development of underdeveloped countries as such. But already, in his paper on the theory of capital (Kaldor 1937), he had come up with the model of a slave economy, in which the rate of growth of the slave population was also the rate of interest obtained on the capital stock of slaves.[1] Moreover, from the 1950s, he engaged intensively in the analysis of general problems of economic growth and the fiscal problems of developing countries.

I agree with Luigi Pasinetti (1986) and Anthony Thirlwall (1987) that the mantle of Keynes fell on Kaldor – rather than on any of the other Keynesians of the Cambridge group – in more senses than one, even though Kaldor was not a member of the group that participated in the forging of Keynes' *General Theory* (Keynes 1936). Like Keynes, Kaldor regarded economics as an essentially fact-based discipline, rather than one in which theories are spun for their elegance.

Like Keynes, again, Kaldor believed that capitalism as a system was highly unstable, but was amenable to control and regulation in the interest of the furtherance of human welfare. There are other similarities in their approach to the subject, such as their treatment of risk and uncertainty, their view of money and the capital market. Even the distinctly Kaldorian theory of income distribution harks back to Keynes' famous analogy with the 'widow's cruse' in Vol. 1 of his *Treatise of Money* (1930).[2] Like Keynes, Kaldor was also engaged in policy discussions practically all his life, and believed that it was necessary for the state to intervene in economic affairs, although both of them regarded capitalism as the only system worthy of their intellectual and moral support.

One of the foundations of a capitalist economy is a class of people who control the means of production and engage in various future-oriented activities, many of which involve the shouldering of risk. Hence, risk-taking and dealing with uncertainty have come to be accepted as major hallmarks of a capitalist economy. Risk-taking behaviour fascinated both Keynes and Kaldor. Keynes' first theoretical work was his *Theory of Probability* (1921), in which he put forward his essentially subjective theory, drawing on the heritage of Thomas Bayes. He regarded insurable risk to be rather uninteresting and theorized about the way people formulated their behaviour in the presence of events that do not repeat themselves in exactly the same fashion. It may be argued that the Marx–Schumpeter theory of innovations characterizing capitalism would require precisely this kind of probabilistic judgement on the part of the entrepreneur.

Kaldor's view of the central role of speculation in a market economy is clearly spelt out in his paper, 'Speculation and Economic Stability' (Kaldor [1939] 1960b). In this paper, Kaldor classifies commodities and their uses into basically two groups, those with positive carrying costs, mainly commodities that are used as working capital, and those with negative carrying costs, mainly fixed capital. He derives a formula connecting current price and expected price:

$EP-CP = i + c - q + r$

where EP and CP are expected and current prices respectively,
i is the rate of interest,
c the marginal carrying cost, and
r the risk premium.

It can be easily shown that the futures price (with the same time period) FP is $FP = EP - r$. 'The possibility of arbitrage, i.e. buying spot and selling futures simultaneously and holding the stock until the date of delivery', prevents the futures price from rising above $EP - r$, while 'speculation . . . prevents it from falling below the amount' (Kaldor [1939] 1960b: 24–26). 'Thus, in addition to the factors mentioned above, the determination of the futures price will also depend, in the real world, on *divergence of opinion*'[3] (ibid.: 29; emphasis in the original).

This insistence by Kaldor and Richard Kahn on divergence of opinion as a condition for the operation of futures markets, including markets in bonds and equities, distinguishes them from those who think of modelling them on the basis of some universally agreed expected price. Kahn was much more consistent in his views in this respect because he disputed the possibility of anchoring the relationship between the short-term and long-term rates of interest in expected values of those rates or changes in those rates, as (Kaldor [1939] 1960b) tried to do (Kahn 1954).

For many economists, Tobin's paper of 1958 is supposed to provide the formal underpinning for the liquidity preference theory of interest (Tobin 1958). But, as Buiter (2003: F587) has pointed out, although the mean-variance approach to behaviour under conditions of risk in asset prices and their returns – pioneered by Markowitz, Tobin, Sharpe and others – has gone from strength to strength, 'it is a remarkable example of a theory that emphatically fails empirically yet is generally considered to yield important insights'. In fact, this genre of theories shares this characteristic with another major neoclassical formulation: general equilibrium theory. Both of these serve an ideological purpose, namely, to demonstrate that the unregulated price mechanism leads to efficient choices, while ignoring the fact that the conditions required for this result to be validated are never to be found in the real world.

The whole branch of finance that works on the hypothesis that deregulated financial markets are efficient has a more sinister effect as well. Deregulation and manipulation of markets worldwide have been major instruments for greatly increased concentration of all assets in a few hands, as so-called technical analysts and investment advisers have herded unwary small investors into turbulent stockmarkets to be slaughtered by well-heeled asset-holders. As in India, in most other countries, governments – acting as agents of the wealthy – have collaborated in this far-from-innocent game of make-believe.

In his 1939 paper, Kaldor also examined the ways in which the prices of bonds and shares behave (Kaldor [1939] 1960b: section II). He summed up his analysis of the price behaviour of long-term bonds in the following manner:

> In the market for long-term bonds, the elasticity of expectations is normally small, and the elasticity of speculative stocks is large, both absolutely and relatively to the elasticity of non-speculative demand and supply (i.e. the elasticity of the supply of savings, and the elasticity of the producers' demand for funds, as a function of the rate of interest). Hence the price in the short period is largely determined by speculative influences (Ibid.: 42).

Kaldor then went on to account for the contrast between the stability in the gilt-edged market and the instability of the share market:

> Shares are also subject to the same influences as bond prices; changes in the expectations regarding future interest rates should affect the one as much as the other. But in addition they are also subject to changes in the expectations concerning the expected level of profits. And here experience suggests that the elasticity of expectations concerning the future level of profits is fairly high; share

prices correlate fairly well with fluctuations in current earnings. (Ibid.: 43)

Although Kaldor provided some of the microeconomic nuts and bolts (to use a phrase from Hahn 1989) for the speculative motive to work, his analysis of the stockmarket did not really advance even as far as Keynes (1936) had taken it in Chapter 12 of *General Theory*, on 'long-term expectations'. It is still salutary to read Keynes' warnings about the competence or capacity of 'professional investors' which is supposed to guarantee equilibration of the stockmarket through competition resulting in 'efficiency'. As he pointed out, the professional investors

> are concerned, not with what an investment is really worth to a man who buys it for 'keeps' but with what the market will value it at, under the influence of mass psychology, three months or a year hence . . . it is not sensible to pay 25 for an investment of which you believe the prospective yield to justify a value of 30, if you also believe that that the market will value it at 20 three months hence.
>
> Thus the professional investor is forced to concern himself with the antici-pation of impending changes, in the news or in the atmosphere, of the kind which experience shows that the mass psychology of the market is most influ-enced. This is the inevitable result of investment markets organized with a view to so-called 'liquidity'. Of the maxims of orthodox finance none, surely, is more anti-social than the fetish of liquidity, the doctrine that it is a positive virtue on the part of investment institutions to concentrate their resources upon the holding of 'liquid' securities. It forgets that there is no such thing as liquidity of investment for the community as a whole. The social object of skilled invest-ment should be to defeat the dark forces of time and ignorance which envelop our future. The actual, private object of the most skilled investment to-day is 'to beat the gun', as the Americans so well express it, to outwit the crowd, and to pass the bad, or depreciating half-crown to the other fellow. (Keynes 1936: 154–55)

It is thus obvious that Keynes regarded the so-called competitive stockmarkets as a predominant case of market failure, and he used the behaviour of American stockmarkets as a telling illustration. This criticism of the working of the stockmarket was not confined to its inefficiency as a signalling device. Keynes also regarded it as a poor conduit for the financing of aggregate invest-ment. The reasons are, again, best given in Keynes' acerbic prose:

> Speculators may do no harm as bubbles on a steady stream of enterprise. When the capital development of a country becomes the by-product of the activities of a casino, the job is likely to be ill-done. The measure of success attained by Wall Street, regarded as an institution of which the proper social purpose is to direct new investment into the most profitable channels in terms of future yield, can-not be claimed as one of the outstanding triumphs of *laissez-faire* capitalism – which is not surprising, if I am right in thinking that the best brains of Wall Street have in fact been directed towards a different object. (Keynes 1936: 159)

Both Keynes and Kaldor recognized the fundamental instability of a capitalist economy and the role that shifts in the preferences of wealth-holders – as between different assets – played in that instability. But both of them, in different ways, believed in the existence of a 'normal rate of interest' – under-written by government bonds – that anchored the long-term expectation of asset-holders. This anchoring would have to be sustained by appropriate government policies. Neither Keynes nor Kaldor believed in the ability of commercial banks, by themselves, to sustain such a policy. Nor did they trust central bankers to do the job. They also recognized that leaving everything to the gyrations of the stockmarket would produce sheer chaos. Thus, interestingly enough, although they remained distrustful of banks as the major controllers of the national economy, the system of financing they wanted was bank-centred, rather than equity-centred – to use a dichotomy that has become current coin in the wake of the Asian financial crisis.

Moreover, they both recognized the ideological roots of the right-wing desire to use monetary policy to control inflation or to cure other economic ills. In 1926, polemicizing against Britain's decision to return to the gold standard at the pre-war parity, Keynes wrote that the underlying monetary policy was 'simply a campaign against the standard of life of the working classes' operating through the 'deliberate intensification of unemployment . . . by using the weapon of economic necessity against individuals and against particular industries – a policy which the country would never permit if it knew what was being done' (Keynes 1925, quoted by Thirlwall 1987: 299). Half a century later, in 1977, in a speech at the House of Lords, Kaldor predicted that monetarism was doomed to failure 'because it could succeed, if it succeeded at all, only by ruining industry, long before it succeeded in making labour more submissive' (Thirlwall 1987: 301).

Both Keynes and Kaldor supported capitalism for the freedom of enterprise and the growth it promised. But they were both convinced that without intelligent public intervention, it functions badly, especially as far as employment and the standard of living of workers were concerned. For the last thirty years, the dominant trend of economic policy, centering on anti-inflationary monetary and fiscal policies, has run in a completely different direction. Both Kaldor and Keynes believed in a kind of dualism of employment and price stabilization, and thought, with David Hume, that moderate inflation was good for growth. In recent years, the emphasis of monetary and fiscal policy has been almost entirely on the control of inflation, no matter what happens to employment or growth.

It is important to note that although monetarism began its triumphant march over the bodies of dismissed and homeless workers from the 1970s, it had been embedded in the stabilization enforced by the IMF on hapless underdeveloped countries from the late 1950s. The basic doctrine was propounded by Jacques Polak, director of research at the IMF, in a paper published in 1957, which has remained the battering ram of the devastation caused by it ever since (see Fine 2005).

Issues of Stability and Sector Proportions

Many of the issues that have cropped up as problems of structural misalignment in the context of programmes of full employment in developed economies and raising rates of economic growth were foreshadowed in Book V of Keynes' *General Theory*, in Kalecki's work dating from before the publication of *General Theory*, and in Kaldor's paper, 'Stability and Full Employment', published in 1938. I shall primarily concentrate on Kaldor's work in this area. Kaldor starts from a situation in which full employment has somehow been achieved. At that point, there is a certain distribution of income between wages and profits. Associated with that distribution, there is also a distribution of GDP between capital goods and consumer goods. It would be entirely a fluke if the distribution of expenditure between consumption and savings matched the outputs of consumer goods and capital goods. If, in this situation, *ex-ante* investment exceeds savings, or, conversely, falls short of savings, forces will be set up to dislodge the economy from the full employment situation. The situation in which savings exceed investment is familiar to everybody: the reaction is very quick, as goods pile up, output is slashed and workers lose their jobs. In the opposite case, prices rise, income is redistributed in favour of the capitalists and eventually result in excess savings. In this paper, Kaldor also brought in the specificity of equipment as a further constraint on the achievement of a balance between the sectoral outputs of goods, the division of expenditure between consumer goods and capital goods, and the *ex-ante* rates of savings and investment. Kaldor wanted to remedy the maladjustment by regulating the propensity to save, through wage subsidies or taxes on wages.

I stumbled upon similar problems in discussing the difficulties of implementing an ambitious growth plan in an economy in which the private sector plays a major role (Bagchi 1970). In an open underdeveloped economy, you can have a coexistence of several apparently contradictory features: excess demand for luxury- and import-intensive goods, balance of payments deficit, deficiency of demand for mass consumer goods and deficiency of demand for capital goods. The high propensity to consume on the part of the capitalist class – belying some of the assumptions of the Cambridge school and of Marxists like Kalecki – was recognized by Kaldor as a serious obstacle against the development of underdeveloped economies with capitalist institutions when he was asked to advise on the right fiscal policy for India and Chile (Toye 1989; Palma and Marcel 1989).

Kaldor made strategic use of the idea of sectoral imbalances impeding the achievement of full employment, stability and growth when he analysed the problems of the world economy. The sectoral relations he examined were between the primary and the manufacturing sectors of a modern economy. There are at least three kinds of difference or asymmetry between the primary and manufacturing sectors.

(i) The former is characterized by diminishing returns, whereas the latter displays both static and dynamic economies of scale.

(ii) In the former prices are demand-determined, whereas prices in the latter sector are supply-based (this distinction goes back to Kalecki).

(iii) The income elasticity of demand for the output of the primary sector is typically less than one, whereas the income elasticities of demand for manufactures (and especially for those that are newly innovated) is generally more than one.

Kaldor had analysed the problems of stabilizing commodity product prices in 1952, when he acted as a consultant of the Food and Agriculture Organization (FAO) to examine the economics of the International Wheat Agreement (Thirlwall 1987: 279). This agreement was a multilateral scheme that had been ratified in 1949. Under it, certain agreements would be purchased by the organization implementing it at a minimum price, whereas any excess would be traded at market prices. The scheme, while not entirely free from moral hazard problems, had the virtue of preserving incentives. Kaldor preferred this kind of scheme to buffer stock arrangements because it preserved incentives while stabilizing prices. Later, he became concerned about the general tendency of primary product prices not only to be unstable, but also to demonstrate a declining trend in relation to prices of manufactures, and he wrote a paper on it in the March 1964 issue of the *Economic Bulletin for Latin America*.

For individual countries, Kaldor opted for what have been called 'positive adjustment policies', preparing for a soft landing or transition of primary producers to industrial employment while the country passes from being an agrarian economy to a situation in which industry dominates the generation of income and employment. After the oil crisis of 1973, he became concerned about the destabilizing effects of sudden changes in the terms of trade of primary versus secondary sectors, and wrote a widely quoted paper on this theme (Kaldor 1976). There, he pointed out that because of the way in which the mark-up or other cost-linked prices of the secondary sector are likely to be affected by sudden increases in the prices of primary products, an inflationary spiral may start in industrial economies, with adverse effects on both income and employment.

> The rise in the price of raw materials and fuels is, according to Kaldor's analysis, passed through the various stages of production into the final price with an exaggerated effect. . . . This initially causes a rise in the profit share (in the value added in manufacturing), which – in countries with strong trade unions – is a strong factor in causing pressure for causing wage increases. Added to this is the price-induced rise in wages caused by the reluctance of workers to accept a cut in standards of living. Through these different mechanisms, the industrial sector resists any compression of its real income by countering the rise in commodity prices through a cost-induced inflation of industrial prices. Furthermore, this inflation will have a *deflationary* effect on real demand for industrial goods, for two reasons. One of them is that the rise in producers' profits is not matched

by a rise in their spending; the other is that the governments of industrial countries will tend to react to increased domestic inflation by deflationary fiscal and monetary measures, that reduce consumer and investment demand (Griffith-Jones 1989: 227)

Because of the asymmetries in pricing situations and income elasticities between the primary and secondary sectors, it is not obvious that a reduction in primary product prices will stimulate the world economy. However, their prices could and did enter the prices of industrial products via the consumption basket of wage earners, and the cost of transport and intermediate goods. Policies or circumstances that caused dramatic changes in primary product prices would affect the price situation in advanced capitalist countries as well, even if changes in unemployment failed to affect prices. Deflation in the primary-producing countries and a reversal of their industrialization process would affect the employment situation in advanced capitalist countries via another route. The capitalists in those countries would threaten to relocate their production in poorer countries unless the workers are prepared to accept lower wages and worse working conditions. The mere threat would often suffice to browbeat trade unions and the governments of those countries (Burke and Epstein 2003). These manoeuvres would transmit further deflationary impulses to the world economy.

From the end of the 1970s in Britain and from the beginning of the 1980s in the USA, neoliberal policies – such as increasing interest rates on loans, especially on loans to developing countries, and concerted attacks on trade unions and workers' rights in general – had the effect of both causing an external debt crisis in the major developing counties, thereby reducing their bargaining power in foreign markets and increasing unemployment rates in the OECD (Organization for Economic Cooperation and Development) countries, and putting their workers on the defensive. Inflation rates in the OECD countries came down significantly, compared to the 1970s. Beckerman and Jenkinson (1986) carried out an exercise to determine the relative roles of changes in primary product prices and increases in unemployment rates in moderating inflation in the 1980s. They argued that

> most of the deceleration of inflation in the OECD countries in general (including Britain) that took place between 1980 and 1982 was due not to the direct impact of higher unemployment on the labour market but to the fall in 'commodity' (that is, primary product) prices from 1980 to 1982, following their very sharp rise (accompanying the second 'oil shock') between 1978 and 1980. (Beckerman and Jenkinson 1986: 39)

In many ways, this is an old story (except for the rise in unemployment in OECD counties). In 1979, I had argued that the drastic decline in the terms of trade of primary producers in the late nineteenth century had played a major role in lowering the cost of living of the working class and industrial costs in general, and thereby promoted the growth of the North Atlantic seaboard during the period of the so-called Great Depression. I would hazard the guess that in view of the rise in the standard of living of the workers of the European countries in the next eighty years, and hence a decline in the proportion of expenditure on food and other agriculture-based commodities, the effect of such a decline on the living standards of the workers of Europe and North America is likely to be far more muted today. But that is not the full story. Oil has become the most important source of energy worldwide; hence, the control of oil has become such a priority for the leaders of the USA and their allies that they are prepared to go to any length, including the murder of millions of hapless people, in order to attain that end, as was demonstrated by their naked aggression against Afghanistan and Iraq. While Kaldor paid far more attention to the inequitable nature of international economic and political relations, both he and Keynes were almost blind to the workings of imperialism and its effects in shaping the contours of the world economy.

Disciplining the Capitalist Class

Both Kaldor and Keynes believed that the function, nay, the duty of a capitalist class is to save and invest. Kaldor often quoted Keynes' statement in the *Economic Consequences of the Peace* to the effect that the Victorian capitalists were allowed ownership of the principal part of the national cake on condition that they consumed very little of it. In 1956, Kaldor found in Chile and India that the wealthy hogged a far larger part of the national income and wealth, but squandered most of it in wasteful consumption. He set about suggesting fiscal measures to try and garner a part of the waste for productive investment by the state, and to introduce incentives under which the capitalists would be both induced and forced to save a larger part of their income. For this purpose, he recommended the introduction of a capital gains tax, an expenditure tax and, in the Indian case, bringing down the marginal rate of personal income tax to a maximum of 45 per cent (Kaldor 1956; Toye 1989).

In the Chilean case, he was only to write a paper for a United Nations journal, the *ECLA Bulletin*, whereas in India, he was brought in as an adviser to the government. He recommended tax reform measures for India, including a comprehensive, self-checking system of reporting covering all accruals of income, and transfers of income and wealth. As it happened, the right wing was so outraged in Chile that his paper could not be published in the *ECLA Bulletin* (Palma and Marcel 1989).

The outcome of his recommendations for India was not much more propitious. The Finance Minister was changed after he had introduced a diluted version of the Kaldor proposals, though the ostensible reason was different, and most of the proposals were buried. The remnants were summarily killed under the new tax reforms of the Rajiv Gandhi era.

Kaldor's tax reform proposals had three basic aims. The first was to encourage investment and discourage wasteful expenditure. The second was to inject a greater degree of equity into the system by taxing people according to their ability to pay. The third was to make it much easier for the tax authorities to check evasion, while not subjecting the tax payer to the arbitrary authority of the tax collector by leaving a large grey area of interpretation. These goals were probably most clearly expressed in his proposals for Indian tax reform (Kaldor 1956).

In order to encourage risk-taking and entrepreneurship, Kaldor proposed that the highest rate of marginal tax on income should be brought down to 45 per cent from rates of 60 per cent and above. But in order to ensure that the increased income accruing to the rich is not squandered in luxury consumption, he proposed a tax on personal expenditure, detailed theoretical arguments for which he had already worked out (Kaldor 1955). The second reason he recommended imposition of an expenditure tax was that although he considered the Haig–Simons definition of income, as the aggregate of all accruals to the purchasing power of a person, to be the only acceptable definition of taxable income, he knew that such a definition required estimation of many components that involved a considerable degree of judgement by the tax authorities. In contrast to that, actual expenditure is easily verifiable, if tax payers are asked to keep accounts of their spending.

Kaldor also wanted the capital of individuals to be brought under the tax net, for the possession of tangible, non-human capital conferred additional borrowing and spending powers on a person. A budding scientist cannot, at least under modern conditions, offer himself as collateral for a loan,[4] but he can pledge an inherited house to obtain credit from a bank. Kaldor therefore wanted an inheritance tax (called estate duty in India) to tap the wealth of those whose only claim to property was that they were well-born. He also wanted a capital gains tax to garner some of the accretion to property values for the benefit of the public.

Finally, Kaldor proposed the taxation of gifts because many wealthy persons wanted to rid themselves of tax liability on their accruals to income and wealth, while endowing their progeny or other near and dear ones with unearned income or property by giving away part of their income or property to the latter. Kaldor did not think that the capital gains tax or the gift tax would damage the incentive to earn, since much of the capital gains made by the rich (such as increases in real estate values caused by population growth and urbanization) had nothing to do with their own efforts. Moreover, he was proposing a drastic reduction of their marginal income tax rates. The clutch of taxes proposed by Kaldor had a self-checking property, for a person could either spend, give away or invest his income, and any of these would show up in an inconsistency if he wittingly or unwittingly tried to evade taxes under one head or another.

There were many reasons why Indian property owners would not have accepted the Kaldor proposals in 1956 or after. The allurement of getting marginal income tax rates reduced was not great enough for most of them since there were many loopholes through which they avoided much of their tax liability. First, under the personal property and inheritance laws that governed most

Hindus, and especially the dominant Hindu business communities, the property was jointly held by several generations, so that, for example, part of the income generated by it could be shown as belonging to a one-year-old grandson of the male head of the family. Second, under company law, a large part of the expenses of the family controlling the firm and their trusted executives could be passed off as business expenses. Third, there was no tax on agricultural land, so that the descendants of landlord and princely families – some of the richest families of India – paid very little personal tax anyway. On top of all this, there was an enormous amount of tax evasion, especially by those who derived their income from trade and industry, rather than from salaries in the organized sector of the economy.

From the 1970s, the climate of opinion in ruling circles in the developed capitalist countries also changed to favour capitalists as much as possible, ostensibly because redistributive measures and the enhanced power of trade unions had damaged the propensity to save and invest on the part of the rich. Kaldor ruefully commented on the climate of opinion in the UK after the election of Margaret Thatcher's government to power in that country:

> Given the hostile attitude of the present Conservative Government to any form of taxation of capital or of the benefits derived from the ownership of property – aided by the argument that during an inflation capital gains are illusory and the tax is a haphazard levy on capital, the long-term capital gains tax, along with the expenditure tax, was in danger of being abolished. (Kaldor 1980: xi–xii)

The message that indulging the rich further was good for economic growth – communicated through the propaganda blitz and structural adjustment measures imposed on the developing countries by the IMF and the World Bank – was heartily welcomed by the ruling classes of these countries, since they had never believed in paying any price for their countries' goods anyway. Kaldor concluded his introduction to the first volume collecting his writings on taxation with the following statement: 'I have become far more sceptical of the possibilities of improving the distribution of income and wealth through taxation or of introducing effective reforms when these are perceived, in anticipation, as affecting adversely the interests of the property-owning classes' (ibid.: xxiii).[5]

Increasing Returns, Capital Gains and Increasing Inequality

All his life, Kaldor was uncomfortable with the notion of equilibrium in economic theory and its application to economic policy. This is shown by the very first papers he published in this area, namely, 'The Determinateness of Equilibrium' (Kaldor [1934] 1960a) and 'The Equilibrium of the Firm' (Kaldor [1934a] 1960a). In these papers, he sought to give far more definiteness to the notion of equilibrium in economic theory than was to be found in the existing literature of the time. In his critical examination of E.H. Chamberlin's theory of monopolistic competition, he had already come across problems posed by increasing returns to scale in reaching an equilibrium configuration of outputs and prices (Wood 1987). But he still thought of increasing returns to scale in static terms, and his view of the determination of prices and quantities in microeconomic settings was basically neoclassical in orientation, as modified by Chamberlin and Joan Robinson. However, after his adherence to Keynesian macro-economics, he became convinced that the neoclassical framework was totally misleading for figuring out aggregate levels of employment and income distribution.

By the beginning of the 1950s, Kaldor realized that marginal productivity theory could not explain the major facts of income distribution obtaining in the real world (Kaldor [1955–56] 1960a). His theories of economic growth were based on the assumption that firms continually exploit increasing returns to scale and innovate as they expand (Kaldor [1957] 1960b; [1958] 1960c; Kaldor and Mirrlees 1962). His critique of the marginal productivity theory erupted into a ringing denunciation of the whole notion of general equilibrium underlying mainstream economic theory in its neoclassical incarnation (Kaldor [1972] 1978, [1975] 1978). Even before this denunciation, he had implicitly turned to classical modes of analysing adjustments to external disturbances or endogenous changes in basic economic parameters, in his paper on the 'Neo-Pasinetti Theorem' (Kaldor [1966] 1978).

In neoclassical analysis, the production functions of firms and the demand curves facing them are taken as given, or, in the case of oligopolies or polypolistic markets,[6] 'conjectural variations' are allowed in the demand schedules. But classical economists recognized that adjustment to any significant change involves investment in fixed or working capital. Adam Smith basically worked with the assumption that most accumulation processes take the form of changes in working capital, although he provided such a path-breaking analysis of the division of labour in a pin factory that necessarily required the employment of fixed capital.

It is not sufficiently recognized that Adam Smith's concept of competition was intended for a world of merchant capital rather than a world of industrial or fixed capital. In the former context, the conditions of capital mobility are established directly through exchange. Commodities whose rates of return are expected to be high are purchased by the merchant. Whether or not his expectations are later borne out at the time of the sale, his capital is restored to liquidity. Since no portion of his capital remains tied up in commodities, he is entirely free to pursue another purchase in whatever area the highest returns are expected. Through the influx and outflow of merchant capital to areas of higher returns from those of lower returns, there is established a uniform rate of profit.

The situation is quite different, however, in a world of industrial or fixed capital. Where finance is committed to production activity, it is at once immobilized. Only that portion of fixed capital used up within the period of production becomes restored to liquidity through the sale of produced commodities (Clifton 1977: 146). In the presence of increasing returns and marginal cost curves, which slope downward even at the point of maximum profit, strategic behaviour plays a major role in establishing the distribution of market shares among different firms.

In his path-breaking paper, 'Speculation and Economic Stability', Kaldor showed that merchants' stocks can play a stabilizing role under certain conditions, but he did not discuss the role of investment in fixed capital in adjustment to disturbances. He briefly analysed this function in his reply to the critique of Pasinetti (1962) by Samuelson and Modigliani (1966). Kaldor clearly formulated the compulsions imposed on individual firms by capitalist competition:

> I have always regarded the high propensity to save out of profits as something which attaches to the nature of business income, and not to the wealth (or other peculiarities) of the individuals who own property. It is the enterprise, not the particular body of individuals owning it at any one time, which finds it necessary in a dynamic world of increasing returns, to plough back a proportion of the profits earned as a kind of 'prior charge' on earnings in order to ensure the survival of the enterprise in the long run. This is because: (i) continued expansion cannot be ensured in an uncertain world, and in the long run, unless *some proportion* of the finance required for expansion comes from internal sources; (ii) the competitive strength of any one enterprise, in a world of increasing returns, varies with the enterprise's share of the market – it declines with any decrease in that share, and improves with an increasing share; hence (iii) in a world of expanding markets, continued expansion (by the individual firm) is necessary merely to maintain the competitive strength of the enterprise. Hence the high savings propensity attaches to profits as such, not to capitalists as such. (Kaldor [1966] 1978: 85)

Kaldor's analytical route to the neo-Pasinetti theorem can provide the core of a theory of the increasing income inequality associated with financial liberalization. He put forward the following equation characterizing the 'equilibrium' in the securities market:

$$s_w W = cG + igK,$$
where s_w is the propensity to save out of wage income,
c is the proportion of capital gains consumed by stock-holders,
G is the value of capital gains, g is the growth rate of capital,
K is the value of capital and
i is the proportion of new investment financed by the issue of new securities.

In an economy in which savings are embodied solely in stocks, the left-hand side gives the total demand for securities by the non-corporate sector. This demand is satisfied by the sale of old securities in the secondary market represented by cG (savings out of dividends distributed to shareholders is included in s_w) and by the issue of new securities in the primary market. Then, a crucial variable has to be introduced, namely, 'the valuation ratio', defined as 'the relation of the market value of shares to the capital employed by the corporations (or the book value of assets)'. After taking into account the change in the value of stocks, as the difference between the valuation ratio multiplied by the growth of capital stock and value of the proportion of investment financed by the issue of new securities, and manipulating the equations, Kaldor arrived at the following two equations that embody his neo-Pasinetti theorem:

$$v = 1/c[(s_w/g)Y/K - (s_w/s_c)(1-i) - i(1-c)].....(1)$$
$$\text{and} \quad \tilde{n} = [g(1-i)/s_c]..........................(2)$$

If v is given, these two equations determine the relation between the rate of growth and the rate of profit, and the distribution of income between wages and profits in a steady state. But suppose v were to be raised exogenously, or if s_c were to decline, how would the rate of profit and the distribution of income be affected?

Answering these questions would require us to first establish the processes through which the values of v or of s_c were to be changed. One set of conditions raising the value of v would be the financial equivalent of what, in military parlance, is called the power of massed reserves. This would work through the processes resulting in economies of scale in production and marketing, processes that Kaldor stressed in his later analyses of economic growth and the resulting movement from disequilibrium to disequilibrium, movements that give rise to cumulative causation.[7]

But equally important would be the economies of massed finance, which have become the major propelling source of changes in v of big firms since the wave of financial liberalization that has swept over the world from the late 1970s. This acceleration in the use of massed finance and the development of a fast-moving market for corporate control has not led to the increase in v, especially relative to the returns to be obtained from investments in bonds and debt instruments. It has also completely upset the stability in the ratio of profits to wages that Kaldor had tried to explain through his innovative growth models.

The stability of the distribution of income between profits and wages was in fact the outcome of the institutional setting of capitalism in the two decades following World War II, and was not a historical constant, as Paul Baran, a more radical critic of capitalism, had pointed out in his reply to the argument that the growth of monopoly capital threatened growth under capitalism (Baran [1959] 1969: 187–88). Contrary to the predictions of some Marxists, the capitalist system has not collapsed under the weight of its contradictions. But it has become an ever-more oppressive system for the majority of mankind and has generated a degree of inequality of economic power unprecedented in recorded history. Contravention of some of the policies that Keynes and Kaldor tried to put in place, and increasing reliance on a necessarily casino-like stockmarket, which they had implicitly or explicitly decried, have contributed mightily to this outcome.

The Reality of Deregulated Stockmarkets and Increasing Inequality

Contrary to the claims of Milton Friedman (1953) and his followers, the stockmarket is not a place that easily corrects mis-pricing of stocks if they depart from their so-called fundamental values (Shiller 1998; Barberis and Thaler 2003). What applies to stockmarkets also applies *mutatis mutandis* to currency markets. In Friedman-type accounts, the 'arbitrageurs' are supposed to take advantage of any mis-pricing of a stock by buying it when it is underpriced and selling it when it is overpriced. But, in fact, due to herd behaviour, or rumours, or the incentives and operations of ill-informed 'noise traders', such mis-pricing continues. Such situations, however, provide corporations or individuals with very deep pockets to clean up after arbitrageurs, noise traders and small investors listening to the advice of their brokers and investment consultants have bitten the dust, and to buy up whole companies or controlling shares in companies.

One major piece of evidence supporting the proposition that the stockmarket does not allocate resources efficiently is the so-called 'equity premium puzzle' (Mehra and Prescott 1985). The puzzle is that practically throughout the twentieth century, a representative selection of US stocks has earned significantly higher rates of return, after reasonable adjustments for risk, than bonds issued by public authorities. If the stockmarket was really an efficient allocator of funds, this premium for stocks should have vanished. One simple explanation is that while small investors have to decide which particular portfolio of private corporation shares to hold in order to get a reasonable return, they consider it much safer to invest their savings in government bonds, because the government is not likely to default. The persistence of this propensity and the consequently higher returns earned by more canny and well-heeled investors are also part of the explanation for the enormously increased concentration of economic power in most economies.

The issues of US hegemony or imperialism rarely enter into mainstream analyses of why a highly indebted US economy run by a highly indebted government continues to attract hundreds of billions of dollars to fund the burgeoning US balance of payments deficit and US government deficit. The main reason is that investors in Japan, Germany or, for that matter, China know that so long as the dollar remains the dominant currency of exchange, and so long as the US government is able and ready to use both its political and military muscle to literally fight off any challenges to dollar supremacy, US Treasury bills will be honoured, however low the return on these bills may be. The recent anger of the US government with Iran and Iraq was sparked not only by their refusal to become its vassals, but also by their plans to shift to the euro as the main currency for trading oil. Ultimately, oil has become the commodity effectively backing the dominant international currency. The US government wants to ensure its monopoly of control over that commodity, even at the cost of violating all international laws governing the declaration of war against other countries.

Keynes had conceived the IMF as an agency for stabilizing international currency exchanges, thereby facilitating growth of the world economy. In Kaldor's case, the cause of industrialization of underdeveloped economies was even more explicit in his agenda for international monetary reform (Griffith-Jones 1989). However, the IMF has become an instrument for impoverishing underdeveloped economies, and has helped make the international economic order even more unequal than it was in the 1970s. After a poor country gets into a debt crisis, the IMF works out a stabilization package. Two conditions are invariably included in that package. First, the government is made to assume the burden of all external debts incurred by the public sector and all the citizens of the country, however illegitimately those debts might have been incurred. In a classic moral hazard situation, the sins of loan-pushing transnational banks and other financial institutions and of the not-so-innocent borrowers in that country are visited on the hapless common people of that country. The second condition that forms a standard part of the IMF stabilization package is a programme imposing severe deflation on the country seeking assistance. This leads to widespread bankruptcy; assets built up over decades are grabbed by foreign 'vulture' capitalists, often transnational corporations that can easily buy them out. Thus the wrecking of the international monetary system Keynes and Kaldor had pleaded for in some of their seminal writings led to an escalation of inequality in an international order already characterized by a high degree of international inequality (Milanovic 2002).

In writing about the pioneers of thinking about economic development, we should pay attention to what they wrote and preached. But we have also to reckon with the undoing of their work during the last quarter of the twentieth century. An attempt to resurrect their perspective will need to confront the enemies of that work, in ideology and policy-making. My contribution is a small step in that direction.

Notes

1 Thirlwall (1987: 73, n. 11) regards this as an anticipation of the von Neumann result on the Golden Rule of growth, but von Neumann had presented his model at a mathematical seminar in Princeton in 1932, although it was published for the first time in German in 1938 (von Neumann 1945–46: 1, n.).

2 Keynes used his so-called 'fundamental equations for the value of money' to argue that there is a peculiarity of profits as against other forms of income: that if entrepreneurs indulge in riotous living, the total profit income from the sale of luxury goods would go up by exactly the amount of profit income thus spent: 'Thus profits as a source of capital increment for entrepreneurs, are a widow's cruse which remains undepleted however much they may be devoted to riotous living. When, on the other hand, entrepreneurs are making losses, and seek to recoup these by curtailing their normal expenditure on consumption, i.e., by saving more, the cruse becomes a Danaid jar which can never be filled up; for the effect of this reduced expenditure is to inflict on producers of consumption goods a loss of an equal amount' (Keynes [1930] 1971: 125).

3 The futures price is the current price of a commodity or an instrument of such a share or an option on a share that is to be delivered at a future date specified in the contract.

4 But under the current neoliberal regime, when government subsidies for education are being drastically slashed, many aspiring scientists and other professionals are entering

the labour market as heavily indebted debt-slaves of banks and other financial organizations.

5 With the benefit of hindsight and with the specific examples of India, Chile and
Turkey in mind, it can be argued that, apart from the general opposition of property-
owning classes to measures of taxation that might harm their interests, there is a
further problem in underdeveloped countries in which landlords still effectively rule
the countryside. In such countries, the landlords *are* the state, and no public policy
measures can ameliorate the condition of the ordinary people if they are perceived as
reducing landlord power. Essentially, confiscatory land reforms are the only means by
which the private non-market power of the landlords can be abolished. It is not an
accident that virtually the only developing countries that have succeeded in disci-
plining the capitalist class and growing fast are those that have abolished landlordism
and compelled everybody, including landlords' families, to obey the law of the land
(Bagchi 2000). Under pressure from reformers and critics, the World Bank has conceded that pro-peasant land reforms are necessary to give peasants the incentives and
resources to act as free economic agents. But the officials following the advice of the
Bank are trying to effect this via the market route. That route has proved to be a blind
alley as far as empowerment of the peasants is concerned, in the Philippines of
Corazon Aquino or the Egypt of Hosni Mubarak, as it did in the Prussia of the
nineteenth century (for a selection of articles critiquing the market route to land
reforms, see Ramachandran and Swaminathan 2002). In Chile and other Latin American countries, the failure to discipline the bourgeoisie has had costly results, even for
the bourgeoisie. The price paid in India was less dramatic and spread over a much
larger number of years and over a vastly larger mass of humanity.

6 Polypoly refers to a market in which there are many sellers but they may not behave
as price-takers because they face a downward-sloping demand curve.

7 Although Adam Smith is credited with discovering economies of scale through his
analysis of the workings of a pin factory, he did not really extend his insight to the
economy as a whole. Josiah Tucker has a much better claim to be regarded as the
pioneer analyst of economies of scale and cumulative causation in the macroeconomic context. Moreover, like Kaldor and Myrdal (1957), in his *Tract* of 1774,
Tucker applied his analysis to the explanation of differentials between rich and poor
countries. Tucker catalogued a better endowment of capital and infrastructure, a
better command of knowledge and information, a superior ability to learn, a higher
propensity to invest, a higher level of wages and, hence, a higher level of domestic
demand, a higher degree of social division of labour leading to high rates of productivity growth, a greater degree of competitiveness among tradesmen and craftsmen,
and a higher endowment of investible capital resulting in a lower rate of interest as
factors allowing a rich country to continue to be more prosperous than a poor country
(Tucker 1774; Bagchi 1994: 84–87). He ended up with what can be characterized as
the Hume–Tucker law: *operose* or complicated manufactures are cheapest in rich
countries, and *raw materials* in poor ones. And, therefore, in proportion as any
commodity approaches one or the other of these extremes, in that proportion will it be
found to be cheaper, or dearer, in a rich or a poor country (Tucker 1774: 36).

References

Bagchi, Amiya K. (1970), 'Long-term Constraints on India's Industrial Growth, 1951–1968', in
E.A.G. Robinson and Michael Kidron, eds, *Economic Development in South Asia*
(London: Macmillan): 170–92.

—— ([1979] 2003), 'The Great Depression (1873–96) and the Third World: With Special
Reference to India', *Social Science Information*, 18 (2); reprinted in G. Balachandran,
ed., *India and the World Economy, 1850–1950* (New Delhi: Oxford University Press):
155–79.

—— (1991), 'Keynes, India and the Gold Standard', in D. Banerjee, ed., *Essays in Economic
Analysis and Policy: A Tribute to Bhabatosh Datta* (Oxford: Oxford University Press):
209–40.

—— (1994), 'Political Economy: A Discourse of Mastery or an Apparatus of Dissent?', *Indian Historical Review*, 20 (1–2): 78–113.

—— (1998), 'Development', in Heinz Kurz and Neri Salvadori, eds, *The Elgar Companion to Classical Economics, A-K* (Cheltenham: Edward Elgar): 213–217.

—— (2000), 'The Past and the Future of the Developmental State', *Journal of World-Systems Research*, 11 (2), Summer/Fall: 398–442; (http://csf.colorado.edu/jwsr)

—— (2002), 'The Mutuality of Private and Public Credit: The Rise and Decline of Public Credit', *Arthaniti* (New Series), 1 (1–2): 32–44.

Banerjee, Abhijit V. and Thomas Picketty (2003), 'Top Indian Incomes, 1956–2000', Department of Economics Working Paper, No. 03–32, Massachusetts Institute of Technology, Cambridge, June.

Baran, P.A. ([1959] 1969), 'Reflections on Underconsumption', in Morris Abramovitz *et al.*, *The Allocation of Economic Resources* (Stanford: Stanford University Press); reprinted in P.A. Baran, *The Longer View*, edited by John O'Neill (New York: Monthly Review Press): 185–202.

Barberis, Nicholas C. and Richard A. Thaler (2003), 'A Survey of Behavioural Finance', in *The Handbook of the Economics of Finance*, Vol. 1, edited by George M. Constantinides, Milton Harris and Rene Stulz (Amsterdam: Elsevier).

Beckerman, Wilfred and Tim Jenkinson (1986), 'What Stopped the Inflation? Unemployment or Commodity Prices?', *Economic Journal*, 96: 39–54.

Boughton, James M. (2002), 'Why White, Not Keynes? Inventing the Postwar International System', IMF Working Paper WP/02/52, International Monetary Fund, Washington D.C.

Buiter, W.H. (2003), 'James Tobin: An Appreciation of His Contribution to Economics', *Economic Journal*, 113, November: F565–F631.

Burke, James and Gerald Epstein (2003), 'Threat Effects and the Internationalization of Production', in Jayati Ghosh and C.P. Chandrasekhar, eds, *Work and Well-being in the Age of Finance* (New Delhi: Tulika Books), 55–98.

Clifton, J.A. (1977), 'Competition and the Evolution of the International Capitalist System', *Cambridge Journal of Economics*, 1 (2): 137–52.

Datta, Bhabatosh (1952), *Economics of Industrialization*, first edition (Calcutta: World Press).

Fine, Ben (2005), 'Financial Programming and the IMF', in Jomo K.S. and Ben Fine, eds, *The New Development Economics: After the Washington Consensus* (New Delhi: Tulika Books; London: Zed Books).

Friedman, Milton (1953), 'The Case for Flexible Exchange Rates', in *Essays in Positive Economics* (Chicago: University of Chicago Press).

Ghosh, Jayati and C.P. Chandrasekhar, eds (2003), *Work and Well-being in the Age of Finance* (New Delhi: Tulika Books).

Griffith-Jones, Stephany (1989), 'Nicholas Kaldor's Contribution to the Analysis of International Monetary Reform', *Cambridge Journal of Economics*, 13 (1), March: 223–35.

Hahn, Frank (1989), 'Kaldor on Growth', *Cambridge Journal of Economics*, 13 (1), March: 47–58.

Harcourt, G.C. and N.F. Laing, eds (1971), *Capital and Growth* (Harmondsworth, Middlesex: Penguin Books).

Hart, Albert G., Nicholas Kaldor and Jan Tinbergen (1964), *The Case for an International Commodity Reserve Currency* (Geneva: UNCTAD).

Heal, Geoffrey (1986), 'Macrodynamics and Returns to Scale', *Economic Journal*, 96: 191–98.

Kahn, R.F. (1954), 'Some Notes on Liquidity Preference', *Manchester School*, Vol. 22: 22–45.

Kaldor, Nicholas ([1934] 1960a), 'The Determinateness of Static Equilibrium', *Review of Economic Studies*, 1, February: 122–36; reprinted in Kaldor (1960a): 13–33.

—— ([1934a] 1960a), 'The Equilibrium of the Firm', *Economic Journal*, 44, March: 70–91; reprinted in Kaldor (1960a): 34–50.

—— (1937), 'The Controversy on the Theory of Capital', *Econometrica*, 5, July.

—— ([1938] 1960b), 'Stability and Full Employment', *Economic Journal*, 48 (192), December: 653; reprinted in Kaldor (1960a): 103–19.

—— ([1939] 1960b), 'Speculation and Economic Stability', *The Review of Economic Studies*, 7, October: 1–27; reprinted in Kaldor (1960b): 17–58.

────── (1955), *An Expenditure Tax* (London: Allen & Unwin).

────── ([1955–56] 1960a), 'Alternative Theories of Distribution', *Review of Economic Studies*, 23 (2): 83–100; reprinted in Kaldor (1960a): 209–36.

────── (1956), *Indian Tax Reform, Report of a Survey* (New Delhi: Ministry of Finance, Government of India).

────── ([1957] 1960b), 'A Model of Economic Growth', *Economic Journal*, 67, December: 591–624; reprinted in Kaldor (1960b): 259–300.

────── ([1958] 1960c), 'Monetary Policy, Economic Stability and Growth: A Memorandum Submitted to the Radcliffe Committee on the Working of the Monetary System', *Principal Memoranda of Evidence*, Cmnd 827, HMSO, London; reprinted in Kaldor (1960c): 128–53.

────── (1960a), *Essays in Value and Distribution* (London: Gerald Duckworth).

────── (1960b), *Essays on Economic Stability and Growth* (London: Gerald Duckworth).

────── (1960c), *Essays on Economic Policy* (London: Gerald Duckworth).

────── ([1966] 1978), 'Marginal Productivity and Macroeconomic Theories of Distribution', *The Review of Economic Studies*, 33 (96): 309–19; reprinted in Kaldor (1978): 81–99.

────── ([1972] 1978), 'The Irrelevance of Equilibrium Economics', *Economic Journal*, 82, December: 1237–55; reprinted in Kaldor (1978): 176–201.

────── ([1975] 1978), 'What is Wrong with Economic Theory', *Quarterly Journal of Economics*, 89 (3), August: 347–57; reprinted in Kaldor (1978): 204–13.

────── ([1976] 1978), 'Inflation and Recession in the World Economy', *Economic Journal*, 86, December: 703–14; reprinted in Kaldor (1978): 214–30.

────── (1978), *Further Essays in Economic Theory* (London: Gerald Duckworth).

────── (1980), *Reports on Taxation I: Papers Related to the United Kingdom* (London: Gerald Duckworth).

Kaldor, N. and J. Mirrlees (1962), 'A New Model of Economic Growth', *Review of Economic Studies*, 29 (3): 174–92.

Keynes, J.M. (1919), *The Economic Consequences of the Peace* (London: Macmillan).

────── (1925), *The Economic Consequences of Mr Churchill* (London: Hogarth Press).

────── ([1930] 1971), *Collected Writings of John Maynard Keynes*, Vol. V, *A Treatise on Money, 1, The Pure Theory of Money* (London: Macmillan, for the Royal Economic Society).

────── (1936), *The General Theory of Employment, Interest and Money* (London: Macmillan).

────── (1971), 'Indian Epilogue', in *Collected Writings of John Maynard Keynes*, Vol. XV, *Activities 1906–1914*, edited by Elizabeth Johnson (London: Macmillan, for the Royal Economic Society).

────── ([1940–44] 1980), *Collected Writings of John Maynard Keynes*, Vol. XXV, *Activities 1940–44, Shaping the Postwar World: The Clearing Union*, edited by D. Moggridge (London: Macmillan, for the Royal Economic Society).

────── ([1941–46] 1980), *Collected Writings of John Maynard Keynes*, Vol. XXVI, *Activities 1941–46, Shaping the Postwar World: Bretton Woods and Reparations*, edited by D. Moggridge (London: Macmillan, for the Royal Economic Society).

Mehra, Rajnish and Edward C. Prescott (1985), 'The Equity Premium: A Puzzle', *Journal of Monetary Economics*, 15 (2): 145–62.

Milanovic, Branko (2002), 'True World Income Distribution, 1988 and 1993: First Calculations Based on Household Surveys Alone', *Economic Journal*, 112: 51–92.

Moggridge, Donald (1992), *Maynard Keynes: An Economist's Biography* (London: Routledge).

Myrdal, Gunnar (1957), *Economic Theory and Underdeveloped Regions* (London: Gerald Duckworth).

Palma, J. Gabriel and Mario Marcel (1989), 'Kaldor on the "Discreet Charm" of the Chilean Bourgeoisie', *Cambridge Journal of Economics*, 13 (1), March: 245–72.

Pasinetti, L.L. (1962), 'Rate of Profit and Income Distribution in Relation to the Rate of Economic Growth', *Review of Economic Studies*, 29: 267–79.

────── (1986), 'Nicholas Kaldor: An Appreciation', *Cambridge Journal of Economics*, 10 (4): 301–04.

Ramachandran, V.K. and Madhura Swaminathan, eds (2002), *Agrarian Studies: Essays on*

Agrarian Relations in Less-Developed Countries (New Delhi: Tulika Books).

Samuelson, P.A. and Franco Modigliani (1966), 'The Pasinetti Paradox in Neoclassical and More General Models', *Review of Economic Studies*, 33: 269–301.

Shiller, Robert J. (1989), *Market Volatility* (Cambridge, Massachusetts: MIT Press).

—— (1998), 'Human Behavior and the Efficiency of the Financial System', in John B. Taylor and Michael Woodford, eds, *Handbook of Macroeconomics*, Vol. 1 (Amsterdam: Elsevier).

Skidelsky, Robert (1992), *John Maynard Keynes, Vol. 2, The Economist as Saviour, 1920–1937* (London: Macmillan).

Spraos, John (1989), 'Kaldor on Commodities', *Cambridge Journal of Economics*, 13 (1), March: 201–22.

Thirlwall, Anthony P. (1987), *Nicholas Kaldor* (New York: New York University Press).

—— (1989), 'Kaldor as a Policy Adviser', *Cambridge Journal of Economics*, 13 (1), March: 121–40.

Tobin, J. (1958), 'Liquidity Preference as Behaviour Towards Risk', *Review of Economic Studies*, 25 (2): 65–86.

Toye, John (1989), 'Nicholas Kaldor and Tax Reform in Developing Countries', *Cambridge Journal of Economics*, 13 (1), March: 183–200.

—— (1997), 'Keynes on Population and Economic Growth', *Cambridge Journal of Economics*, 21 (1), January: 1–26.

Tucker, Josiah (1774), *Four Tracts on Political and Commercial Subjects*, second edn (Gloucester, UK; printed by J. Rivington, London: St. Paul's Churchyard).

Tversky, Amos and Daniel Kahneman (1992), 'Advances in Prospect Theory: Cumulative Representation of Uncertainty', *Journal of Risk and Uncertainty*, 5: 297–323.

von Neumann, John (1945–46), 'A Model of General Economic Equilibrium', *Review of Economic Studies*, 13: 1–9.

Wood, Adrian (1987), 'Nicholas Kaldor (1908–1986)', in John Eatwell, Murray Milgate and Peter Newman, eds, *The New Palgrave Dictionary of Economics*, Vol. 3 (London: Macmillan): 3–8.

Karl Polanyi as a Development Economist

Kari Polanyi Levitt

Not too many years ago, it would have been unthinkable for Karl Polanyi to be included in a collection of pioneers of development economics. Indeed, he would have been surprised because none of his writings addressed issues of growth or development. When I first encountered the early literature of development economics in the late 1950s, in a collection of essays edited by Agarwala and Singh (1958), published in Delhi, I hastened to share my enthusiasm with my father. He did not discourage my newfound interest in the subject, but his response was characteristic. 'Development, Kari? I don't know what that is.'

He was then engaged, in collaboration with Columbia graduate students, in studies of economic life in primitive and archaic societies. At the time I failed to understand what led him to undertake this research, which seemed to me so distant from the contemporary world. Only years later did I appreciate that his research in economic anthropology was motivated by his determination to prove that the nineteenth-century market economy was unique: 'Never before in human history has the principle of gain been elevated to the organizing principle of economic life' (Polanyi [1947] 1968: 43). His extensive research into non-market exchange in primitive and archaic societies challenged the preconceptions of anthropologists and historians who imposed – on pre-capitalist societies – concepts of scarcity and price-making markets derived from the claims of economics to universal validity. To rid the study of economies of what he once called 'our obsolete market mentality', he posited three general patterns of integration of economic activity: reciprocity, redistribution and exchange. These patterns were universal in the sense that they could be found in all systems of organization of economic life including contemporary market economy. Polanyi's approach was comparative. There was, in his work, no suggestion of progress or any implication that modern societies are more advanced or more developed than those of the past.

But his unforgettable reaction to my discovery of the new subject of development economics did not reflect indifference to the emerging nations of post-colonial Asia and Africa. On the contrary, it was his hope that his warning of the destructive effects of subordinating society to the requirements of the market economy could save humanity from disasters more profound than anything experienced to date. In a letter to a friend of his youth, Bé de Waard, in 1958, six years before his death, he wrote:

> My life was a world life – I lived the life of the world. But the world stopped living for several decades, and then in a few years it advanced a century! So I am only now coming into my own, having somewhere lost 30 years on the way – waiting for Godot – until the world caught up again, caught up to me. In retrospect, it is all quite strange, the martyrdom of isolation was only apparent – ultimately, I was only waiting for myself. Now the scales are weighed against us – against you, against me – because in ten years, I would stand vindicated in my own lifetime. My work is for Asia and Africa, for the new peoples. The West should bring them spiritual and intellectual assistance; instead the West is destroying the tradition of the nineteenth century and is even demolishing its Victorian ideals. . . . My ideas at last are drawing opposition and that is a good sign, I would dearly love to live to fight for them, but man is a mortal being. (Cited in Polanyi Levitt and Mendell 1987)

In 1947, Polanyi believed that universal capitalism was discredited everywhere except in the United States. He could not have imagined that the liberal economic order of 1870 to 1914 would be greeted in the 1990s as a model for the globalization of universal capitalism (Polanyi 1945). Fifty years would have to pass before the originality of Karl Polanyi emerged from relative obscurity to be embraced in so many quarters as a definitive critique of the fateful effects of the subordination of society to economic market criteria.[1] Not until the Asian crisis of 1997 and disasters of instant market capitalism in Russia would his work be cited in thousands of speeches, papers, articles and policy statements. Many authors have provided excellent expositions of the principal thesis of *The Great Transformation* and its relevance to contemporary globalization. But none would have given him more satisfaction than to be identified as the most effective critic of the neoliberal project for the twenty-first century by a senior fellow at the Cato Institute, a leading right-wing think-tank.

> He has emerged in recent years as a kind of patron saint of globalization's critics. George Soros notes his intellectual debt in his acknowledgments at the beginning of *The Crisis of Global Capitalism*. Dani Rodrik, of Harvard University and author of *Has Globalization Gone Too Far?*, refers to him frequently. John Gray, a professor at the London School of Economics who wrote *False Dawn: The Delusions of Global Capitalism*, titled his first chapter 'From the Great Transformation to the Global Free Market'. These arguments are an almost perfect inversion of the truth. The tragedies of the twentieth century stemmed, not from an over-reliance on markets, but from a pervasive loss of faith in them. (Lindsey 2001)

Without doubt, Polanyi's critique of the nineteenth-century market economy and its fateful consequences resonate most strongly with critics of globalization. But, interestingly, *The Great Transformation* is now required reading in

international development studies. Although economists have been slow in acknowledging his contribution, he is found in the company of such pioneers of development economics as Gunnar Myrdal, Arthur Lewis, Albert Hirschman, Amartya
Sen and Samir Amin, together with institutionalists – old and new – in a course
on 'Ideas in Development' at Johns Hopkins.[2]

A World Life

Polanyi's life was indeed a 'world life'. There was a constant theme in
his world of thought in a life marked by three emigrations. It was his insistence
that there are no impersonal historical forces that absolve us from personal respon-
sibility for the fate of fellow human beings. Ideas matter – when people cease to
believe in the legitimacy of the powerful, their power is eroded.

Polanyi was born in 1886 in Vienna, but the family moved to Budapest
shortly thereafter and his formative years were Hungarian. He grew up in a
comfortable upper middle-class family. His father was a civil engineer and a
successful railway contractor until a prolonged season of bad weather ruined the
business and the family descended into genteel poverty. His mother, daughter of
a rabbinical scholar from Vilna, then in Russia, was known for her role in host-
ing gatherings of Budapest's literary, artistic and intellectual elite. The Polanyi
children received a superb home education, including instruction in Latin and
Greek, English, French and German. Karl graduated from the University of
Budapest in 1912 with a doctorate in law, the only university qualification he
ever had. He was prominent in Hungarian intellectual life as the founding president of the Galilee Circle, a student movement that undertook educational activities on a remarkable scale of 2,000 classes per year. The ideology was one of
western enlightenment, opposed to obscurantism, clericalism and the moribund
political order of the Hungarian monarchy.

He was 28 in 1914 when he enlisted in the Austro–Hungarian army as a
cavalry officer and served on the Russian front.[3] He was hospitalized and in
1919 he emigrated to Vienna, where he was soon followed by a large exodus of
Hungarians fleeing the White Terror. Among them was Ilona Duczynska; they
were married in 1923. The Russian Revolution of 1917 was fighting for its existence in a prolonged civil war. Polanyi joined the wide-ranging debate on how a
socialist economy could be constructed. The model he favoured was a functional
form of guild socialism associated with the English social historian G.D.H. Cole
and the Austro-Marxist, Otto Bauer. He engaged in a debate on the feasibility of
a socialist economy with Ludwig von Mises, mentor of Friedrich von Hayek, in
the pages of the premier German language social science journal, *Archiv Fur
Sozialwissenchaft und Socialpolitik*. It was in this context that he studied the
works of the leading exponents of the Austrian school of economics. For many
years, he struggled to construct a socialist economic model that would combine
the economic criterion of technical efficiency with social and cultural requirements and democratic decision-making. Eventually, he abandoned this exercise
and found, in history and anthropology, a more effective means of developing

insights regarding the place of the economy in society. He remained, to the end of his life, a socialist. In a letter written a few days before his death, he said: 'The heart of the feudal nation was privilege; the heart of the bourgeois nation was property; the heart of the socialist nations is the people, where collective existence is the enjoyment of a community culture. I myself have never lived in such a society.'[4]

From 1924, Polanyi's position as a senior editor of *Oesterreichische Volkswirt*, the leading financial and economic weekly of Central Europe, placed him in the eye of the storm of economic and political upheavals on the continent. From this observation post, he followed the attempts by the western powers to restore the pre-1914 economic order and its eventual breakdown in 1931, when the collapse of a major bank in Vienna triggered a financial crisis that spread westward to England and the United States. 'Conservative Twenties, Revolutionary Thirties' summarizes these experiences.[5]

In 1933, when the deteriorating political climate did not permit the journal to keep a prominent socialist on their editorial staff, Polanyi left for England, but continued to write for the journal. Kari joined him in 1934. Ilona stayed back to engage in the struggles of the then illegal opposition to Austrian fascism until 1936, when she also came to England (Polanyi Levitt and Mendell 1987).

In his initial years in England, Polanyi was associated with a small group of intellectuals and religious leaders who called themselves the Christian left. He contributed an essay on 'The Essence of Fascism' and co-edited *Christianity and the Social Revolution* (1935). Among other contributors was Joseph P. Needham (1954). To this group, he brought a continental perspective and introduced them to Karl Marx's *The Economic and Philosophic Manuscripts of 1844*.[6] In 1937, recommendations by R.H. Tawney and G.D.H. Cole assisted him in obtaining employment as a tutor with the Workers' Education Association (WEA), teaching courses on international relations and on English social and economic history, a subject entirely new to him. His encounter with the conditions of working class life on overnight stays with the families who accommodated him was a profound culture shock. He contrasted the inferior status of the English working-class in the richest country of Europe with the social and cultural achievements of the workers of socialist Red Vienna in impoverished post-1914 Austria. The lecture notes for his WEA classes[7] upon the frame upon which he later developed *The Great Transformation*. Although the book was written at Bennington College, Vermont, in 1941 to 1943, it was in England that he found the origins of the disasters that befell Europe from 1914 to 1945.

From 1947 to his retirement in 1953, Polanyi taught a course in General Economic History as a visiting professor at Columbia University, and from 1953 to 1957, he co-directed an Interdisciplinary Research Project with Conrad Arensberg on the economic aspects of institutional growth. The results of this research were published as *Trade and Markets in Early Empires* (1957). *Dahomey and the Slave Trade* was published posthumously with the assistance of Abraham Rotstein in 1966. A former student, George Dalton, produced the invaluable collection of essays by Karl Polanyi titled *Primitive, Archaic and Modern Economies* (1968), and Harry Pearson edited a posthumous volume of Polanyi's writings, *The Livelihood of Man* (1977).

In 1950, the Polanyis made their home in Canada in Pickering, Ontario, because Ilona was blacklisted from entering the United States on the grounds of former communist activities in Hungary (1917 to 1920) and in Austria (1934 to 1936). In 1961, Karl initiated the journal *Co-existence* as a vehicle for dialogue across the cold war divide. The editorial board included the eminent economists Joan Robinson, Gunnar Myrdal, Oskar Lange, Jan Tinbergen, P.C. Mahalanobis, Ragnar Frisch and Shigeto Tsuru. The first issue appeared shortly after his death in 1964 (Schlesinger 1964). Both Karl and Ilona died in Canada and now rest in a cemetery in Budapest.

The most frequently cited biographical source on the life of Karl Polanyi is a chapter in Peter F. Drucker's memoirs, 'The Polanyis' (Drucker 1978: 123–40).[8] In this highly entertaining exercise of imagined recollections of his friend Karl and other members of the family, almost none of the facts are correct; indeed, some are manifestly absurd.[9] Drucker was perceptive in noting that the Polanyis sought 'a new society that would be free and yet not "bourgeois" or "liberal"; prosperous and yet not dominated by economics; communal and yet not a Marxist collectivism'. But he could not have been more wrong in dismissing Karl Polanyi as a 'minor figure' whose 'failure . . . signifies the futility of the quest for . . . the perfect – or at least the good – society', or his research on the economic organization of past civilizations as a retreat 'into academic busyness' (Drucker 1978: 138).

The Great Transformation

The Great Transformation, first published in 1944, is the best known and most important of Karl Polanyi's works, now translated into fifteen languages. In it his thesis was that the economic and social upheavals and political tensions resulting from the utopian attempt to restore the nineteenth-century liberal economic order, including the gold standard, after World War I, were the essential cause of the world economic crisis and of the demise of democracy in most of the states of continental Europe. Like Keynes, he understood that the gold standard was a social mechanism designed to restructure the domestic economies of debtor countries in the interest of *rentier* financiers. His account of the vulnerability of the small and weak peripheral states of Central and East Europe to a pull on the 'golden thread' reads like a preview of the IMF (International Monetary Fund) stabilization programmes of the 1980s.

> There was hardly an internal crisis in Europe that did not reach its climax on an issue of the external value of the currency. By means of deflation, mass dismissal of public servants, wage repression and persistent unemployment, currencies were stabilized and fixed in terms of gold, to guarantee debt service to foreign bondholders.

Polanyi remarked that, 'Students of politics now grouped countries not according to continents but according to the degree of their adherence to a sound currency' (Polanyi 1944: 24). In the succession states of Central Europe international creditors instituted regimes of external supervision under the auspices of the League of Nations operating from Geneva. The League of Nations employed no more than a few hundred people. Today, the IMF and the World Bank employ many thousands of highly paid professionals and consultants to institute a long list of macro and microeconomic measures designed to impose balanced budgets and 'free markets' on indebted developing countries. *Plus ca change.*

Describing the role of international finance in restoring rightist regimes in Europe, Polanyi noted:

> In Belgium, France, and England the left was thrown out of office in the name of sound monetary standards. An almost unbroken sequence of currency crises linked indigent Balkans with the affluent United States through the elastic band of the international credit system which transmitted the strains of the imperfectly restored currencies first from Eastern to Western Europe, and then from Western Europe to the United States. (Polanyi 1944: 23–24)

Europe leaped from crisis to crisis until an unsustainable pyramid of debt collapsed in 1931. National fascisms, Soviet five-year planning and the New Deal were protective reactions to save societies from economic and social disintegration.

Like Marx, who came to England a century before him, Polanyi found the 'Origin of Our Times' – the original title of *The Great Transformation* – in the birthplace of industrial capitalism, in nineteenth-century England.

> Market society was born in England – yet it was on the Continent that its weakness engendered the most tragic complications. In order to comprehend German fascism, we must revert to Ricardian England. The Industrial Revolution was an English event. Market economy, free trade, and the gold standard were English inventions. These institutions broke down in the 1920s everywhere – in Germany, Italy or Austria the event was merely more political and dramatic . . . the factors that wrecked that civilization should be studied in the birthplace of the Industrial Revolution, England. (Polanyi 1944: 30)

Fictitious Commodities

Contrary to a commonly held belief, there was nothing natural or inevitable about the nineteenth-century market system. As Polanyi demonstrated, *laissez-faire* liberalism was designed by the early English political economists and instituted by the power of the state. In a frequently quoted passage, Polanyi concluded that '*laissez faire*' was planned', while the protective reaction against the discipline of the market was 'spontaneous' (Polanyi 1944: 147). The extension of price-making markets to embrace the fictitious commodities of land, labour and money was an innovation more revolutionary than the mechanical inventions of early industrial capitalism. Land, labour and money are 'fictitious' commodities because, unlike true commodities, they are not produced for sale. Natural resources, including land, are god–given; people do not have children to provide workers for the labour market; and money is a social convention. While commodity money has been used as currency, modern money is essentially a book-keeping entry validated by the sanctity of contract and codified by law. Historically, money was the first to be liberated from regulation prohibiting usury, for centuries deemed sinful by Christian doctrine.

The divorce of agricultural producers from their means of subsistence by the privatization (enclosure) of communal lands created a new underclass of vagabonds and paupers. The threat to social stability was countered by measures of poor relief and wage subsidy. The critical step in the creation of an industrial proletariat in nineteenth-century England was the abolition of poor relief by the draconian New Poor Law of 1834, which gave legal sanction to the degradation of wage labour. It was instituted by the reform of parliament of 1832, which subordinated the landed oligarchy to the urban and industrial bourgeoisie. The majority of the population had no voice and no vote. Trade unions were out-lawed. The result was an unleashing of productive forces and accumulation of capital. But wages failed to rise above subsistence levels until the second half of the nineteenth century. With reference to Ricardo and Marx, Arthur Lewis based his model of economic development with unlimited supplies of labour on early English industrialization. The classical economists were concerned with capital accumulation, economic growth and the distribution of incomes from produc-tion. They largely ignored the dispossession, displacement and human degrada-tion by the destruction of social relations in which economic livelihood, social status, pride in craft and cultural expression had previously been embedded.

Polanyi insisted that the creation of a self-regulating market by the commodification of land, labour and money required nothing less than the subordi-nation of society to the requirements of the market economy. His central thesis was that the nineteenth-century liberal economic order was 'economic' in a dif-ferent sense from that in which all societies have been limited by the material conditions of existence. It was 'economic' in the distinctive sense that it chose to base itself on a motive never before raised to the level of justification of action and behaviour in everyday life, namely, individual gain (Polanyi 1944: 30). Prior to the rise of industrial capitalism, markets were never more than accesso-ries of economic life. In that regard, the generalized market economy of modern capitalism stands as an exception. As 'improvement' (read efficiency) conquered 'habitat' (read 'security'), and labour, land, money and the essentials of life became commodified, the economy acquired an existence of its own, driven by 'economic' laws of its own, whether conceived in neoclassical or Marxist terms.

The Double Movement

Regarding the creation of the self-regulating market, Polanyi warned, in a frequently cited passage, that:

Such an institution could not exist for any length of time without annihilating the human and natural substance of society; it would have physically destroyed man and transformed his surroundings into a wilderness. Inevitably, society took measures to protect itself, but whatever measures it took impaired the self-regulation of the market, disorganized industrial life and thus endangered society in yet another way. (Polanyi 1944: 3)

The reference here is to the 'double movement' of the explosive spread of market economy and checks to its expansion by protective civic, social and national movements. Polanyi interpreted legislation regarding public health, factory conditions, social insurance, public utilities, municipal services and trade union rights in Victorian England as countervailing measures to check the societal effects of the unfettered expansion of capital. He noted that, on the continent, governments of widely different political complexions enacted similar measures, including protection of industries and agriculture threatened by ruinous competition. These measures were instituted by state interventions at the national level. Following World War I, social conflicts arising from draconian financial requirements to conform to the rules of the gold standard could not be mediated by the democratic process, and resulted in the rise of authoritarian and fascist regimes in most of continental Europe. It must be understood that Polanyi's 'double movement' is not a self-correcting mechanism to moderate the excesses of market fundamentalism but an existential contradiction between the requirements of a capitalist market economy for unlimited expansion, and the requirements of people to live in mutually supportive relations in society.

When the world emerged from World War II to construct the international institutions that framed the post-war era, it was generally accepted that the market economy would have to serve national objectives of full employment and social security. Polanyi foresaw a world of regional blocs of diverse social and economic systems. The tide, it appeared, had turned against the unrestricted domination of the economy by capital. The historical swing of the pendulum had restored social control over the economy. This was the 'great transformation' that closed the book on the economic liberalism of the English classical political economists.

The Bretton Woods international financial order permitted policy space for industrial countries to pursue full employment and social security financed by redistributive fiscal arrangements. Developing countries were able to engage in import-substituting industrialization and long-term economic planning. As Polanyi reminded us, however, the measures taken by society to protect itself could impair the functioning of the market and set in motion a counter-attack by capital to free itself from social constraints. This, indeed, is what has happened since the 1970s, when declining productivity and profits, low or negative real interest rates favouring debtors, and a wave of political radicalism in the South prompted capital to reverse the pendulum. A macroeconomic regime change precipitated the Latin American debt crisis of the 1980s, and the Reagan and Thatcher administrations dismantled the gains made by labour in the first three post-war decades.

The liberalization of trade and capital in the last quarter of the twentieth century has once again unleashed capital from regulation – now on a global scale. The dictates of financial capital are once again governing markets. Combined with the predominance of transnational corporations, the democratic political process in national societies is being undermined and corrupted. Indeed, provisions of the World Trade Organization (WTO) regarding investment, competition, government procurement and intellectual property are specifically designed to bind states to supranational agreements to protect investors from legislation at the national level. The struggle to protect society from the disintegrating forces of the market economy has moved to the international arena, as illustrated by the anti-globalization movement. Inequality has escalated to unprecedented levels, but there are no international institutions to moderate the polarizing effects of the liberalization of capital. Fiscal resources that sustained the welfare state in the industrialized countries are eroding. Indebted developing countries are in the grip of conditionalities which do not permit them to follow strategies of economic development that were successful in the past.

A prolonged period of relative economic stability and strong economic growth in Europe and North America encouraged a reading of Polanyi's 'double movement' as a kind of self-correcting mechanism. Such illusions were shattered in the 1990s. The surge of portfolio capital seeking high returns and capital gains in the emerging markets of Asia and Latin America precipitated a series of severe financial and economic crises most dramatically in the high-growth economies of Asia.

The lessons of *The Great Transformation* were recovered, and Polanyi emerged from relative obscurity to feature in academic discourse and journalistic comment. Among the first to cite Polanyi was Dani Rodrik. His position was that proposals to construct a new financial architecture for the global economy were doomed to frustration because global capitalism is inherently impracticable, and, indeed, we have never truly had a global capitalist system. The real question, he suggested, was, how to make the world safe for different brands of national capitalism to prosper side by side. Until we understand this, we cannot formulate workable solutions.

> To understand why, it helps to go back to *The Great Transformation* by the economic anthropologist Karl Polanyi, which was first published in 1944. Polanyi took issue with the nineteenth-century liberal idea of a self-regulating market. He argued that markets could not exist outside the web of social relations for long without tragic consequences. Indeed, he interpreted the turmoil of the interwar period and its aftermath – the collapse of the gold standard, the decline into protectionism and bilateralism, the rise of fascism and national socialism, and ultimately World War II – as the result of societies rising to protect themselves from the onslaught of the unregulated market.
>
> Polanyi's enduring insight is that markets are sustainable only insofar as

they are embedded in social and political institutions. These institutions serve three functions without which markets cannot survive: they regulate, stabilize, and legitimate market outcomes. That is why every functioning society has regulatory bodies that prevent unfair competition and fraud, monetary and fiscal institutions that help smooth out the boom–bust cycle, as well as social insurance schemes that help bring market outcomes into conformity with a society's preferences regarding the distribution of risks and rewards. It is trite but true to say that none of these institutions exists at the global level. (Rodrik 1998)

In outlining a rules-based national economic order, Rodrik recalled that the objective of the architects of the Bretton Woods institutions was not growth of international trade *per se* but stability of the international economic order. Rodrik was not alone in his appreciation of the importance of *The Great Transformation*. Joseph Stiglitz composed a preface to the 2001 edition of the book, in which he castigated the market fundamentalist ideology and practices of the International Monetary Fund. In a contribution to a collection called *Rethinking Development Economics*, José Antonio Ocampo presented an alternative view of development and corresponding global arrangements. Drawing on Polanyi's insight, he maintained that 'the economic system must be subordinated to broader social objectives' (Ocampo 2003: 101).

The Disembedded Economy

The instability, insecurity and serious financial crises associated with globalization have led scholars and policy-makers, including the World Bank, to embrace institutional reform and good governance. It is generally agreed that attempts to introduce instant capitalism in post-Soviet Russia failed because they were not underpinned by the essential legal and social institutions of civil society. The term 'embedded economy' has gained currency in policy discourse and Polanyi is frequently cited in this connection. In the 1990s, a second generation of the Washington Consensus added institutional reforms of good governance to the standard list of macro and microeconomic prescriptions. Structural adjustment programmes were enhanced to target poverty reduction by means of poverty reduction strategy papers (PRSPs). The assumption here is that corruption is uniquely attributable to politicians, that countries would benefit from the introduction of western political institutions and practices, and that empowerment of civil society could substitute for the traditional role of the state. In reality, the rolling back of the state has *dis*empowered civil society. Agglomerations of private economic power, including private mercenaries, have undermined public authority and the rule of law. The result has been to diminish the capacity of societies to determine the allocation of their own resources in accordance with their particular national objectives. The governance reforms imposed by creditor agencies are problematic. Poverty reduction is essentially subordinated to the macroeconomic requirements of fiscal discipline and debt service. The ownership of the programmes remains in Washington. As never before, the economic livelihood of people is beyond national control, instanced by collapsing commodity prices, financial crises triggered by footloose capital, relocation of production facilities to cheaper sources of labour and destruction of domestic food production by liberalized imports. In this regard, globalization has disembedded economic life on an international scale.

The concept of the disembedded economy is central to Polanyi's contention that the nineteenth-century liberal economic order – the template of contemporary globalization – was economic in a different sense from the way economic livelihood was organized in all previous societies. In describing the economy as a distinct and separate sphere of human activity, Polanyi wrote:

> The disembedded economy . . . stood apart from the rest of society. . . . In a market economy the production and distribution of material goods in principle is carried on through a self-regulating economic system of price-making markets. It is governed by laws of its own, the so-called laws of supply and demand, and motivated by fear of hunger and hope of gain. (Polanyi 1968: 78–115; Polanyi, Arensberg and Pearson 1957)[10]

Social relations of extended family, community and all other ties of traditional society are displaced by special economic institutions such as private property and the economic motive of individual gain. Because the disembedding of the economy was socially unsustainable, Polanyi suggested that society protect itself from impersonal market forces in a variety of ways.

Block dismisses the disembedded economy and contends that Polanyi's real discovery was the 'always embedded economy'. He maintains there was a shift from Polanyi's earlier Marxist influence to a later revision of his views, and only time did not permit him to revise the manuscript of *The Great Transformation* to resolve this contradiction: 'Polanyi glimpsed, but was not able to name or elaborate the idea of the always embedded market economy' (Block 2001).[11] By discarding the disembedded economy, Block moved Polanyi into the mainstream of socio-economic discourse. The effect is to obscure the radical implications of the existential contradiction between a market economy and a viable society. There is a suggestion here that Polanyi was influenced by Marxism in the turbulent inter-war years, and that there was an ideological shift during the writing of the book in the United States from 1941 to 1943. Such an interpretation misses the point. It fails to understand what Polanyi accepted from marx and what he rejected.

Polanyi shared Marx's fundamental insight into the historically limited nature of the organization of economic life by the universalization of the market principle. His account of the societal consequences of the commodification of money, land, labour and, indeed, the essentials of life, recall the alienation theme in the writings of Marx. What he rejected was the Ricardian labour theory of value and the economism of historical materialism. Whereas Marx anticipated the eventual breakdown of the capitalist order on account of inherent *economic* contradictions, Polanyi emphasized the contradiction between the requirements of capitalism for limitless expansion and the human requirement to be sustained by mutually supportive social relations. In Polanyi's account of this existential contradiction, the outcome is not determinate. There is no grand design of progress. There are no impersonal historical forces that inevitably move humanity forward.

As we enter the twenty-first century, we witness societal disintegration manifested in genocidal wars, displaced populations, the HIV/AIDS pandemic, ethnic and religious conflicts, and irreversible damage to the natural environment that sustains life on earth. Our world is arguably more turbulent and dangerous than Polanyi's. The impulse of social protection of societies threatened by the concentration of economic, financial and, increasingly, military power may be mobilized by appeals to solidarities as diverse as class, race, ethnicity, caste, religious belief or nationalisms. The rhetoric of populist politics may lean to the left or the right. Where the conflict between the 'economic' and the 'social' cannot be resolved, there is chaos. In the so-called failed states, social and civic relations of mutual support have disintegrated (Putzel 2002). It is not by coincidence that Polanyi's warning of the fateful consequences of liberating capitalist market relations from social control has such resonance today.

The Place of the Economy in Society

In 1947, at the age of 61, Polanyi received his first appointment to a university teaching position. His course on General Economic History in the graduate faculty of Columbia University presented the opportunity to extend the study of economic institutions from modern to historical and traditional societies (Polanyi 1977).[12] His research on economic institutions in archaic and primitive societies was motivated by his determination to establish the unique nature of a market economy. He set out to prove that in all of previous human history, individual gain had never been elevated to the organizing principle of economic life; 'ranging over human societies we find hunger and gain not appealed to as incentives for production'. He explained that we have been conditioned to respond to economic motives of individual gain that are in no way inherent in human nature. 'The nineteenth century thought of hunger and gain as economic motives simply because the organization of production under a market economy works only as long as people have reason to subordinate all human requirements to the activity of earning a living' (Polanyi 1947: 109–17).

Polanyi maintained that the methodology of economics was flawed by its market bias, and that economic anthropologists and historians brought to their empirical research assumptions of market relations drawn from their experience of living in a market society. In 'Carl Menger's Two Meanings of Economics', an intellectual attack on the market bias implicit in economics, Polanyi distinguished between the formal and substantive meanings of economics. The formal meaning pertains to the logic of the means–ends relationship in conditions of scarcity, as in 'economizing'. The substantive meaning pertains to man's relation to land in providing the essentials of life. The two meanings, he wrote, 'have nothing in common'. The formal definition of economics is an application of the logic of choice under the constraint of scarcity; the substantive definition relates to the organization of the economic livelihood of real people in real societies. 'The substantive meaning implies neither choice nor insufficiency of means; man's livelihood may or may not involve the necessity of choice and if choice there be, it need not be induced by the limiting effect of "scarcity"' (Polanyi 1957: 243).

Reciprocity, Redistribution and Exchange

We first encounter reciprocity and redistribution in Chapter 4 of *The Great Transformation*, drawn from Polanyi's reading of the anthropological writings of Malinowski and Thurnwald. To introduce a measure of order into the endless variations of the organization of economic life, Polanyi posited three forms of integration: reciprocity, redistribution and exchange. To be effective as integrative mechanisms, reciprocity requires reciprocal movements between designated symmetrical groupings, as in kinship relations; redistribution of goods in and out of a centre requires centricity and is generally accompanied by hierarchy; and exchange requires a system of price-making markets. These patterns of integration do not derive from the summation of individual acts but are conditional on the existence of specific institutions. They do not represent stages of development; no sequence in time is implied. However, 'economic systems' may be classified according to the dominant form of integration, corresponding to the manner in which labour and land are instituted in society to produce the material requirements of life. Thus, in communal societies, kinship relations of reciprocity predominate in the allocation of land and labour; in the flood-water empires, land was largely distributed and sometimes redistributed by palace or temple, and so, to some degree, was labour; and the rise of the market to a ruling force in the economy can be traced by noting the extent to which land and food were mobilized through exchange, and labour turned into a commodity free to be purchased in the market (Polanyi 1957: 255). We note Polanyi's consistent reference to man and nature, labour and land, toil and soil as the ultimate economic resources of every society, and the institutional modalities regarding land are as significant as those regarding labour.

In the history of economic thought, man and nature as the original sources of wealth is a forgotten contribution of the Austrian school of economics. The emphasis on labour as the ultimate source of value derives from English political economy, elaborated by Ricardo and appropriated by Marx. Natural resources acquire value only when labour is applied to their extraction or use. In neoclassical economics, they have value only if they are scarce; hence the well-known paradox, that air and water have no value because they have no exchange value, and diamonds are valuable because they are scarce. The environmental cost of the commodification of natural resources has attracted environmental economists to Polanyi's critique of the market economy and market society.[13]

Polanyi rejected the Marxist historical 'stages' of slavery, feudalism and capitalism based on the predominant labour regime as historically untenable. Polanyi's three patterns of integration have an interesting correspondence with Samir Amin's three modes of production: the primitive communal, tributary and capitalist. It must be noted that elements of all three patterns of integration are found in every society. Reciprocity relations of kinship persist in varying degrees to modern times; redistributive institutions may be found in communal societies and play an important role in all variants of national capitalism; and markets, as Polanyi noted, are not a new phenomenon.

The Economistic Fallacy

As suggested in the introduction of this chapter, Polanyi's venture into economic institutions in pre-capitalist society was undertaken to reveal the fallacy of economic motives and economic determinism. 'If the term "economic" is used as synonymous with "concerning production" we maintain that there do not exist any human motives which are intrinsically "economic" as to the so-called economic motives it should be said that economic systems are usually not based on them' (Polanyi 1947). Regarding economic determinism, Polanyi wrote: 'The market mechanism . . . created the delusion of economic determinism as a general law for all human society. Under a market economy of course this law holds good. Indeed, the working of the economic system here not only "influences" the rest of society but actually determines it' (Polanyi 1977: 12). Similarly, there is nothing natural about scarcity.

The implication is that an economy based on fear of hunger and love of gain is socially unsustainable because it violates basic human nature and the fundamental requirements of people to be sustained by family, community and other social relations. A comprehensive presentation of Polanyi's general theory of economic institutions is to be found in 'The Economy as an Instituted Process'. It ranges over money uses, forms of trade and non-market exchange, and concludes with an appeal for the social sciences to develop a wider frame of reference to which the market itself is referable, based on a substantive approach to the analysis of economic institutions and economic organization.

'The Economy as an Instituted Process' is perhaps the most comprehensive account of Polanyi's attempt to construct a general theory of the organization of economic livelihood. In this approach, based on a substantive definition of economics, as 'man's relation to land in providing the essentials of life', the market as the principal integrative mechanism is a special case. His unpackaging of the triad of trade, market and money from the baggage of assumptions drawn from the modern market economy and formalized in mainstream economics, opened a large and promising area of research of economic institutions in archaic and primitive societies.

Because the self-regulating market is, as Polanyi illustrated, an unattainable ideal fraught with social and ecological disaster, social institutions constrain and regulate the market, and public goods are provided by the state whose fiscal operations also finance more or less comprehensive redistributive measures. Reciprocity exists beyond relations of kinship in social obligations of all kinds. International trade is not exclusively commercial and may be motivated by political arrangements of mutual advantage. It is generally subject to international agreement. National currencies are a form of special purpose money, particularly where there is exchange control. Informal arrangements of local special purpose money may facilitate exchange within a community. Barter is a form of non-market exchange and non-market elements are present in a variety of cooperative associational or non-profit activities. When the formal economy breaks down or otherwise fails to clear markets, non-market exchange plays a crucial role in the survival strategies of individuals, communities and enterprises.

Students of development may be better able to appreciate Polanyi's insistence on the importance of non-market economic relations in the organization of economic life and its immediate relevance for countries under pressure to institute painful measures of economic liberalization. When the state is unable to mediate conflict, support individual and community creativity, provide economic and social infrastructure, or ensure that the gains of economic growth are shared by all, the benefits of growth will be captured by middle and upper-income earners. Market forces of polarization will dissemble the economy from traditional social relations, and people will seek solidarities of community, ethnicity, religious belief or other cultural bases of perceived exclusion. Polanyi's rejection of economic motives of individual gain as fundamental to human nature and his research into a diversity of patterns of economic organization suggest that economic livelihoods can be instituted in a great variety of ways. This, however, is incompatible with the universalization of the market principle. It implies a civilizational transformation in accord with the fundamental need of people to be sustained by social relations of mutual respect.

Notes

[1] A Google search for Polanyi turns up some 30,000 hits.

[2] The Paul Nitze School of Advanced International Studies at Johns Hopkins University offered the course on 'Ideas in Development' in 2003.

[3] For a useful collection of papers on the Polanyi family and Karl's contribution to Hungarian intellectual life, presented at the centenary conference in Budapest in 1986, see Polanyi Levitt, ed. (1990).

[4] From a letter written to Rudolph Schlesinger, editor of the journal *Co-existence*, founded by Karl Polanyi in 1964.

[5] For historical documentation, including memoirs on the life of the Polanyis in Vienna in the 1920s, see McRobbie and Polanyi Levitt, eds (2000).

[6] This was first published in Germany in 1931, and smuggled out of the country to Switzerland when the Nazis came to power.

[7] Available in the archive of the Karl Polanyi Institute of Concordia University in Montreal.

[8] Drucker came from Vienna to the United States, where he became a leading authority on the modern corporation.

[9] Kenneth McRobbie's systematic study, 'Reading and Anti-Polanyi', has found that of over 100 'facts', only thirteen are correct.

[10] Polanyi (1968) returned to a central theme of *The Great Transformation*.

[11] We can make systematic use of Polanyi's insight in *The Great Transformation* once we have 'unpacked' the text and shown the tensions between Polanyi's original Marxist architecture for the book and the new ideas he developed as he was writing them.

[12] Polanyi (1977) was constructed from lecture notes for this course by Harry W. Pearson.

[13] Herman Daly (1996) and others.

References

Agarwala, A.N. and S.P. Singh, eds (1958), *The Economics of Underdevelopment* (New Delhi: Oxford University Press).

Block, Fred (2001), 'Karl Polanyi and the Writing of the Great Transformation', paper presented at the Eighth International Karl Polanyi Conference on 'Economy and Democracy', Mexico City, Mexico.

Daly, Herman E. (1996), *Beyond Growth: The Economics of Sustainable Development* (Boston: Beacon Press).

Drucker, Peter F. (1978), 'The Polanyis', in Peter F. Drucker, *Adventures of a Bystander* (New York: Harper and Row): 123–40.

Duczynska, Ilona (1978), *Workers in Arms: The Austrian Schutzbund and the Civil War of 1934* (New York: Monthly Review Press).

Halperin, Rhoda (1994), *Cultural Economies: Past and Present* (Austin: University of Texas Press).

Lindsey, Brink (2001), 'The Decline and Fall of the First Global Economy', *Reason*, December.

McRobbie, Kenneth and Karl Polanyi Levitt, eds (2000), *Karl Polanyi in Vienna, The Contemporary Significance of the Great Transformation* (Montreal: Black Rose Books): 255–328.

Needham, Joseph (1954), *Science and Civilization in China* (Cambridge: Cambridge University Press).

Ocampo, José Antonio (2003), 'Development and the Global Order', in Ha-Joon Chang, ed., *Rethinking Development Economics* (London: Anthem Press).

Polanyi, Karl (1944), *The Great Transformation: The Political and Economic Origins of Our Time* (Boston: Beacon Press).

—— (1945), 'Universal Capitalism or Regional Planning', *The London Quarterly of World Affairs*, 10 (3): 86–91.

—— ([1947] 1968), 'Our Obsolete Market Mentality', *Commentary*, 3, February: 109–17; reprinted in George Dalton, ed., *Primitive, Archaic, and Modern Economies* (Garden City, New York: Doubleday).

—— (1947), 'On Belief in Economic Determinism', *The Sociological Review*, 39: 96–102.

—— (1957), 'The Economy as an Instituted Process', in Karl Polanyi, C.M. Arensberg and Harry W. Pearson, eds, *Trade and Markets in the Early Empires* (Glencoe, Illinois: Free Press).

—— (1968), 'Aristotle Discovers the Economy', in George Dalton, ed., *Primitive, Archaic, and Modern Economies* (Garden City, New York: Doubleday): 78–115.

—— (1977), *The Livelihood of Man*, edited by Harry W. Pearson (New York: Academic Press).

Polanyi, Karl, C.M. Arensberg and Harry W. Pearson, eds (1957), *Trade and Market in the Early Empires* (Glencoe, Illinois: Free Press).

Polanyi Levitt, Kari, ed. (1990), *The Life and Work of Karl Polanyi* (Montreal: Black Rose Books).

Polanyi Levitt, Kari and Marguerite Mendell (1987), 'Karl Polanyi, His Life and Times', *Studies in Political Economy*, 22, Spring: 7–39.

Putzel, James (2002), 'Politics, the State, and the Impulse for Social Protection: The Implication of Karl Polanyi's Ideas for Understanding Development and Crisis', Working Paper no. 18, London School of Economics, London, October; http://www.crisisstates.com/Publications/wp/wp18.htm

Rodrik, Dani (1998), 'A Global Fix: A Plan to Save the World Economy', *The New Republic*, 2 November.

Schlesinger, Rudolf, ed. (1964), *Co-existence*, November (London: Pergamon Press).

Alexander Gerschenkron and Late Industrialization

C.P. Chandrasekhar

The inclusion of an assessment of Alexander Gerschenkron in a volume concerned with the contributions of pioneers in the analysis of the economics of 'development' may appear paradoxical. To start with, Gerschenkron was concerned with the historical process through which the developed countries of today came to occupy their spaces in the pantheon of industrialized nations. He could not, therefore, seen as a theorist concerned with the economic dynamics of countries that have institutional features characteristic of those which are identified as underdeveloped. Secondly, Gerschenkron's work focused on Europe and excluded even present-day developed countries like Japan, besides the vast number of backward and ex-colonial countries in Africa, Asia and Latin America.

Yet, the literature on the economics of development is replete with references to his work, especially his celebrated essay titled 'Economic Backwardness in Historical Perspective' (Gerschenkron 1962). This interest is not misplaced. A theme that recurred in Gerschenkron's historical research was the combination of factors that provided the spur for the industrial transformation of backward societies. Inasmuch as that investigation sheds light on the problems of industrial transformation in the developing countries since World War II, his work can and did provide support to the literature on development.

Gerschenkron was pre-eminently an economic historian concerned with the analysis of observed empirical reality. In the essay referred to above, he declared that:

> Historical research consists essentially in application to empirical material of various sets of empirically derived hypothetical generalizations and in testing the closeness of the resulting fit, in the hope that in this way certain uniformities, certain typical situations, and certain typical relationships among individual factors in these situations can be ascertained. None of these lends itself to easy extrapolations. All that can be achieved is an extraction from the vast storehouse of the past of sets of intelligent questions that may be addressed to current materials. (Gerschenkron 1962: 6)

This method, he brought to bear on the historical experience of modern Europe. In the process, he achieved two goals. He challenged a number of arguments that had been advanced earlier regarding the nature and determinants of development of individual nations in the region, especially their economic development. And, despite his modest statement of the nature of the historian's quest, he derived a set of strong generalizations on the distinctive features of those development processes and the factors that accounted for them.

What concerns us most when assessing Gerschenkron's influence on development economics is the former – his discussion of the nature and determinants of industrial transformation of backward economies. In this area, the first conclusion Gerschenkron arrived at was that Marx's generalization – that 'the industrially more developed country presents to the less developed country a picture of the latter's future' – was only partially true, and possibly trivially so.[1] What was more relevant for him was that most often, the industrialization process in a backward country was substantially different – not just in terms of speed, but also in nature – from that in an advanced country. This obviously meant that countries that were different – in terms of the degree of their backwardness – would also be characterized by different processes of industrialization.

One set of distinctive features of late industrialization identified by Gerschenkron relates to the size, technological level, sequence and variety of new industries that are created in the course of the industrial transformation of a country. There is a 'tendency on the part of backward countries to concentrate at a relatively early point of their industrialization on promotion of those branches of industrial activities in which recent technological progress had been particularly rapid'. This

> required, in nineteenth century conditions, increases in the average size of plant. Stress on bigness in this sense can be found in the history of most countries on the European continent. But industrialization of backward countries in Europe reveals a tendency toward bigness in another sense. The use of the term 'industrial revolution' has been exposed to a good many justifiable strictures. But, if industrial revolution is conceived as denoting no more than cases of sudden considerable increases in the rate of industrial growth, there is little doubt that in several important instances industrial development began in such a sudden, eruptive, that is 'revolutionary', way. (Gerschenkron 1962: 10)

This *discontinuity*, Gerschenkron argued,

> was not accidental. As likely as not, the period of stagnation (in the 'physiocratic' sense of a period of low rate of growth) can be terminated and the industrialization processes begun only if the industrialization movement can proceed, as it were, along a broad front, starting simultaneously along many lines of economic activities. This is partly the result of the existence of complementarity and indivisibilities in economic processes. (ibid.)

At one level, the statement that late industrialization has characteristics that are distinctive – a high rate of initial industrial growth or an industrial spurt, a higher average degree of capital intensity (in terms of both capital–

labour and capital–output ratios) than was characteristic of early industrializers like Britain, a change in the sequence in which industries emerged, and a near-simultaneous emergence of multiple industries – is almost definitional. These are natural outcomes of what are conventionally considered the benefits of late entry. There already exist a range of productive techniques in the form of a shelf of blueprints that can, in principle, be accessed by backward economies, even if at a cost. Late industrializers, as the cliché goes, need not reinvent the wheel. Nor are they excessively burdened by outmoded capital stock that has yet to be written off, which is a penalty paid by the early starter. This encourages the exploitation of productivity increases associated with newer technologies. But since such technologies are more capital-intensive than those used by early industrializers in the initial stages of their industrialization process, the average capital intensity and level of investment in late industrializers tend to be much higher.

Further, given the industry-wide externalities associated with modern industry (Dobb 1959), the presence and growth of certain industries become a prerequisite for the success of others. As a result, the process of late industrialization must imply a degree of syncopation and a near-simultaneous creation of a wider range of industries than was true of the first industrializers. In particular, a range of heavy industrial sectors that process industrial raw materials, provide intermediate goods or are in the nature of infrastructure, need to be created rather early, to facilitate the industrialization process. All of this raises the investment–income ratio even further.

These inevitable features of late industrialization, therefore, do not challenge the fundamental notion that the developing countries can see in the developed countries, an image of their own future. All they point to is that because technology does not regress and technological transfer is possible, it is ensured that the route followed by late industrializers to a developed status would differ in form from that taken by early industrializers.

There was a second, and more interesting, aspect of the industrialization process in late industrializers that Gerschenkron garnered from history. This related to the then (and even now) prevalent notion that there are certain 'prerequisites' – in the sense of certain realized 'initial conditions' – which need to be satisfied for the successful industrial transformation of a country. These include: (i) the existence of a class of would-be investors who have accumulated adequate sums of capital for undertaking capital-intensive investments in industry; (ii) the availability of a large enough and disciplined army of labourers who – being divorced from land and devoid of capital assets – have nothing to sell but their labour power and can be employed in industry; and (iii) a large enough market for manufactures, which could provide the incentives for and viably sustain industrial investment.

Marx's analysis of the processes of capitalist development and the primitive accumulation of capital was immensely insightful inasmuch as it examined how all of these 'prerequisites' were ensured in the course of the transformation from feudalism to capitalism, yielding the initial conditions needed for an industrial revolution. He also dealt with the role that the pre-capitalist regions of the world, which were initially brought under the ambit of capitalism and then colonized, played in accelerating and reducing the domestic costs of industrial transformation of countries like Britain. An elaboration of the full implications of the role the colonies played, however, had to wait for the analyses of writers like Rosa Luxemburg and Lenin.

An important insight gleaned from the discussion of prerequisites by later analysts of the problems of development of underdeveloped countries was the crucial role of the 'agrarian transition' and, therefore, of agrarian reforms in their capitalist transformation and industrialization. Gerschenkron summarized this perception, even if only to disagree:

> Without such reforms, it is said, an industrialization in Europe could not begin at all. Only if the peasants were free from the trammels of an institutional framework which limited their mobility could industry receive the labour it needed. Only a flourishing peasant agriculture emerging from a properly conceived and correctly administered agrarian reform could constitute a large and growing market for industrial goods and sustain the demand for them. Only a so reformed agriculture could supply the growing industry with foodstuffs and, in less developed countries also engage in exports of agricultural produce and thereby insert a rather fixed item into the balance of payments, so as to provide foreign exchange for imports of machinery and for the service of industrialization loans. (Gerschenkron 1970: 100)

This and other perceptions influenced generations of development economists who, when analysing why underdevelopment persists in much of the so-called 'developing world', focused on the ways in which colonialism consolidated non-capitalist agriculture, and on how this factor, along with the failure of most post-colonial states to transform agriculture, made the process of capitalist transformation gradual, uneven, incomplete and inadequate to generate and sustain an independent industrial base.

The reasons why the 'initial conditions' described above – which were delivered in large part by agrarian transition and colonial expansion – were seen as prerequisites for industrialization should be obvious. Given the levels of investment required for an industrial revolution in a late industrializing country, accumulation of adequate sums of capital in the hands of investors is imperative. The need for a 'free' labour force, with access to food for consumption, for the emergence and growth of a new segment of economic activity is obvious. And the importance of a large enough market for manufactures is self-evident.

Gerschenkron distanced himself from this notion of prerequisites. To an extent, he (1970: 8) accepted that no industrialization seems possible in a country 'as long as certain formidable institutional obstacles (such as the serfdom of the peasantry or the far-reaching absence of political unification) remained' (Gerschenkron 1970:8). His difficulty with analyses based on prerequisites was not that they were wrong or even of little importance in understanding the experience of England, but that they were interpreted absolutely, mechanically and dogmatically when applied to other countries (ibid.: 102). His fundamental objection was to a 'stage scheme' of development, which required all countries to pass through the same or similar stages in the course of their emergence as industrialized economies.

Gerschenkron argued that some of the problems that the prerequisites argument focused upon were partially dealt with by the very context and character of late industrialization. And, to the extent that they were not, countries responded to the absence of these so-called prerequisites with institutional substitutions of various kinds that allowed them to overcome the barriers to industrialization. It was because of this that 'these beautiful exercises in logic have been defeated by history'.

Late industrializers, Gerschenkron implicitly reminded us, were not only beneficiaries of the fact that productive technologies in many areas had already been developed and exploited, but also of the fact that there existed countries and individuals who had profited immensely from capitalist development and industrialization. This provided late industrializers with access not just to technologies, but also to technological expertise and capital from abroad. Thus, foreign technology transfer[2] and foreign investment allowed countries to both access new technologies and partially overcome the problem of inadequacy of capital for investment. What was more, these technologies were capital-intensive in character. Hence, the size of the required free labour force was much smaller than would otherwise have been the case.

> The advantages inherent in the use of technologically superior equipment were not counteracted but reinforced by its labour-saving effect. This seems to explain the tendency on the part of backward countries to concentrate at a relatively early point of their industrialization on promotion of those branches of industrial activities in which recent technological progress has been particularly rapid. (Gerschenkron 1962: 9)

The real constraint was access to an adequate quantity of skilled labour, which could be imported or trained, rather than of unskilled labour.

But this was not all. Gerschenkron believed that even the other supposed 'prerequisites' – such as prior accumulation of capital or an agrarian transition – were not absolute necessities, inasmuch as in the course of development, countries that had overcome 'formidable institutional obstacles' and were set for industrialization would find 'institutional substitutions' that ensured a breakthrough. The effects of the advantages of late industrialization, of the 'basic factors' discussed above, were 'greatly reinforced by the use in backward countries of certain institutional instruments and the acceptance of specific industrialization ideologies'.

It is in the elaboration of these institutional instruments that we find one of the most useful of Gerschenkron's contributions. Principal among these was his discussion of the role played by certain institutional adjustments in the financial sector, in the success of late industrializers like France and Germany. Basing his arguments on the roles played by Crédit Mobilier of the brothers Pereire in France and the 'universal banks' in Germany, Gerschenkron argued that the creation of 'financial organizations designed to build thousands of miles of railroads, drill mines, erect factories, pierce canals, construct ports and modernize cities' was hugely transformative. Financial firms based on old wealth were typically in the nature of rentier capitalists, and limited themselves to flotations of government loans and foreign exchange transactions. The new firms were 'devoted to railroadization and industrialization of the country', and, in the process, influenced the behaviour of old wealth as well.

As Gerschenkron argued:

> The difference between banks of the credit mobilier type and commercial banks of the time (England) was absolute. Between the English bank essentially designed to serve as a source of short-term capital and a bank designed to finance the long-run investment needs of the economy there was a complete gulf. The German banks, which may be taken as a paragon of the type of the universal bank, successfully combined the basic idea of the credit mobilier with the short-term activities of commercial banks. (Gerschenkron 1962: 13)

The banks, according to him, substituted for the absence of a number of elements crucial for industrialization:

> In Germany, the various incompetencies of the individual entrepreneurs were offset by the device of splitting the entrepreneurial function: the German investment banks – a powerful invention, comparable in economic effect to that of the steam engine – were in their capital-supplying functions a substitute for the insufficiency of the previously created wealth willingly placed at the disposal of entrepreneurs. But they were also a substitute for entrepreneurial deficiencies. From their central vantage points of control, the banks participated actively in shaping the major – and sometimes even not so major – decisions of the individual enterprises. It was they who often mapped out a firm's paths of growth, conceived far-sighted plans, decided on major technological and locational innovations, and arranged for mergers and capital increases. (Gerschenkron 1968: 137)

Thus, the lack of an adequate period of prior accumulation and of an adequately evolved entrepreneurial class did not constitute constraints in these instances because of the institutional substitution in the realm of finance that made up for those inadequacies. The state, too, through its role in fostering development, was seen to serve as an institutional substitute. While, in Austria, Italy, Switzerland, France and Belgium, banks played a major role in triggering industrial transformation, this was not true, according to Gerschenkron, of the European continent as a whole, for two reasons. Excluding countries like Denmark where no such process of industrial transformation occurred due to the paucity of natural resources and 'the great opportunities for agricultural improvement', there were others, like Russia, 'where the basic elements of back-wardness appear in such an accentuated form as to lead to the use of essentially different institutional instruments of industrialization' (Gerschenkron 1962: 16).

Despite the emancipation of serfs in Russia in 1861, for almost a quarter of a century, the rate of growth remained relatively low.

> The great industrial upswing came when, from the middle of the eighties on, the railroad building of the state assumed unprecedented proportions and became the main lever of a rapid industrialization policy. Through multifarious devices such as preferential orders to domestic producers of railroad materials, high prices, subsidies, credits, and profit guarantees to new industrial enterprises, the government succeeded in maintaining a high and, in fact, increasing rate of growth until the end of the century. Concomitantly, the Russian taxation sys-tem was reorganized, and the financing of industrialization policies was thus provided for, while the stabilization of the rouble and the introduction of the gold standard assured foreign participation in the development of the Russian industry. (Gerschenkron 1962: 19)

Overall, industrialization took place in Russia

> through a number of specific substitutions. The demand of the peasants was substituted for by the demand of the State for capital goods. The inadequate labour supply was substituted for by the introduction of modern labour-saving technology. The insufficient increases in productivity in agriculture were substituted for by pressure on the income levels of the peasantry. And the cases of substitution of this kind were not confined to the effects of the conditions of agriculture. They extended to the whole of the industrial economy, the importa-tion of technology and qualified personnel from abroad being a substitute for the missing prerequisite of indigenous knowledge and deficiency in educational background. Just as to some extent both the exaggerated size of plants and the role of government bureaucracy substituted for the inadequate supply of entre-preneurs. (Gerschenkron 1970: 104)

The role of the state was crucial because the scarcity of capital, stan-dards of honesty in business and public distrust of the banking system were so great that banks could not play the role they did in countries like Germany. In sum, given the greater backwardness of Russia, the state was a second-order institutional substitute as compared to banks in Germany. Institutional substitu-tions of this kind ensured that there were really no binding prerequisites for industrialization in a country, except for fundamental institutional obstacles like serfdom or lack of unification.

There are three elements of Gerschenkron's approach that need to be noted. First, once fundamental institutional obstacles are overcome in a country, and if other circumstances do not militate against industrialization, as in Den-mark, independent of the degree and nature of its backwardness, it is presumed that there willl be a set of institutional substitutions that ensure its industrial transformation. In that sense, there is a degree of automaticity or inevitability about industrialization in backward economies. Not surprisingly, Gerschenkron believed that

> past historical experience may justify a measure of optimism with regard to the general prospects of industrialization of backward countries. What is meant is not simply that past industrialization occurred in the face of considerable obstacles and deficiencies. In viewing the historical record one cannot be failed to be impressed with the ingenuity, originality, and flexibility with which backward countries tried to solve the specific problems of their industrial development. There is no *a priori* reason to suppose that the underdeveloped countries which today stand on the threshold of the industrial revolutions will show less creative adaptation in compensating for the absence of factors which in more fortunate countries may be said to have 'preconditioned' the initial spurts of rapid industrial growth. (Gerschenkron 1962: 51)

The second noteworthy feature is the link he establishes between the degree of backwardness of a country and the nature of institutional substitution adopted.[3]

> The more backward a country, the more likely its industrialization was to proceed under some organized direction; depending on the degree of backwardness, the seat of such direction could be found in investment banks, in investment banks acting under the aegis of the state, or in bureaucratic controls. So viewed, the industrial history of Europe appears not as a series of mere repetitions of the 'first' industrialization but as an orderly system of graduated deviations from the industrialization. (ibid.: 44)

Thus Gerschenkron had his own version of a stage scheme, despite his dismissive remarks about the stage schemers, among whom he included Marx on the one side and Rostow on the other.

Finally, he used this stage scheme to arrive at a notion of non-linear substitutions.

> Geographically seen, that is to say, spatially speaking, all these substitutions, their numbers and intensity can be explained in terms of the rising degree of backwardness of the areas concerned. To do so, gives us first of all an opportunity to bring some order into the apparent chaos, to establish, that is, a morphology or typology of the development. But the approach yields more than just a spatial ordering of events. As we follow the course of the industrial spurt over time, we see how under the impact of diminishing backwardness also the pattern of substitutions begins to change and substitutions characteristic of a high degree of backwardness begin to be replaced by substitutions that have been used in areas of medium backwardness. In this fashion, temporally seen, the original morphology becomes more complex, is given a causal twist, and its

organizing principle of the degree of backwardness becomes a causal principle, explaining for us the nature of the processes of industrial change. (ibid.)

In sum, there is not just an automatism about substitutions, but, given the relationship between the substitution that is resorted to and the stage of backwardness, there is a basic tendency towards successful industrialization built into the system. In terms of final destination, Gerschenkron returned to the Marxian dictum that the industrially mo.e developed country presents to the less developed country a picture of the latter's future. It is only the processes that are different.

These features of Gerschenkron's argument imply that, except in unusual and rare circumstances, an industrial revolution is inevitable in a backward country. Differences across countries would relate to the factors required to initially trigger an industrial 'revolution', to differential delays in the start of the spurt that initiates industrial transformation, and to differences in the time taken to complete the process of industrialization.

It hardly bears stating that history has proved that such 'optimism' is unwarranted. There are a large number of countries which, despite long years of experience with factory-based production, have yet to witness the economic dynamism that processes of industrial transformation delivered in the developed countries of today. In fact, even at the time when he was writing, if Gerschenkron had extended his vision to the then ex-colonial countries of the world, he would have found reason to be sceptical about the potentialities for capitalist industrialization in many countries.

India, for example, which, given its geographical size and population, constituted a viable market for a complex of industries, had by the time of freedom from colonial rule in 1947 experienced close to a century of factory-based industrial production. Yet, the industrial sector accounted for a small share of national income and employment, reflected an extremely limited degree of diversification, and was dominated by primitive forms of production and backward technologies. This was also true of a large number of underdeveloped countries in Asia, Africa and Latin America, whose experiences with the nature and timing of imperial conquest were very different. Further, though there was evidence of a post-independence spurt in industrialization in India engineered by an interventionist state, that state did not evolve 'automatically' but as a result of a struggle for freedom which saw in industrialization a means to strengthen political freedom with economic independence. Finally, the spurt in industrialization notwithstanding, a number of failures of that Indian state, including the failure to ensure an agrarian transition and to create the *prerequisites* for successful industrialization based on the domestic market, meant that industrial growth faltered after the mid-1960s and that, even today, the country can hardly be characterized as one that has undergone a successful industrial transformation.

Ignoring the lessons of these experiences involved a two-fold neglect. First, it neglected the role played by the inducement to invest offered by the market in these colonies, and by the drain of surpluses from them in stimulating and financing investment in the metropolitan centres and the regions of recent settlement in the capitalist world. The growth that such investment triggered, together with the role of 'development finance' institutions and the state that Gerschenkron correctly stressed, also helped processes of industrialization in other developed countries which were themselves not colonies or which did not have the benefit of a colonial hinterland.

Second, it neglected the economic devastation wrought by colonialism in the periphery, by leaving behind structures and institutional obstacles that hindered industrial advance. It was in countries where external forces (as in South Korea and Taiwan) or internal movements (as in China) removed these structural constraints and institutional obstacles that successful industrialization of the kind seen in the present-day developed countries was substantially achieved. Where these structures remained in place, even if in modified form, neither did the state display the capability to trigger successful industrialization nor could institutional substitutions, such as institutions of development finance, break through the barriers that defined and determined backwardness.

Thus, besides all else, neglect of the role of empire in advancing the industrialization of the metropolis and reproducing backwardness in the periphery, whether due to the Eurocentric focus of Gerschenkron's analysis or his ideological predilections or to both of these, resulted in excessive optimism about the possibilities of successful industrialization across the world. That having been said, it is necessary to take note of the importance Gerschenkron attributed to two forces that were crucial for late industrialization: a financial structure that, in form and purpose, was different from that which prevailed in England during its industrialization; and an interventionist state that either abolished or neutralized the effects of structures that were bottlenecks or hindrances to successful industrialization.

It is the crucial role of these forces that the dominant paradigm influencing policy in developing countries has challenged and substantially diluted. Neoliberal reform in the age of finance includes policies of financial reform that seek to dismantle the specific structures of development finance created by 'backward' countries to deal with the constraints on development set by international and national inequalities in asset and income distribution. It hardly bears stating that it also seeks to dilute and do away with interventionism that substitutes for, or regulates, a market which fails to deliver adequate and sustainable growth, replacing it with state policy that enhances operation of the market mechanism.

Of the forces that Gerschenkron saw as necessary for industrialization by late industrializers, the second has been stressed by a number of writers and constitutes the fulcrum of analyses of the role of the developmental state, while the first has received far less attention than it deserves. Unfortunately, financial liberalization – which reduces controls on the entry and functioning of financial intermediaries, deregulates interest rates, does away with directed credit programmes, breaks down the walls separating different financial markets, and dilutes prudential regulation and supervisory intervention – also alters the structure of the financial sector. In fact, in most contexts, the result of intervention is to make the domestic financial sector increasingly mimic the structure that has come to characterize the US and UK markets since the 1980s.

This development is significant for three reasons. First, differences in financial structures of individual countries have been the norm, historically, across the globe, making the current trend towards homogenization of financial structures an oddity, even if not an anomaly. Second, there is strong evidence not only of a deep relationship between financial structures – the mix of financial contracts/instruments, markets, interventions and institutions – and growth in general, but also of an important role for specific kinds of financial structures in explaining the success of late industrialization in contexts as diverse as Germany and Japan, on the one hand, and South Korea and Taiwan, on the other. Third, the emergence of the currently 'fashionable' Anglo–Saxon model is a recent phenomenon, at least in the US.

The relationship between financial development and real economic growth is indeed complex. In the final analysis, given production conditions, a rise in the rate of 'real capital formation leading to an acceleration in the rate of physical accumulation' is at the core of any development process. And, once the Keynesian revolution made it clear that lack of adequate savings can never be a binding constraint on investment and growth, it appeared that the role of the financial sector in mobilizing and channelling savings was a secondary one and inevitably fulfilled. This view was emphasized by Joan Robinson in the pithy statement, 'where enterprise leads finance follows'. According to this view, economic development creates demands for particular financial arrangements, and the financial system responds automatically to these demands.

But, as Maurice Dobb and others have made clear, the maximal rate of investment that can be achieved along any growth trajectory is not independent of the evolution of the composition of investment along that path. And where private investors have an important role in investment decision-making, there is no reason to expect that markets will help realize the appropriate investment allocation or even the maximal investment rate associated with any initial investment allocation.

It is in this context that the facilitating role of the financial structure intervenes. Especially where private investment decision-makers have an important or leading role in investment, an appropriate financial structure, *inter alia*, can help move the system to allocate investments required to realize the feasible maximal rate of growth, and to ensure that the feasible rate is closely approximated.

By alluding to or focusing on factors such as these, Gerschenkron drew attention to an often neglected aspect of factors supporting successful industrialization. As the effects of neoliberal financial reform unfold, Gerschenkron's insights into the role of financial structures in late industrialization have gained substantially in significance. It is for those insights that he deserves a place in a book devoted to pioneers of the economics of development.

Notes

[1] The resemblance here to Trotsky's theory based on the 'law of combined and uneven development' has often been noted. Arguing against the view that all countries undergo the same pattern or pass through the same stages of development as the advanced nations, Trotsky held that backward countries were not merely primitive and subordinate, but also developing, through the appropriation or imposition of advanced forms of technology and production from the developed countries. In so developing, they avoided many of the features characteristic of intermediate stages of development which the developed capitalist countries had earlier been through. But Gerschenkron did not see himself as indebted to Trotsky. Rather, as his grandson Dawidoff (2002: 186) puts it: 'He saw his historical synthesis of industrial development as the great proof of his scholarly supremacy. Nobody else had such an approach to economic history. Intellectually it made Shura his own man. He was not a Marxist or a Keynesian, nor was he obviously indebted to John Stuart Mill or Max Weber. He was the advantages of backwardness.' Given Gerschenkron's cultural, geographical and intellectual roots, however, there is reason to be sceptical of that judgment.

[2] Gerschenkron (1970: 19–20) illustrated the role that foreign assistance can play with an instance from Russia, wherein Old Believers – who did not correspond to those endowed with Weber's Protestant ethic – contributed significantly to early industrial development. 'A German, Ludwig Knoop (1821–94), was the little Bremen apprentice to commerce, who after a year in Manchester came to Russia (in 1839) in his English re-incarnation as the representative (or rather an assistant to a representative) of Lancashire. The talented youngster, one of the great entrepreneurial figures of the century, began as an importer of yarn and cloth, but very soon undertook to supply complete equipment to Russian cotton spinneries and later to weaving sheds. In addition, he brought from Lancashire skilled labour, foremen and engineers. Over his lifetime he managed to establish in this fashion some 120-odd factories – surely one of the most remarkable examples of a massive borrowing of foreign technology.'

[3] E.H. Carr (1967) criticized the idea that certain industrialization processes were reflective of 'backwardness' on the ground that this implied setting 'a norm for industrialization' suggestive of 'romantic nostalgia' for the English industrial revolution, following which, applying the 'criterion of backwardness inevitably generated the result' that certain substitutions were reflective of a certain degree of backwardness. Gerschenkron (1970) dismissed this as a distortion of his view.

References

Carr, E.H. (1967), 'Some Random Reflections on Soviet Industrialization', in C.H. Feinstein, ed., *Socialism, Capitalism, and Economic Growth: Essays Presented to Maurice Dobb* (Cambridge: Cambridge University Press).

Dawidoff, Nicholas (2002), *The Fly Swatter: How My Grandfather Made His Way in the World* (New York: Pantheon Books).

Dobb, Maurice (1959), *An Essay on Economic Growth and Planning* (New York: Monthly Review Press).

Gerschenkron, Alexander (1962), *Economic Backwardness in Historical Perspective: A Book of Essays* (Cambridge, Massachusetts: The Belknap Press of Harvard University Press).

—— (1968), *Continuity in History and Other Essays* (Cambridge, Massachusetts: The Belknap Press of Harvard University Press).

—— (1970), *Europe in the Russian Mirror: Four Lectures in Economic History* (Cambridge: Cambridge University Press).

Raúl Prebisch and Arthur Lewis
The Two Basic Dualities of Development Economics

Kari Polanyi Levitt

Raúl Prebisch (b. 1901) and Arthur Lewis (b. 1913) contributed two basic dualities to development economics: the centre–periphery paradigm, and the transfer of labour from a traditional to a modern capitalist sector in conditions of unlimited supplies of labour. Both Prebisch and Lewis advocated industrialization, albeit for somewhat different reasons. *Latin America and its Principal Problems*, published in 1950 by the United Nations Economic Commission for Latin America (UNECLA, or CEPAL in Spanish), also known as the CEPAL Manifesto, explained the mechanisms that underlie a secular deterioration of the terms of trade of peripheral commodity-exporting economies.

The Latin American experience of import-substituting industrialization as a response to the breakdown of international trade and investment in the 1930s and 1940s was the basis on which Prebisch advocated industrialization as a means of capturing the gains of technological progress for the peripheries. The argument hinged on the asymmetry of structures of commodity and labour markets in centres and peripheries, which enables labour to share the gains of productivity with capital in the metropole, whereas the weak bargaining position of labour in the peripheries retards the adoption of labour-saving technology and such productivity gains as accrue to export sector are passed on to the metropole in the form of low prices. The document was prepared by Prebisch working with a team of young Latin American economists under his direction.

The case for industrialization as argued by Lewis was posited on the comparative advantage of labour-surplus countries in manufacturing activity. It was presented in *The Industrial Development of the Caribbean* (1951), based on the success of 'Operation Bootstrap' in Puerto Rico. Lewis advocated industrialization for the production of manufactured goods for domestic, regional and metropolitan markets – a radical position at a time when the West Indies and other colonial economies were exclusively designed to provide agricultural and other primary commodities to the metropole. But it was Lewis' article, entitled 'Economic Development with Unlimited Supplies of Labour' (1954), and the controversies that ensued in the academic literature that contributed to the establishment of development economics as a specialized field of study in the academy. The article addressed the mechanisms of transfer of surplus labour from traditional activities in agriculture and a variety of domestic services to a modern accumulating capitalist sector in conditions of unlimited supplies of labour. In this model, wages in the modern capitalist sector are determined not by the productivity of labour but by its opportunity cost. It is not generally appreciated that in the open version of the Lewis model, where the modern sector exports to the metropole and surplus labour is freely available from external sources, the benefits of productivity increases are captured by the metropole in a manner resembling the Prebisch analysis.

Raúl Prebisch: The Originality of CEPAL Developmentalism

When Raúl Prebisch was appointed executive director of the newly created United Nations Economic Commission for Latin America (ECLA) in 1948, he brought with him long years of experience as an 'insider' government technocrat in Argentina, where he was well connected with the agrarian oligarchy by family ties (Sikkink 1988a: 93). In 1933 he attended the World Economic Conference in an official capacity, and had occasion to observe that the currency of international trade was power. He concluded that Argentina, as an important but vulnerable trading nation, would have to chart new paths with an active role for the state, abandoning the academic baggage contained in western textbooks current at the time. During the Great Depression, 'we stopped accepting with reverence the theories developed there (the metropole), and as a result of passing through so many vicissitudes, we began to seek our own developmental path' (Prebisch 1982: 151). During the war, when access to traditional European markets was severed, 'we had to improvize defence measures which were the beginning of an autonomous development effort'. Prebisch started his professional life as a firm believer in the tenets and truths of neoclassical economics, acquired by self-study and taught as a part-time university professor. The experience of the Great Depression caused him to reject these theories. Intellectual emancipation from the dominant ideologies of the North became a lifetime vocation.

> Thirty years ago, the periphery had begun a tenacious and difficult attempt to emancipate itself intellectually. It was learning to question those theories developed in the centres that did not fit with the basic interests of peripheral development. The return to conventional theories in recent years has represented an attempt to counteract this effort aimed at independent thinking about development. The seductiveness of these theories is very powerful, and it clouds their proponents' view of reality so they are unable to perceive clearly the interplay of internal and external interests behind these new manifestations of conventional thinking. (Prebisch 1982: 151)

In 1943, Prebisch was dismissed from his post as director of the central bank of Argentina by Peronist politicians hostile to his close connection with agrarian export interests. By that time, he was Latin America's best-known banker and economist, and an internationally respected figure. In the same year, he received an extended consultancy from Mexico's central bank, followed by offers of similar consultancies in several other Latin American countries. His Argentinian nationalism was modified to embrace the rest of Latin America.[1] Throughout these years, he continued to lecture and research at the University of Buenos Aires. In 1947, he published his book on Keynes, whose work he had encountered in Europe in the 1930s.

In 1948, following the election of Juan Peron, Prebisch was effectively exiled from Argentina, and accepted an invitation from the ECLA to complete the draft of the *First Economic Survey of Latin America* for the Havana meeting in 1948. While preparing his presentation for this meeting, he encountered Hans Singer's United Nations study on terms of trade, and reworked his paper. The result was *The Economic Development of Latin America and its Principal Problems* (Prebisch 1949), acclaimed as an indigenous economic paradigm with a vocabulary for viewing Latin America within a single conceptual and policy framework.

It has been said that, in a sense, Prebisch 'created' Latin America. A careful reading of these two documents reveals the major themes of Prebisch and ECLA. The 'Manifesto' was not available in English translation for several years, but Prebisch became known to the English-speaking economics profession through 'Commercial Policy in the Underdeveloped Countries' (1959). In the United States, the reception was hostile (Sikkink 1988a: 91). Prebisch was branded as a heretic and radical to be treated with suspicion. It was implied that he understood neither economics nor the practical world of business. This was indeed ironic, given his credentials as an experienced central banker.

Centre–Periphery Paradigm

The trade relationship between central and peripheral countries is the original centrepiece of the Prebisch doctrine. It distinguishes Latin American structuralism from classical political economy and Keynesian growth theory, which treat capitalist accumulation as an endogenous phenomenon within a closed economy. The centre–periphery system is a single economic system whose bipolar evolution favours technological development of the central metropolitan countries. It is the historical outcome of the way in which technical progress is propagated in the world economy.

In the peripheries, technical progress penetrates only where the industrial centres need imports of low-cost foodstuffs and raw materials, thus creating an outward-directed, externally propelled development of these countries. Modern techniques form islands of high productivity within previously existing socio-economic structures, because new techniques are introduced only in the primary export sectors or in infrastructure directly servicing them. In Latin America, this occurred in the last quarter of the nineteenth century.

On the basis of this definition, important regions of the third world – principally in Asia – are not, and never were, peripheries. The centre–periphery analysis thus applies to Latin America and the Caribbean, most of Africa, and a limited number of Asian countries. Underdevelopment is not the absence of economic growth. In the period from 1870 to the Great Depression of 1930, there was substantial economic growth in Latin America and other raw material-supplying peripheries. But after 1930, the primary export model broke down and was no longer capable of generating growth.[2]

We summarize the following differences between central and peripheral economic structures, implicit in the early ECLA studies.

Production Structures

Centres: articulated, diversified and integrated with multiple domestic linkages.

Peripheries: disarticulated, fragmented and specialized with few domestic linkages.

Productivity

Centres: capitalism has penetrated the whole of society and productivity is relatively homogeneous.

Peripheries: islands of high productivity in a sea of low productivity activity; a wide range of heterogeneous productivities.

Income Distribution

Centres: moderate range of wage labour incomes.

Peripheries: large spread between highest and lowest wage labour incomes.

Peripheral Dependence

The centres generate and the peripheries receive technology and consumption styles. The centres generate business cycles and macroeconomic policies; the peripheries receive external shocks, which they cannot absorb without creating external and internal disequilibria due to their fragile and vulnerable economic structures.

Terms of Trade

There are three versions of propositions concerning the deteriorating terms of trade of peripheral export economies.

(1) The adverse movement of the double factoral terms of trade simply states that trade between a (peripheral) country with a slow rate of productivity growth, and an industrialized country with a higher rate of productivity growth, will inevitably result in progressive deterioration of the terms of exchange of the input or effort of the former in relation to that of the latter. It will be reflected in an ever-growing divergence of real living standards, which will occur even where commodity terms of trade are constant. This is the phenomenon of 'unequal exchange', noted also by Lewis, and explained in an excessively complicated theory by Emmanuel (1972).

(2) The point of departure of the 'cyclical' explanation of the deteriora-

tion of commodity terms of trade was the observation that, in the 1930s, the prices of peripheral commodity exports declined by more in the course of the downswing of the business cycle than they gained in the upswing, whereas the prices of manufactured goods were relatively stable. The major share of the 'fruits of technical progress' accrued to the central countries because productivity increases in the exports of peripheral countries resulted in falling prices, whereas productivity rents in central countries were captured by labour and capital in the form of higher wages and profits. In the upswing of the cycle, unionized workers in central economies could capture productivity increases as rising wages; in the downswing, they were able to resist reduction in money wages. In surplus labour countries, however, wages are flexible because labour has little or no bargaining power.

This explanation turns on differences in labour and goods markets in central and peripheral countries: monopolistic in the former and competitive in the latter type of economies. In central countries, industrialists can respond to a weakening of demand by cutting back output rather than reducing prices, as would be the case if markets were truly competitive. Peripheral commodity exporters, by contrast, operate in highly competitive markets, where weak demand results in falling prices. Indeed, it may be necessary to increase supply to compensate for falling prices, further weakening the capacity of peripheral producers to capture technological rents.

(3) The third or 'industrialization' version of the deteriorating terms of trade thesis turns on differences in the income elasticity of demand for imports between central and peripheral trading partners. The rate of growth of metropolitan demand for agricultural and mineral commodity imports declines with rising incomes and technological change, whereas import demand in peripheral countries undertaking industrialization is income-inelastic because imports of capital and intermediate goods are essential industrial inputs. A similar theory was developed independently by Hans Singer (1950; see also Singer 1971). The theoretical argument explaining deteriorating commodity terms of trade is frequently referred to as the Prebisch–Singer theory.

In the 1950s and 1960s, decades of strong growth in the capitalist world economy, the business cycle was dormant and trade acted once more as an engine of growth. Deteriorating terms of commodity trade appeared to have receded into the annals of economic history. Since the end of the commodity boom of the mid-1970s and acceleration of the technological 'dematerialization' of production, primary commodity prices have gone into continued and severe decline (Ocampo and Parra 2005). Terms of trade are back on the agenda.

Peripheral Industrialization and Structural Bottlenecks

The CEPAL analysis recognized that industrialization in export-dependent economies would manifest tendencies to external disequilibrium in the form of a 'trade gap', due to weak external demand for primary commodity exports, and strong demand for imported intermediate and capital goods. Where import volumes are constrained to decline due to lack of foreign exchange to pay for them, production levels also decline, as does aggregate consumption. This is the burden of the 'two-gap' model, and the basis for the case for medium-term official development finance for countries undertaking industrialization programmes. Additionally, it was recognized that imported capital-intensive technology was likely to be labour-displacing, thus pushing down wage levels and limiting the growth of purchasing power of the masses of the population. Foreign exchange was not the only structural bottleneck. Land tenure patterns inherited from the era of agro-export outward-directed development, lack of infrastructure, fiscal systems that failed to tax elites and the inelastic supply of domestic foodstuffs were recognized as serious problems to be addressed.

In *Toward a Dynamic Development Policy for Latin America* (Prebisch 1963), Prebisch elaborated the case for industrialization as a means to raise productivity and labour incomes. The policy prescriptions included overall economic planning and programming, abolition of feudal land tenures, radical income redistribution, regional and sub-regional economic integration, and measures to encourage industrial exports to the centres.

External finance would continue to be needed to supplement domestic savings. A case was also made for international cooperation to stabilize commodity prices and for the introduction of preferential market access for the less developed countries. These last-mentioned items became part of long drawn-out negotiations within the framework of UNCTAD, resulting in the Generalized System of Preferences (GSPs) and a (very modest) Commodity Fund.

The End of Easy Import Substitution

In the 1960s, industrialization in Latin America was moving toward stagnation, diagnosed as 'the end of easy import substitution'. Slow growth was accompanied by internal (inflation) and external (balance of payments) disequilibria, as well as persistent unemployment. Regressive income distribution, chronic unemployment and extreme poverty in the shanty towns surrounding rapidly growing cities contributed to rising social tensions and radical political protests. The American response to the challenge of the Cuban revolution came in the form of the Alliance for Progress. The United States dropped previous opposition to economic planning, and a growth industry of technocratic planning on paper flourished within international agencies and at major US universities.

Prebisch at UNCTAD

In 1964, Prebisch departed for Geneva, to take up duties as Director-General of the newly established United Nations Conference on Trade and Development (UNCTAD). The key document was *Toward a New Trade Policy for Development*, which estimated a $20 billion 'trade gap' between developed and developing countries. The developed countries were hostile. The Secretariat was understaffed. Prebisch was overworked and frustrated. The G-77 group of developing countries was divided within itself. Latin American solidarity had disintegrated. ECLA was no longer a regional leader, as it had been before 1964. Latin American regional integration was failing. Brazil, now controlled by the colonels, was 'playing on two pianos' – the General Agreement on Tariffs and Trade (GATT) and UNCTAD. Latin American relations with the United States deteriorated after the invasion of the Dominican Republic in 1965. As a negotiating forum, UNCTAD I failed to satisfy Prebisch's expectations; UNCTAD II promised no improvement. In 1968, the Southern bargaining power was weaker and the Northern hostility to UNCTAD greater than in 1964. Prebisch resigned. In 1970, he presented *Change and Development: Latin America's Great Task* (Prebisch 1970) to the Tenth Annual Meeting of the Inter-American Development Bank. In retrospect, it was his opinion that in the ten years he spent in the service of international institutions and numerous North–South dialogues, 'Nothing important was achieved then or later' (Prebisch 1982: 150).

In the mid-1970s, as the world entered an economic crisis described by him as 'more profound, complex and difficult than the Great Depression', Prebisch returned to Santiago where he founded the *CEPAL Review*. From 1977 to his death in 1986, he contributed an important series of articles, restating and elaborating his original analysis of the problems of peripheral capitalism. He challenged the revival of monetarism and neoclassical economics, with the explicit intent of stemming the galloping tide of the appeal of economic liberalism to younger generations of Latin American economists. In his later writings, Prebisch insisted that we must reach beyond the narrow framework of economic theory. Economic factors cannot be separated from social structures (Prebisch 1984: 184). Peripheral industrialization has been greatly delayed, and took place during successive crises of the centres, accentuating the tendency of the periphery to imitate the centres, grow in their image and likeness, adopt their lifestyles and technologies, ideas and ideologies, and reproduce their institutions. This pattern of industrialization shaped the social structure of the periphery, tending to exclude those at the bottom from the benefits of economic growth. This explains why peripheral society becomes increasingly conflictive, and tends eventually to fall victim to serious economic and political crises. The argument turns on the origins and distribution of the 'economic surplus' that arises from the heterogeneous social structure of Latin American economies. As a result, large numbers of people are engaged in low productivity activity, unable to capture the gains of high productivity activity that accrue to a small fraction of the labour force, and to privileged social strata which imitate the consumption patterns of the centres. This is detrimental to reproductive capital accumulation, produces premature diversification of demand and is accompanied by disproportionate siphoning off of income by the centres, principally through transnational corporations: 'the surplus is based on sheer economic, political and social inequity'.

Democratization and labour unions can assist by asserting redistributive pressures, but as long as high-income groups can defend their high levels of consumption, competition between the state and organized labour for the remaining surplus will result in inflation, as monetary authorities yield to pressures to increase the money supply. 'The transformation of the system seems to me inevitable if we are to combine development with social equity and political advance. However, the most widely disseminated doctrinal options do not appear to be of much use for guiding this transformation.' Presbisch rejected both neoclassical economic liberalism and orthodox socialism, the latter because it stifles the democratic process. Social democracy was also dismissed, 'as it usually drifts to mere redistribution and the crises associated with it, offering no way out'. He pleaded for a synthesis of socialism with genuine economic liberalism – socialism to ensure the social use of the surplus; economic liberalism because individual decisions of what to produce and consume should be left to the market (Prebisch 1984: 191). Prebisch's view of the relationship of state and market is summarized as follows:

> The quest for an economic incentive, inasmuch as it spurs the initiative of enterprises and individuals, is a powerful generator of efficiency and growth, but it does not solve the serious problems which technology has brought with it as regards the environment, natural resources and social equity. This is where the state has an absolutely fundamental role to play, in a manner compatible with the market, with its great economic and political importance.
>
> This is not all however. The economic incentive increasingly goes beyond the sphere of business and penetrates into areas that it should never enter, because it perverts great values and degrades human fellowship. (Prebisch 1981: 24)

In the 1960s, CEPAL 'developmentalism' came under increasing attack from reformist and radical Latin American economists on the grounds that these strategies were aggravating income inequalities, and that there was little or no 'trickle down'. It is important to note, however, that the vigorous debates concerning the nature of Latin American dependence and underdevelopment were conducted by Latin American social scientists – some structuralist, some Marxist – sharing a common vocabulary and common experiences. The 'developmentalism' of Prebisch and the early CEPAL economists was an eclectic and heterodox confection of economic theories, including Keynesian macroeconomics – with an important difference. It was the difference that constituted its originality, and its continuing relevance to the analysis of open economies dependent on the vicissitudes of international trade and capital movements. As early as 1949, Prebisch observed that in the central countries, the volume of investment is the dynamic element in economic growth, and can be regulated by fiscal and monetary policy. In the peripheral economies, exports are the dynamic element, but they can neither be regulated nor controlled by the periphery (Prebisch 1949: 14). Forty years later, it remains true that third world countries dependent on exports for economic growth have no control over the external environment, and little voice in the international institutions that govern their access to credit.

Arthur Lewis: The Classical Model in a Tropical Setting

Like Prebisch, the impact of the Great Depression on the peripheral economy – in this case the West Indies – was a formative influence on Arthur Lewis. He was born in 1913, and grew up in St Lucia, a small island in the Caribbean archipelago that has produced two Nobel laureates: the poet and painter Derek Walcott, and the economist Arthur Lewis. His mother was a school-teacher and his father a customs official in a British colony dominated by the sugar industry. He completed his secondary education at the age of 14, too young to take up the Island scholarship that had been awarded to him to proceed to a British university of his choice. He spent the intervening four years as a junior clerk in the public service. He did not want to be a doctor or a lawyer, the two conventional routes to upward social mobility. He tells us that he wanted to be an engineer, 'but neither the colonial government nor the sugar plantations would hire a black engineer' (Lewis 1984: 1). At age 18, Lewis enrolled at the London School of Economics to obtain a Bachelor of Commerce degree. There he encountered economics, a subject neither he nor anyone in St Lucia had ever heard of before; it seemed, however, to be a preparation for employment in business or public administration.

London in the 1930s and 1940s was an intellectual centre of anti-colonial struggles and a meeting ground of personalities, many of them future leaders of newly independent nations of Africa and Asia. 'In London, meeting fellow anti-imperialists from all over the world, I launched upon a systematic study of the British colonial empire and its practices – colour bars, prohibiting Africans from growing coffee in Kenya so that they were forced into the labour market to work for cash to pay their taxes, and all the rest' (Lewis 1984: 13). Lewis addressed the problems of the West Indies in a number of papers and pamphlets, including a submission to the Moyne Commission, set up following a labour unrest throughout the West Indies in the late 1930s, and an economic plan for Jamaica advocating radical land reform.

Lewis was an outstanding scholar, and was appointed assistant lecturer – the first black appointment made by the London School of Economics. He lectured the first-year course on Economic Analysis and the author was fortunate to be among his undergraduate students in 1942. He was appointed full professor at Manchester University in 1948, at the age of 35. It was at that time that he returned to a question he had asked himself since he was growing up in St Lucia: why do workers in the sugar industry work so hard for so little pay, while workers in industrial countries enjoy better working conditions and receive far higher pay?

> My interest in the subject (economic development) was an off-shoot of my anti-imperialism. I can remember my father taking me to a meeting of the local Marcus Garvey Association when I was seven years old. So it is not surprising that the first thing I ever published was a Fabian Society pamphlet, called *Labour in the West Indies*, which gave an account of the emergence of the trade union

movement in the 1920s and 30s and, more especially, of the violent confronta-
tions between the unions and the government in the 30s. (Lewis 1984: 12)

This was not Lewis' only publication for the Fabian Society, an intellectual arm of the British Labour Party, associated with figures such as Sidney and
Beatrice Webb and George Bernard Shaw. His writings included 'Principles of
Economic Planning', an essay on the management of a mixed economy. With
early nineteenth-century England in mind, Lewis theorized that economic growth
required a capitalist sector able to internalize capital accumulation by ploughing
back profits to expand employment. With reference to 'comparative advantage',
he argued that a small and densely populated country like Jamaica should specialize in manufacturing, and import food from countries that have a comparative
advantage in agriculture like the United States or Canada. Foreign investors
should be encouraged to introduce modern technology ('tricks of the trade') and
access to external markets. At a time when colonial authorities were hostile to
any form of industrialization, this was quite radical. It is a mistake, however, to
enlist Lewis in support of the currently fashionable demonization of industrial
production for the domestic market. Practically speaking, industrialization had
to start by addressing the domestic market, whether in Jamaica or in Africa,
where Lewis, as the first economic advisor to the newly established state of
Ghana, recommended import substitution combined with agricultural development. We also note Lewis' increasing insistence on the need to increase productivity in the domestic food-producing sector as a precondition for successful
economic development.

The search for solutions to the development problems of 'tropical' countries was a constant preoccupation. It led Lewis to research the historical evolution of the international economy, from the *Economic Survey* (Lewis 1949a) to
his major research on primary commodity producers, published as *Growth and
Fluctuations, 1870–1913* (Lewis 1978). The results of the research were bril-
liantly summarized in his four Schumpeter lectures, published as *The Evolution
of the International Economic Order* (Lewis 1977). In 1955, Lewis had produced
The Theory of Economic Growth, one of the first book-length texts on the subject. His most important single work was 'Economic Development with Unlimited Supplies of Labour', first published in the *Manchester School* in 1954 (see
also Lewis 1958). In this article, Lewis constructed a model to address his two
major concerns – how to start the process of economic growth in an underdeveloped country, and how to escape from adverse terms of trade. We suggest that it
is the intersect of these two themes that lends the Lewis model its originality and
explanatory power, and links his earlier work with his later work.[3]

Lewis tells us that in August 1952, walking down a street in Bangkok,
the explanation of the dual problem of economic underdevelopment and adverse
terms of trade revealed itself to him: 'So in three minutes I had solved two of my
problems with one change of assumption'. It was necessary only to reject the
neoclassical assumption of a fixed supply of labour in favour of an infinitely

elastic supply of labour to the capitalist sector, in the traditions of Smith, Ricardo and Marx. The reinvestment of profits from the employment of labour would yield a rising share of investment in national income: 'It occurred to me that this model would also solve another problem which had bothered me since undergraduate days: what determines the relative price of steel and coffee?' (Lewis 1984: 132). The open version of the Lewis model explains why the factoral terms of trade will continually shift against a surplus labour country.

The Lewis model is essentially Ricardian. A 'traditional' non-capitalist sector of peasants, petty artisanal producers, domestic servants and other kinds of Smithian 'unproductive' labour, augmented by female entry into the labour force and by population increase, provides the capitalist sector with 'unlimited supplies' of labour, at a wage somewhat above the subsistence level as determined by average per capita production in the traditional sector. As the capitalist sector expands, employment and output increase, and the share of profits (savings) in national income rises. Eventually, as surplus labour is exhausted, the wage rate rises. At this point, the economy crosses the boundary from a dual to a single integrated labour market, and real wages rise with increasing productivity, in accordance with conventional growth models. The model is drawn from Lewis' reading of the English experience, where the real wage did not rise substantially in the first fifty years after the industrial revolution.[4]

Lewis' 'capitalist' sector is defined in functional Smithian or Marxian terms as employing 'productive' labour (Smith) or using 'reproducible capital" (Marx) by the ploughing back of profits. Capitalist production is not necessarily industrial, 'as anybody familiar with a plantation economy must know' (Lewis 1972: 76). The traditional sector is not exclusively agricultural but includes what is now known as the urban informal sector, and women's work, paid or unpaid. Nor is the capitalist sector necessarily privately owned. The model can equally be applied to a socialist economy of state-owned enterprises, as is clear from Lewis' references to its applicability to the rise of the savings rate in the Soviet Union in the 1930s. It is implicit in the model – whether applied to a private or public capitalist sector – that capital accumulation and economic growth depend on an institutional framework which ensures that the entire national surplus in excess of the subsistence wage bill is devoted to investment in the expansion of the capitalist sector; 'all the benefits from increasing returns goes into the capitalist surplus' (Lewis 1954: 436).

The model is classically production-oriented. Aggregate demand plays no role. Wages in the capitalist sector do not rise so long as there is surplus labour. There are no savings in the traditional sector. All savings are from capitalist profit. Capitalists are motivated to invest in the expansion of production by 'animal spirits'. Inequality of income is both a necessary condition and a result of economic growth. Lewis was attacked on all these grounds, but most particularly for his assumption of 'zero marginal product' in the traditional sector. In 'Reflections on Unlimited Labour', Lewis conceded that considerable confusion and 'irrelevant and intemperate controversy' was caused by his earlier reference to 'zero marginal product of labour' in the traditional sector, and explained that all the model requires is an excess supply of labour at the subsistence wage (Lewis 1972: 77).

The Lewis model comes in three versions: a closed model with no trade between the traditional (labour reservoir) sector and a fully self-sufficient modern capitalist sector; a closed model where an industrial modern sector trades with a traditional agricultural food-producing sector; and an open economy version whose capitalist sector trades both with the traditional sector and with the outside world. The first version of the closed model has two turning points: one, as the supply price of labour begins to rise, and two, and the more important one, when all surplus labour is exhausted and the economy enters a new phase of rising real wages and self-sustaining growth.

In the second version of the closed model, the rate of accumulation of the capitalist sector may be checked by adverse internal terms of trade in the form of a rise in the real cost of providing the subsistence basket of food for workers in the capitalist sector. This version was worked out in detail by Fei and Ranis (1961). The Fei–Ranis model is essentially a model of balanced growth between agriculture and industry. This is the version that has attracted most attention in the development literature with considerable explanatory powers concerning the process of growth and modernization in closed economies.

The third or open version of the Lewis model has received less attention in the literature than it deserves. This version, which addresses the dual problems of underdevelopment and deteriorating terms of trade, is arguably the most significant contribution of Arthur Lewis to an understanding of the contemporary world. In his studies of economic history, Lewis observed that the revolution in transportation and communication gave 'the capitalists the option of importing whatever cannot be produced locally'. In the open version of the model, the capitalist sector exchanges an export commodity (coffee) with a product of a fully developed country (steel). So long as labour is in surplus and its opportunity cost is low, the price of coffee will also be low.

> It is the factoral terms of trade that determine the commodity terms, and not the other way around. The factoral terms have moved continually against the LDCs since the beginning of the nineteenth century. The basic way to stop this is to raise the productivity of LDC farmers producing for the domestic market, thereby increasing the supply price of export crops. Productivity increases in the capitalist sector are not shared by the labour they employ. If the capitalist sector sells its product in external markets, as in the case of plantation economy, the productivity increase is shared by the capitalists and foreigners who benefit from the low prices of imports from labour surplus countries. (Lewis 1977:12)

The conclusion that Lewis drew from this model is that low wages and poverty in a labour-surplus economy will persist so long as the opportunity cost of labour to the capitalist sector remains low. This applies equally to agricultural and to manufactured exports from 'labour-surplus' countries.

In a series of lectures in honour of Schumpeter published as *The Evolution of the International Economic Order* in 1977, Lewis maintained that 'the absence of industrialization in tropical countries in 1870–1914, was not due to any failure of trade to expand, but rather to their terms of trade'.

> The factoral terms of trade offered some countries (Australia, Canada) the opportunities for full economic development. The factoral terms available to the tropics, on the other hand, offered the opportunity to stay poor – at any rate until such time as the labour reservoirs of India and China might be exhausted. (Lewis 1977: 12, 19)

Solutions are to be found not in reform of trade relations but in transformations of domestic structures, particularly in the increase in productivity of the domestic food sector. Lewis concluded his Schumpeter lectures with the following words:

> The development of the LDCs does not, in the long run, depend on the developed countries, their potential for growth would be unaffected even if all the developed countries were to sink under the sea. The LDCs have within themselves all that is required for growth. They should not have to be producing primarily for developed country markets. International trade cannot substitute for technological change, so those who depend on it for their major hope are doomed to frustration. The most important item on the agenda of development is to transform the food producing sector, create agricultural surpluses to feed the urban population, and thereby create the domestic basis for industry and modern services. If we can make this domestic change, we shall automatically have a new international order. (Lewis 1978b: 171)

In his Nobel lecture, 'The Slowing Down of the Engine of Growth' (1980), Lewis advocated trade and cooperation between developing countries with less reliance on trade with the industrialized countries, because the 'engines of growth' of the latter would slow down at the end of the twentieth century. They have indeed slowed down, but world trade has not slowed and is now growing faster than world output, driven by an intensification of international competition. Developing countries are forced to compete ever more fiercely with each other and their economies are restructured to become ever more export-dependent; while the increasing volume of cheap labour exports are driving down prices and depressing the real wages and purchasing power of the working classes in industrial and developing countries alike. The relationship of trade and development, so central to the writings of Lewis, remains a major unresolved problem of the contemporary world.

Conclusion

The theories of Prebisch and Lewis, as described above, attracted criticism in the 1960s and 1970s from younger Latin American and Caribbean economists who considered them excessively conservative. However, in the 1980s, when development economics was attacked as a structuralist heresy akin to socialism, Prebisch castigated the ideologues of neoliberalism, and Lewis, in his Nobel lecture (1980), repeated the warning that those who depend on trade as an engine of growth are doomed to failure and that countries must engage in trade on their own terms. He also repeated his conclusion that the first priority is the application of technology for increasing of the production of domestic food and other essential material requirements of the population. In an autobiographical note written late in life, we hear echoes of Marcus Garvey in Lewis' statement that 'I took it for granted that anything the Europeans could do we could do.' Prebisch warned a younger generation of Latin American economists of the seductive neoliberal discourse of Hayek and Friedman, and admonished them for their enthusiastic adoption of 'the flagrant manifestation of the hegemony of the centres: the intellectual dependence of the periphery'. 'The centres are simply not interested in our achieving a socially satisfactory form of development.'

> Let Milton Friedman understand! Let Friedrich Hayek also understand! A genuine process of democratization was moving forward in our Latin America, with great difficulty, and frequent delays. But its incompatibility with a system of accumulation and distribution of income is leading toward crisis. And crisis brings about an interruption in the process and the suppression political freedom; just the right conditions for the promotion of the unrestricted play of the laws of the market. What a paradox! You praise political freedom and individual rights. But you don't realize that in these lands of the periphery, your preaching can only bear fruit through the suppression of freedom and the violation of those rights. Because not only do the ideologies you preach perpetuate and aggravate social inequalities, they also conspire flagrantly against the efforts that must be made to reach new forms of understanding and articulation between North and South. The damage you are doing with your dogmas is immeasurable. (Prebisch 1981: 174)

Since the Asian crisis of 1997, there has been growing recognition of the bankruptcy of neoliberal policies, and of the need to revisit the development experience and the propositions of an earlier generation of development economists. We suggest that the insights of Prebisch and Lewis into the mechanisms of peripheral capitalism – or, as Lewis called them, 'tropical primary exporting economies' – have lost none of their relevance. Although the experiences that gave rise to their work were the Latin American and Caribbean ones, the explanatory power of their insights embraces the totality of contemporary North–South relations.

Notes

[1] For Prebisch's generation, Argentina's reference point in the international economic order lay outside of Latin America. Argentina was by far the most prosperous of the countries of Latin America, on a par with Canada and Australia in terms of GNP per capita. After visits to these two countries, with their surprisingly small provincial capital cities, and to race-divided and self-important Washington, Prebisch felt more

comfortable comparing the capital of Argentina with that of New York or with the capitals of western Europe (Pollock and Zuntz 1978).

[2] See Rodriguez (1977) for a useful retrospective on the ECLA centre–periphery system.

[3] The 'development' component of Lewis' problematic was 'to provide a mechanism explaining the rapid growth in the proportion of domestic savings in the national income in the early stages of an economy whose growth is due to the expansion of capitalist forms of production'. The 'terms of trade' component was to answer the question 'why tropical produce is so cheap. Take for example the case of sugar. This is an industry in which productivity is extremely high . . . the rate of growth of productivity is unparalleled by any other major industry in the world – certainly not by the wheat industry. Yet the workers in the sugar industry continue to walk barefoot and to live in shacks while workers in wheat enjoy among the highest living standards in the world' (Lewis 1954).

[4] According to data available to Lewis, the rate of savings in Britain rose from about 5 per cent before 1780 to 7 per cent in the early 1800s, and 12 per cent by about 1870, at which level it stabilized. The model also gives a pretty good explanation of the sharp rise in the rate of savings in the Soviet Union in the 1930s (Lewis 1972: 75–77).

References

Emmanuel, Arghiri (1972), *Unequal Exchange* (New York: Monthly Review Press).

Fei, J.C.H. and Gustav Ranis (1961), 'A Theory of Economic Development', *American Economic Review*, 51: 698–710.

Lewis, W.A. (1939), *Labour in the West Indies* (London: Fabian Society).

—— (1944), 'An Economic Plan for Jamaica', *Agenda*, 3 (4): 154–63.

—— (1945), Memorandum of Evidence to the West Indian Royal Commission (London: CO Public Records Office).

—— (1949a), *Economic Survey, 1919–39* (London: George Allen and Unwin).

—— (1949b), *The Principles of Economic Planning* (London: Allen and Unwin).

—— (1951), *The Industrial Development of the Caribbean* (Port of Spain: Kent House).

—— (1954), 'Economic Development with Unlimited Supplies of Labour', *Manchester School*, 22, May: 139–91.

—— (1955), *The Theory of Economic Growth* (Homewood, Illinois: Irwin).

—— (1958), 'Unlimited Labour: Further Notes', *Manchester School*, 32: 1–32.

—— (1972), 'Reflections on Unlimited Labour', in L.E. diMarco, ed., *International Economics and Development: Essays in Honour of Raúl Prebisch* (New York: Academic Press): 75–96.

—— (1977), *The Evolution of the International Economic Order* (Princeton: Princeton University Press).

—— (1978), *Growth and Fluctuations, 1870–1913* (London: Allen and Unwin).

—— (1980), 'The Slowing Down of the Engine of Growth', *American Economic Review*, September: 555–64.

—— (1984), 'Autobiographical Note', in William Breit and Roger W. Spencer, eds, *Lives of the Laureates: Thirteen Nobel Economists*, third edition (Cambridge, Massachusetts: MIT Press).

Ocampo, J.A. and M.A. Parra (2005), 'The Commodity Terms of Trade and Their Strategic Implications for Development', in Jomo K.S., ed., *The Long Twentieth Century, Volume 1: Global Economic Dimensions* (New Delhi: Oxford University Press).

Pollock, David and Michael Zuntz (1978), 'The United States and Latin American Development: Some Thoughts on the Problems of a Newly-Emerging "Middle-Income" Region', Norman Patterson School of International Affairs, Carleton University, Ottawa.

Prebisch, Raúl (1949), *The Economic Development of Latin America and Its Principal Problems* (New York: United Nations).

—— (1959), 'Commercial Policy in the Underdeveloped Countries', *The American Economic Review*, 49 (2), May: 251–73.

—— (1963), *Toward a Dynamic Development Policy for Latin America* (New York: United Nations).

—— (1970), *Change and Development: Latin America's Great Task* (Washington D.C: Inter-American Development Bank).

—— (1981), 'Dialogue on Friedman and Hayek, from the Standpoint of the Periphery', *CEPAL Review* (Santiago de Chile), 15, December.

—— (1982), *La obra de Prebisch en la CEPAL* (Mexico: Fondo de Cultura Económica).

—— (1984), 'Five Stages in My Thinking on Development', in G.M. Meier and Dudley Seers, eds, *Pioneers in Development* (New York: Oxford University Press): 173–91.

Rodriguez, Octavio (1977), 'Sobre la concepción del sistema centro-periferia', *Revista CEPAL* (Santiago de Chile), 3.

Sikkink, Kathryn (1988), 'The Influence of Raúl Prebisch on Economic Policy-Making in Argentina, 1955–1962', *Latin American Research Review*, 23 (2): 91–114.

—— (1988b), 'Response', *Latin American Research Review*, 23 (2): 128–31.

Singer, H.W. (1950), 'The Distribution of Gains between Investing and Borrowing Countries', *American Economic Review*, 40 (2): 478ff.

—— (1971), 'The Distribution of Gains Revisited', in Alec Cairncross and Mohinder Puri, eds, *The Strategy of International Development* (London: Macmillan).

Sir Hans Singer

Advocating a Fair Distribution of Fruits of Progress

Kunibert Raffer

Writing a chapter on Sir Hans Singer is both a pleasure and a problem. The pleasure is obvious, and the problem was succinctly expressed by D. John Shaw (2002: xix): 'To cover all his work adequately would have required much more than one volume.' Shaw's well-researched biography of some 350 pages, however, is considerably longer than this chapter. Starting with an article in the *Review of Economic Studies* (1935), Singer's list of publications is impressive. Shaw counted 450 publications, disregarding United Nations internal reports and book reviews. Five *festschriften* have been published in his honour (Shaw, ed. 2001: 2). Another is forthcoming.

By necessity, this chapter is an eclectic summary, bearing the risk of not doing full justice to Singer. It starts with Singer's *weltanschauung*, the foundations of his views on economic theory and policy, to facilitate better understanding his work. The main strands of Singer's thinking follow, starting with the Prebisch–Singer thesis (PST), which may be seen as their basis. Its finding – that real trade does not provide Southern countries with sufficient resources to finance developmental needs – led to advocating industrialization, diversification and soft financing, and explains Singer's contributions to the issue of food aid.

A *Weltanschauung* Where People Matter

If one wanted to summarize Singer's thinking in one catchphrase, 'redistribution of the fruits of growth' (Shaw 2002: 165), 'assuring equitable participation in economic improvements', or, more simply, 'economics as though people mattered' would be good choices. His first influences were his father Heinrich, a doctor who often treated the poor without charge, and the local rabbi, Dr Norden. At Bonn, Schumpeter and Spiethoff influenced his economic formation. 'The PST was greatly influenced by Schumpeter in his emphasis on technical innovation as a stimulus to new investment' (Singer 1998a: 20; cf. 1997: 129ff). The Prebisch–Singer thesis extended the concept of 'creative destruction'. New technologies influence the terms of trade by replacing or economizing on primary commodities. Globally, this creates divergence.

His work at the Pilgrim Trust, his support for Beveridge's welfare state idea (Singer 1943) and his Keynesianism shaped Singer's later work. He connected his work in the UK and at the UN: 'Obviously, a partisan of the social welfare state would be attracted by the thought and possibilities of a global welfare state represented by the United Nations in these hopeful first days of naive utopianism' (Singer 1984: 276). While mainstream economists concentrated on allocative efficiency, Singer's interest was 'from the beginning' more 'in the direction of distributive justice, or rather distributive efficiency' (ibid.: 280). There is a direct connection from his work on unemployment and the welfare state to his concern with a fair distribution of benefits from trade and investment, basic needs and the problems of children.

Working for the International Labour Organization's World Employment Programme, Singer often thought of his work on unemployment in Britain, particularly during the Kenya Employment Mission (1971–72). This programme was 'one of the formative influences on development thinking and policy in the 1970s' (Jolly 1998: 173). The report of the ILO mission to Kenya was the first international report recognizing the positive aspects of the informal sector, and recommending how its contributions could be made more effective. It was the 'forerunner' of the basic needs approach (ibid.: 174). Jolly (1998) recounts how the mission's head, Singer, sketched the idea that the incomes of the poorest must increase more rapidly than they would by growth and trickle-down alone. Redistributing from growth would mean adding to the incomes and assets of the poor without having to take away from anyone else, an idea that ran counter to the dominant perception of the Kuznets curve. Thus, reducing inequality by redistributing from growth, as formulated in the Kenya report, gave rise to the strategy of redistribution with growth, based on the joint IBRD/IDS study of the same name that even spoke of trickle-up effects from greater incomes of the poor. Arguing in favour of investing in the poor became acceptable.

Keynes influenced Singer's (1997) thinking profoundly. Singer appreciated and supported Keynes' efforts to ensure that the conditions of the 1930s, bringing about mass misery, mass unemployment, Hitlerism and war, would 'never again' occur. To ensure this, Keynes had drafted a proposal from which the Bretton Woods system emerged, extending his ideas to the global economy. Implementing Keynes' proposals – including the International Trade Organization, the international tax on balance of payments' surpluses, the control of speculative capital flows (still a membership right in the International Monetary Fund's Articles of Agreement, although the IMF keeps members from exercising it) and a world currency based on thirty primary commodities – would have avoided many problems. Keynesianism thus remains relevant (Singer 1998b: 108). Unfortunately, Keynes did not prevail and the truncated Bretton Woods system could not prevent further deterioration. The foreign exchange gap of the South, which prevented application of Keynesian expansionist policies internationally, would not have developed if Keynes' ideas had not been distorted by US interests, and would have been facilitated by stable commodity prices, adjustment pressure on surplus countries and adequate provision of international liquidity (Singer 1997: 145ff; cf. Shaw 2002: 253).

Singer became an outspoken critic of neoliberalism, feeling great concern about the resurgence of the policies of the 1930s, which had brought about rising inequality, leading in turn to the rise of rightist parties and, especially in developing countries, outright misery. While advocating such policies at the IDS, John Williamson (1996: 15) 'was challenged by Hans Singer to identify the policy changes that I regarded as so welcome'. Williamson made a list summarizing ten policy prescriptions, which 'we' find recommendable. Answering Singer's question 'who is we?', Williamson answered this would be 'we in Washington'; thus the Washington Consensus. When East Asia's financial debacle of 1997–98 damaged the reputation of neoliberalism, Singer (1998b) hoped that the pendulum might soon swing back towards Keynesianism. In his latest (co-authored) book, Singer advocates reforms for a more equal world order, that is, economic proposals as though people matter (Raffer and Singer 2001: 236ff).

The Prebisch–Singer Thesis

Productivity growth was universally assumed to be higher in industrialized countries (ICs, or the centre) than in Southern countries (SCs, or the periphery). Standard microeconomic concepts, economies of scale, learning by doing in manufacturing and increasing marginal costs of expanding raw material production supported this view. Historically, British terms of trade during the first half of the nineteenth century did, in fact, deteriorate (Singer 1989b: 323), reflecting the falling prices of manufactures and increasing primary commodity prices, as textbooks predict. The net barter terms of trade (NBToT) of SCs were assumed to have improved with the increasing marginal costs of primary commodity production distributing productivity gains globally. This is necessary for actual trade to be as beneficial as the textbook model predicts, that is, prices have to equal marginal costs in the long-run perfect market equilibrium. It was taken for granted that the world market functioned like the textbook model.

The Prebisch–Singer thesis (for its genesis, see Toye and Toye 2003) rocked the boat of professional complacency, exposing an apparent contradiction between theoretical expectations and practical outcomes. The US even attempted to close the Economic Commission for Latin America (ECLA), where Prebisch worked (ibid.: 463). For diplomatic reasons, ECLA tried to distance itself publicly from Prebisch, whom it privately supported wholeheartedly, by breaking with the UN practice of not signing UN documents. Thus, Prebisch's contribution was published under his own name, while Singer's was not.

The secularly deteriorating net barter terms of trade of SCs, observed by Singer (1950) and Prebisch (1950), destroyed the established orthodox logic of mutually beneficial world markets. If international markets and trade behaved according to academic models, Southern net barter terms of trade would have to improve. Empirical analysis showed the opposite to be true. Real trade was not as beneficial as claimed by theory. This conclusion also holds with constant net barter terms of trade if the centre's rate of technical progress is higher than the periphery's. Prices would not be aligned to marginal costs, and southern double factoral terms of trade would deteriorate. Prebisch talked of 'syphoning off productivity gains', while Singer's (1950) title emphasized the distribution of gains. Singer's interest derived from the problem of growth that increases inequality and disparities, and the question of whether world markets would perpetuate the division of labour militarily enforced by colonialism (Toye and Toye 2003: 448).

Before 1950, some ICs had also been quantitatively important primary commodity exporters. Well before the rise of industrial production in some SCs, however, the periphery virtually only exported raw materials. With a few exceptions, SCs have remained relatively dependent on them. Singer (1989b) presents quantitative evidence that the prices of primary commodities exported by ICs fell by 0.73 per cent annually during 1954–72 (in constant export unit values), while those of SC raw material exports fell by 1.82 per cent (both coefficients significant at 1 per cent). Thirlwall and Bergevin's (1985) evidence supports this conclusion. The prices of primary commodities (excluding oil) exported by SCs experienced a pronounced and significant negative trend, while those exported by ICs showed no significant trend.

Singer and Prebisch presented the following reasons for this inequality-exacerbating drive of real world markets, sometimes wrongly called different versions.

- *Market power.* Workers (trade unions) and entrepreneurs in ICs have sufficient market power to keep IC prices from falling with technical progress. The gains from technical progress are unevenly distributed due to higher factor incomes at the centre. Conversely, the lack of such market power forces SC export prices down. This 'para-market' assumption has been strongly criticized (cf. Spraos 1983: 23f) by orthodox economists, who blame the Great Depression of the 1930s on union power and wage stickiness. While the Washington Consensus and neoliberalism put the blame for most, if not all, evils on the 'stickiness of factor markets', this argument is conveniently ignored when it suggests that differential market power exacerbates inequality through trade.
- *Trade cycles* in the centre are cushioned and therefore less threatening to incomes. Raw material prices are more volatile, falling steeply during recessions, which adds momentum to the declining relative prices trend.
- *Trade cycles* in the centre are cushioned because people are better able to preserve their incomes. Raw material prices are more volatile, falling steeply during recessions, which adds momentum to the declining terms of trade trend.
- *Low income elasticities of primary commodity exports* limit the growth prospects of SC exports. Manufactures were virtually not exported around 1950. Initially attacked, this view is now generally accepted, as reflected in the phrase 'de-coupling growth from raw material consumption'.
- *Low demand elasticities.* Lower prices of primary commodities do not strongly increase demand. Strong expansion of raw material exports thus creates excess supply.

- *The necessity of importing products* which cannot be produced locally, such as machinery. The control of sophisticated technology embodied in these exports remains concentrated in the centre (Singer 1989b: 326). The low income elasticities of imports by the centre and the high income elasticities of SCs needing imports to develop both produce disequilibria. The periphery is incapable of earning the resources needed for imports and of producing the investment goods it needs. Current account deficits and foreign exchange gaps result, with indebtedness usually following. Protectionism by the centre increases these disequilibria by restricting peripheral export revenues further, while protectionism by the periphery reduces them. Diversification is needed to close the gap between earning capacity and developmental import needs.
- *Oversupply of labour* in the SCs keeps wages down. Arthur Lewis' labour market dualism thus complements the Prebisch–Singer thesis.

Cultural dependence – resulting in the wastage of scarce resources for luxury consumption, or of imports of little or no developmental importance and increasing the gap between revenues and developmental import needs – and debt pressure, forcing countries to sell, were added later.

Retaining productivity gains is the central problem. In a closed economy, real income can increase either by nominal incomes increasing at constant prices or by prices falling with productivity improvements at constant nominal incomes. Internationally, however, only prices transmit productivity gains. Competitive markets would make export prices fall in line with marginal costs. Export prices of countries experiencing stronger productivity gains would fall more, thus improving net barter terms of trade for countries with slower productivity growth. The Prebisch–Singer thesis' factor market argument simply means that the centre's productivity gains are largely absorbed by higher incomes, while those of the periphery tend to be transmitted via lower prices.

Debating Statistical Significance

The debate, however, soon focused on technical and statistical questions: the quality of historical data; whether prices appropriately reflected product quality improvements of manufactures or changes in transport costs affecting prices; whether the case rested unduly on British net barter terms of trade; and, eventually, on the interesting technical question as to whether a negative trend can be proven statistically. Both Singer (1950) and Prebisch (1950) drew attention to quality problems in Singer's historical data. Many problems, presented as though they had just been discovered, 'were already acknowledged at some length in the United Nations paper [written by Singer] . . . which Prebisch had indicated as the source of British data' (Spraos 1983: 45). After listing several counterarguments that 'appear to be damaging', Streeten (1981: 217) concluded: 'The core of the doctrine may well survive the onslaughts. This core is that in the world economy there are forces at work that make for an uneven distribution of the gains from trade and economic progress generally, so that the lion's share goes to the lions.'

Over decades, many new econometric methods have been used to test the Prebisch–Singer thesis. Sapsford and Chen (1998: 28f) compiled an overview from 1950 to 1998, concluding that with 'ten out of the top twelve studies listed' supporting it, the Prebisch–Singer thesis stood the test of time extremely well, although estimated annual rates of deterioration differed. Oil is usually omitted as a special case after 1973. Most importantly, none of the econometric studies found increasing Southern net barter terms of trade, nor was this ever claimed. Grilli and Young's (1988) alternative data set, widely used after 1988, also showed a negative trend. Criticizing the shortcomings of time-series analysis, Chen and Stocker (1998) used a partial equilibrium model for related goods and principal component analysis to re-examine the Prebisch–Singer thesis, with their results (for 1900–86) clearly supporting it.

Obviously, econometric results may be influenced by the time periods chosen, which leads to the question of structural breaks. With reservations regarding their quality, Spraos (1983: 68) concluded that for data up to the publication of the Prebisch–Singer thesis, 'evidence points to a deteriorating trend', albeit at a smaller rate. Extending the series into the 1970s, however, he concluded that no significant trend can be found, a conclusion he later qualified after plummeting raw material prices in the 1980s. Sapsford (1985) extended Spraos' analysis into the early 1980s. Analysing the time-series from 1900, and accounting for the wartime break of World War II, he found the Prebisch–Singer thesis strongly borne out for both the pre-war and post-war periods, and for the whole time-series since 1900. There was a clear downward trend before the war, and then, a strong upward shift brought about by it. The net barter terms of trade started from a much higher level after this discontinuity but immediately deteriorated again perceptibly.

The only serious challenge to the Prebisch–Singer thesis, by Cuddington and Urzúa (1989), criticized the method of trend estimation, rejecting the World War II break in favour of one structural break after 1920, presumably reflecting the end of the prolonged expansion after World War I. Thus, there was a one-time structural shift and no evidence of an 'ongoing, continual downtrend' (ibid.: 441). Sapsford, Sarkar and Singer (1992) challenged this conclusion on technical grounds, and showed that the extreme drop in 1920–21 of the more recently constructed Grilli–Yang series, on which it rests, is absent in earlier material. They found an annual trend decline of 0.6 per cent for 1900–85. A statistical debate over whether prices fall continuously or whether one of several trend-less series follows another after structural price drops is theoretically interesting but of little practical relevance. In both cases, revenues decline over time and diversification is indicated.

It is sometimes argued that income terms of trade are much more important than net barter terms of trade. If additional exports (over)compensate the effect of falling net barter terms of trade (which is not necessarily so due to demand elasticities), the same or more resources can be earned. This is quantitatively true, but may hide another problem. If falling net barter terms of trade are not caused by increased productivity but simply reflect falling export prices, double factoral terms of trade deteriorate. More must be produced and exported to earn the same revenues (or to keep the income terms of trade constant), similar to people having to work longer hours after wage cuts. Even with constant income, they might not be totally indifferent to lower hourly wages.

In 1994, several IMF publications corroborated the trend of declining terms of trade. Reinhart and Wickham (1994: 175) concluded that 'the recent weakness in commodity prices is mostly secular, stressing the need . . . to concentrate on export diversification and other structural policies', even seeing scope for stabilization funds. Borensztein *et al.* (1994: 7) found 'some evidence that the downward trend has steepened in the recent past'. The large decline of real commodity prices during the previous decade should be regarded as largely permanent. Also, price volatility had increased steadily and considerably since the 1960s. The growth of supply is seen as one price-depressing factor, an effect of the IMF's structural adjustment policies forced on debtor nations and repeatedly criticized by Singer. These findings by the IMF staff, an institution highly critical of the Prebisch–Singer thesis over several decades, seem to have contributed to closing the debate. Nearly half a century after its original publication, the Prebisch–Singer thesis stands vindicated.

Trade Policies for Development

Singer saw his seminal paper as a policy guide urging diversification away from primary commodity production (cf. Shaw 2002: 57). The gap between necessary imports and limited capacities to earn foreign exchange had to be closed. Early proponents of the Prebisch–Singer thesis, including Singer and Prebisch, were often accused of advocating import-substituting industrialization in opposition to production for export. This erroneous understanding produced protracted and fierce debates. Singer clarified:

> But the whole debate which the critics of Prebisch now conduct in terms of outward versus inward orientation, or of export promotion versus import substitution is an absurd and silly discussion. Obviously we want both, as Raúl Prebisch pointed out so clearly . . . we want a combination of import substitution and export promotion. . . . In other words what is needed is an interplay between inward-oriented or import substitution efforts (where regional cooperation also has a great role to play) and export promotion. (Singer 1986: 4f)

Prebisch (for example, 1984) repeatedly advocated export subsidies to overcome the disadvantages of infant exporters, thinking, however, that they might meet stronger opposition from ICs than infant industry protection. Import-substituting industrialization would thus be a second best solution, as the emphasis has always been on industrialization. Protection should make up for cost disadvantages, to be eventually phased out in line with productivity improvements of domestic SC industries. Balassa's (1984: 308) assertion that 'One finds no prescription for export expansion . . . in any of the contributions to the Prebisch–Singer thesis' is, politely put, highly misleading. Singer (1986: 6) stresses that Prebisch's ideas were realized in South Korea, which implemented Prebisch's preferred option of supporting exporters, and that many Korean economists were well aware of this. Pointing out that import substitution had become very popular and 'part of the established wisdom' in 'the name of rural development and promotion of domestic food production', Singer (1984: 288) felt that the objections were 'perhaps more to industrialization than to import substitution'.

Prebisch (1976: 66) clearly stated that there is no inherent or irreversible intrinsic quality condemning raw materials to deteriorating net barter terms of trade. Deterioration occurs when increases in production outstrip demand growth, or when the periphery wants to sell more than the centre wants to buy, which can equally well happen with manufactures (cf. Prebisch 1959: 258f), though Prebisch never fully included manufactures into his analysis. By contrast, Singer extended his empirical research to manufactures (Sarkar and Singer 1991). As it turned out, shifting away from commodities to manufactures did not necessarily solve the problem. In comparison with manufactured exports of ICs, the type of manufactures exported by SCs 'shared some of the disadvantages pointed out by Prebisch–Singer for primary commodities in relation to manufactures' (Singer 1989b: 327). The terms of trade of manufactures improved less for SCs than for ICs. Singer therefore concluded that both commodity and country effects exist, reinforcing each other. He attributed the deterioration of the terms of trade during 1954–72 to three distinct factors: falling terms of trade of primary products vis-à-vis manufactures, a fall in the prices of manufactures exported by SCs relative to manufactures exported by ICs, and the higher proportion of primary commodities in periphery exports.

While the net barter terms of trade cannot fall below the Ricardian limbo's floor in the textbook – this would mean that exporters sell at a lower price than they could get at home – this may happen if the unrealistic assumption of constant returns is changed *ceteris paribus*. Graham (1923) did so, assuming decreasing productivity for the agrarian product (wheat) and economies of scale for watches. Under this assumption, the limbo widens. The net barter terms of trade can deteriorate beyond the limbo's initial floor. Graham's raw material exporter loses by specializing according to comparative advantage, experiencing the development of underdevelopment. Graham's paradox gives further theoretical weight to the policy conclusions of the Prebisch–Singer thesis. Together with Raffer's theory of unequal exchange, the nucleus of a more realistic trade theory emerges (Raffer 1994).

Soft Financing and the United Nations

The collapse of the ITO after its successful negotiation in 1948 caused Singer – who at one point was also drawn into the preparatory work for the Bretton Woods conference (Shaw 2002: 35) – to be pessimistic about future prospects for convergence in the world economy, even though the position of raw material-exporting SCs was favourable at that time: 'the dice were loaded against one of the trade partners'. Singer thought that Keynes would have objected to establishing the Bretton Woods institutions without the trade pillar (Singer 1984: 279; Shaw, ed. 2001: 102). He opposed the official 'Trade not Aid' policy of the ICs. If trade did not supply the necessary resources for development, financial transfers were needed. Seeing both foreign direct investment and commercial bank lending as potentially self-defeating alternatives, Singer advocated aid and soft financing as the only alternative, an idea 'born and developed at the same time as the work on terms of trade with a clear intellectual link between the two'; it was the 'natural avenue to which the interest of the United Nations, and my own with it, turned . . . because of trade pessimism' (Singer 1984: 296). One must recall that the Overseas Development Agency (ODA) was tougher before 1970 than nowadays. 'ODA loans' were frequently made, with a spread over the interest rate at which the 'donors' themselves could borrow. Pure business investments were often recorded as 'aid' (Raffer and Singer 2001: 69ff). Important 'donors' objected to better ODA terms. Advocating soft aid was thus 'subversive' (Singer 1984: 296), as Singer personally learnt during the McCarthy days.

Singer (ibid.: 297) became one of the 'irresponsible wild men' at the United Nations, attempting to create a major soft financing mechanism. With the end of the ITO, this became even more urgent. Singer (1993) identified the ITO, the missing third pillar of trade, as the reason why the Bretton Woods system – with its relatively interventionist rules in the financial sector – eventually collapsed, and the failure to establish a system of democratic global economic management by the UN General Assembly and ECOSOC as another cause. It is interesting that Bretton Woods had developed from Keynes' proposals drafted as the Allies' countermove against the proclamation of a 'New Order' by the German Minister of Economics and president of the Reichsbank, Walter Funk, when Hitler was triumphant (Raffer and Singer 2001: 1; cf. Laughland 1997). Funk's centrepiece was a European Economic Community (Europäische Wirtschaftsgemeinschaft, EWG), whose structures were strikingly similar to what exists presently in Brussels. Cynics might be tempted to say that, in the end, Keynes lost out to Funk.

Attempts to establish soft financing started in 1949 with UNEDA (United Nations Economic Development Administration), proposed by V.K.R.V. Rao, a fellow student and friend of Singer's at Cambridge, in the Sub-Commission on Economic Development, which Singer served as a UN staff member. UNEDA was immediately blocked by the US and the IBRD (International Bank for Reconstruction and Development). Then, the idea of a UN Fund for Economic Development was propagated. When it was realized (apparently by Singer) that the acronym UNFED might not be a good omen, it was changed to SUNFED by adding the word Special. Inspired by the Marshall Plan, SUNFED should have administered large-scale soft aid. The 'long opposition of the World Bank not only to involving the UN in financial aid but even to the principle of soft aid, also served to prevent this idea materializing' (Singer 1989a).

The idea of multilateral aid gained US support during the Kennedy era for political reasons (including Castro's coming to power), though in a very different form. There was no question of a UN-controlled (S)UNFED. Like the Bretton Woods twins, the new institution was to be established under firm Northern control, in marked contrast to the Inter-American Development Bank (IDB) established with a voting majority of borrowing countries in 1959. The OECD (Organization for Economic Cooperation and Development) officially confirmed Singer's feeling about the importance of control: 'The developed countries preferred this to the alternative proposal, a special fund ensconced in the United Nations, because the structure of the World Bank ensured weighted voting in their favour' (OECD 1985: 141). It is, after all, the North's bank, not the World Bank. Finally, in 1961, President Kennedy proposed that the 1960s be designated the UN's Decade for Development. Singer drafted the proposals for action for the Secretary General's report (Shaw 2002: 104).

The IBRD immediately dropped its reservations about soft aid, once it became clear that the IBRD, and not the UN, would administer it. Thus, the International Development Association (IDA) was established as the bank's soft loan window. Mason and Asher (1973) credited the UN's wild men with preparing the ground for the IDA. Reid (1973: 134) suggested that the pressure for SUNFED was used by several poor countries to get some form of soft financing. Singer (1984: 299) was 'quite satisfied with this distribution of roles as "fall guys" for Eugene Black and IDA'. Soft financing was now established as 'sound practice', though not at the UN. The UN got a 'valuable consolation prize' in the form of the Special Fund. Singer was in charge of its preparation until the arrival of its first managing director, Paul Hoffman, the former administrator of the Marshall Plan. In 1965, the UN Special Fund and the UN Expanded Programme for Technical Assistance (EPTA) were amalgamated to form the United Nations Development Programme (UNDP).

The idea of a Marshall Plan for the South was taken up again in 1958 by Bruno Kreisky, who advocated the idea quite vocally as Austria's Federal Chancellor after 1970 (Raffer and Singer 1996: 62). Like the earlier idea to emulate the Marshall Plan to finance development on concessional terms, it did not gain enough support. The World Development Fund proposed by the Brandt Commission suffered a similar fate. As in the case of SUNFED, the IBRD objected strongly.

Singer was aware that insufficient soft financing, combined with insufficient export revenues, would produce a debt problem. His scepticism regarding hard financing by commercial lenders, expressed immediately after World War II when the situation of SC exporters was still quite good, was unfortunately proved right by the debt crisis. The Pearson Report (Pearson *et al.* 1969) prepared at the request of the IBRD's president – drew attention to Southern over-indebtedness caused by structural disequilibria, and proposed debt cancellations. Singer's concerns about structural disequilibria were already vindicated in the 1960s. However, the Euromarket lending spree, taking off at the very time when the Pearson Report was published, covered up the problem (for details, cf. Raffer 2004).

Singer made quite a few contributions on the debt problem, criticizing the neoliberal turn to 'structural adjustment'. Pointing out the fallacy of composition (individual efforts to gain market shares by lowering one's price do not work successfully if all exporters do so) was, of course, to be expected. But he also joined those demanding 'some degree or method of debt reduction' during the 1980s (reprinted in Shaw, ed. 2001: 123), seeing the inevitability of some form of debt work-out arrangement for countries well before the HIPC Initiative or the IMF's SDRM proposal. He identified three factors – equivalent to a 'multiple taxation of export earnings' (Singer 1989c) – that made the situation untenable at the time of his analysis: debt service represented a 30 per cent tax on Latin America's export earnings, terms of trade deteriorated by at least 20 per cent over the previous decade, and exports declined by another 20 per cent due to slowed-down IC growth – 'a total cut of . . . over half of export earnings'. Debt pressure contributed to terms of trade losses. To the extent that higher export volumes were bought at the expense of deteriorating terms of trade – the usual 'structural adjustment' procedure – this represented a case of mesmerizing growth.

Singer drew lucid parallels to the German transfer problem analysed by Keynes: 'Today, the Latin American countries in paying *their* reparations (debt service) demonstrate the validity of Keynes' views' (Shaw, ed. 2001: 128, emphasis in original). Germany's hyperinflation, which Singer personally experienced when young, could also be seen in debtor countries. Singer concluded that the complete Bretton Woods system imagined by Keynes would have prevented this problem. If Keynes' world currency based on the average price of thirty commodities, including gold and oil, had become reality, the 'oil shock' of 1973 – which 'did little more than restore the real price of oil' (ibid.: 102) – might not have happened. Bretton Woods might have survived. Singer also emphasized that while important, oil price increases were definitely not the only reason for the debt crisis (Raffer and Singer 2001: 133). He supported the proposal of a fair and transparent arbitration procedure based on US Chapter 9 insolvency (Raffer and Singer 1996: 203ff; 2001: 243ff), and seconded Paul Streeten's (1994) idea of copying one interesting feature of the Marshall Plan: regional cooperation and self-monitoring by recipients.

Singer, who had already written a study on children in development for the United Nations (International) Children's (Emergency) Fund (UNICEF) in 1972, was invited by Richard Jolly to join a team of experts analysing the effects of the crisis on children in 1984. Jolly's team produced a seminal report documenting how children suffered under the recession during the early 1980s (UNICEF 1984). It called for changes in adjustment policies and conditionalities to protect the living standards of the most vulnerable. 'In many ways the study set the scene for another seminal study by UNICEF on Adjustment with a Human Face (Cornia, Jolly and Stewart 1987)' (Shaw 2002: 187). Singer has repeatedly advocated reform of the UN (see ibid.: 221ff, or, for example, Raffer and Singer 2001:

254ff). With particular urgency, he has advocated making the IBRD and IMF 'special agencies of the UN', as had been initially planned in 1944.

Food Aid

Food aid, in particular, has always been of very strong interest to Singer. This followed logically from his research on the effects of international trade on SCs. Singer *had* already identified commercial food imports as one important development barrier:

> The major proportion of the imports of the underdeveloped countries is in fact made up of manufactured food (especially in overpopulated underdeveloped countries), textile manufactures, and manufactured consumer goods. The prices of the type of food imported by the underdeveloped countries, and particularly the prices of textile manufactures, have risen so heavily in the immediate post-war period that any advantage which the underdeveloped countries might have enjoyed in the postwar period from favourable prices realized on primary commodities and low prices for capital goods has been wiped out. (Singer 1950: 481)

When soft financing via the UN was blocked, food aid remained a realistic option to get more resources. Singer has repeatedly emphasized its element of additionality: 'If you talk about financial aid, you are the taxpayer's enemy, if you talk about food aid, you are the farmer's friend' (Singer 1994: 51) – an important distinction in ICs with strong agrarian lobbies. Substantial parts of Marshall aid to Europe were in the form of food aid, which contributed to making it attractive. US food aid under PL 480 encouraged Singer (1984: 301) to see the possibilities of an international aid programme more optimistically. Singer was involved in the creation of a multilateral food aid facility and the establishment of the UN World Food Programme.

Singer (1991: 111) pointed out that, economically, the bulk of food aid was, in fact, financial aid; over half was sold in recipient countries to provide balance of trade support as such food aid is directly equivalent to foreign exchange resources released because recipients can save the costs of commercial food imports. Financed from the same budget as ODA in Britain, it was seen as inferior to other aid. In most other countries, however, it is at least seen as largely additional, a form of disposing of agricultural surplus financed from agrarian budgets, thus not affecting ODA budgets. Unlike in the case of ODA, an internationally binding agreement, the Food Aid Convention, was achieved. Much of it is grant aid, and much goes to the particularly poor.

Singer's focus on food aid may be traced to his continued interest in distributive justice as it provides a nutritional safety net to the poor by, paraphrasing Amartya Sen, 'entitling' them to food. Connecting secularly falling terms of trade with the need of the poor to get food, Singer overcame what Sen (1983: 754) called 'perhaps the most important thematic deficiency of traditional development economics', well ahead of many others. Sen saw this deficiency reflected in the neglect of people, their needs and their right to live decently, which should be the ultimate concern of development.

Although an outspoken advocate of food aid, Singer has never been uncritical, always drawing attention to problems and shortcomings, mainly implementation problems (cf., for example, Raffer and Singer 1996: 73ff; Shaw, ed. 2001: 199ff). Food aid may discourage local farmers if administered wrongly. It can, but need not, cause disincentives. Singer especially recommended triangular transactions: donors buy food in other SCs to be shipped as aid to recipient SCs. This may also have the advantage of not encouraging shifts away from local consumption patterns in the way Northern imports would. Singer saw the creation of the World Trade Organization (WTO) as a major opportunity to increase the quantity of food available under the Food Aid Convention (Singer 1994; Singer and Shaw 1995). This would cushion the WTO's adverse effects on net food importers. Singer and Shaw (1995: 329) proposed 'a sub-committee on food aid' within the Committee on Agriculture. Although Article 16 of the Agreement on Agriculture demands measures in favour of net-importing SCs, such proposals were not welcome.

In Lieu of a Conclusion

This chapter attempts to summarize Singer's main contributions, aware of the problems of condensing his theoretical work and policy advice into the space available. Rather than trying to further condense the chapter in a short conclusion, one might end by quoting a distinguished economist, Sir Alec Cairncross (1998: 13f), Singer's fellow student at Cambridge:

> There are few of the developing countries that he has not visited and still fewer that he has not advised. He must have addressed a wider variety of academics in a wider variety of places about a wider range of subjects than any other economist, living or dead. He has moved from continent to continent, expounding, advocating, and devising strategies of economic development. His influence has been felt as much by word of mouth in the succession of countries where he has lectured as through the pile of working documents and published papers that survive like a spoor of his travels.

Appendix: Biographical Note

Hans Wolfgang Singer was born on 29 November 1910 at Elberfeld, now part of Wuppertal, Germany. The choice of his first names reflects the family's favourite poet, Goethe. His father, Heinrich, was a doctor. Serving as an officer during World War I, he earned the Iron Cross. Being Jewish, he was murdered after the Nazis took over. In 1929, Singer started studying medicine at Bonn, but soon changed to economics. His aborted medical studies produced an invaluable reward: he met his later wife, Ilse Lina Plaut, at the medical faculty.

Singer became a member of a discussion group of students Joseph Alois Schumpeter gathered around himself. He started his PhD thesis on the theory of economic development with Schumpeter. After Schumpeter left for Harvard, Arthur Spiethoff became his supervisor and Singer his research assistant. The thesis' focus changed to urban economics.

Singer, Wolfgang Stolper and August Lösch, the founder of modern location theory and regional economics, dominated the faculty association (*Fachschaft*) of students, giving it a clear anti-Nazi position. One incident characterizes Singer's courage. When vicious anti-Semitic insults against him were smeared on the faculty's bulletin board, Singer added a remark asking the anonymous person to sign because otherwise this person would not only be 'a swine, but also a coward' (Stolper 1998: 522). This eventually brought about a farce: the student who had written the smears was kicked out of the Student-SS – not for writing them but for denying it.

When the Nazis seized power, Singer had to flee via Switzerland to Turkey. A letter from Richard (later Lord) Kahn invited him to Cambridge. Schumpeter had recommended him to Keynes, proposing Singer for a scholarship. After an interview by a small committee, whose members included Keynes and Pigou, and whose secretary was Austin Robinson, he got one of two grants for refugees.

This grant allowed him to return to Germany to marry Ilse Plaut. The couple left quickly again for England. As a refugee, Ilse Singer could not pursue her medical studies. Nevertheless, she became a well-known figure in her own right. During the war, she worked for the resettlement of German refugees in Manchester. In New York, she was actively involved in protests against the discrimination of women through a branch of the Women's International League for Peace and Freedom, and worked voluntarily for an organization for better housing and against discrimination of black people (Shaw 2002: 90). Just before moving back to England, the Singers suddenly became unpopular with their neighbours because they had sold their house to a charming young couple – who were black. Ilse Singer's voluntary activities selling UNICEF cards made her an institution at the annual conferences of the Development Studies Association. Many members bought their annual supplies from her. She raised funds for fifty years. As a feminist, she joined the Greenham Commons Protest. She died on 3 March 2001, after 67 years of marriage (Jolly 2001).

Enrolled at King's College, Singer became a member of Keynes' Monday night discussion club. His dissertation on urban ground rent earned him one of the first PhDs in economics at Cambridge. His first employment was with the Pilgrim Trust. On Keynes' recommendation, Singer (1997: 138) was recruited as one of three young men to investigate the causes and effects of unemployment. The team lived with unemployed families, an early case of participatory research, from which two books resulted (Oakeshott, Owen and Singer 1938; Singer 1940). Singer (1997: 139) sees an obvious connection between studying depressed areas in Britain and in developing countries, for example, northeast Brazil, northern Thailand, or Kenya. After working at the University of Manchester (1938–44) and a brief internment as an enemy alien (1940), Keynes recommended him for a post at the Ministry of Town and Country Planning (1945–46). A series of twelve articles on the German war economy appeared in consecutive issues of *The Economic Journal* during 1940–44, at the invitation of Keynes. Appointed lecturer at the University of Glasgow, Singer was released on a provisional two-year assignment to the UN in 1947.

Numerous activities, visiting missions, official reports, consultancies to various governments and international organizations followed. He played an important role in the establishment of the UN Special Fund, the World Food Programme (WFP) and the

African Development Bank, where he served as chief economist during the initial stages (Shaw 2002: 119, 275). His work in favour of a more equal world at the UN, especially his efforts to establish (S)UNFED, triggered sharp attacks by Senator McCarthy and his followers, a 'deliberate and orchestrated character assassination' using false and misleading information (Shaw 2002: 90). His support of Beveridge (and the welfare state), and his prior work in the UK and for the British Labour government were 'cited' as proof of his left-wing 'aims' to disrupt the US. Singer considered leaving the UN, but, fortunately, this period blew over. At that time, neither of the Singers were members of a political party.

Retiring from the UN in 1969, Singer joined the newly founded Institute of Development Studies (IDS) as a Fellow, and was appointed Professor at the University of Sussex. He influenced and shaped the IDS over decades. He became an Emeritus Professor at Sussex University in 1975, but continued working at the IDS where he continues to be a Fellow. He has received half a dozen honorary degrees, and countless distinctions and honours. In 1994, Hans Singer was knighted in recognition of his achievements as an academic and as a practitioner of economic policy. The WFP honoured him with its Food for Life Award in 2001. Economists from the South 'have put his name forward on several occasions to receive the Nobel prize for economics' (Shaw 2002: 261). Like Joan Robinson, he might never receive it.

For valuable comments on the draft and information on facts, I am deeply indebted to Sir Hans Singer. I am very grateful to Paul P. Streeten and D. John Shaw for their most helpful comments.

References

Balassa, Bela (1984), 'Comment', in Meier and Seers, eds (1984: 304ff).

Borensztein, Eduardo, Mohsin S. Khan, Carmen M. Reinhart and Peter Wickham (1994), *The Behaviour of Non-Oil Commodity Prices*, IMF Occasional Paper No. 112, International Monetary Fund, Washington DC.

Cairncross, Alec (1998), 'The Influence of Trade on Economic Development', in Sapsford and Chen, eds (1998: 12ff).

Chen, John-ren and Herbert Stocker (1998), 'A Contribution to Empirical Research on the Prebisch–Singer Thesis', in Sapsford and Chen, eds (1998: 86ff).

Cornia, G.A., Richard Jolly and Frances Stewart, eds, (1987), *Adjustment with a Human Face, Protecting the Vulnerable and Promoting Growth, A Study by UNICEF*, 2 vols (Oxford: Clarendon Press).

Cuddington, John T. and Carlos M. Urzúa (1989), 'Trends and Cycles in the Net Barter Terms of Trade: A New Approach', *Economic Journal*, 99 (396): 426ff.

Graham, Frank D. (1923), 'Some Aspects of Protection Further Considered', *Quarterly Journal of Economics*, 37: 199ff.

Grilli, E.R. and M.C. Young (1988), 'Primary Commodity Prices, Manufactured Goods Prices and the Terms of Trade of Developing Countries: What the Long Run Shows', *World Bank Economic Review*, 2 (1): 1ff.

Jolly, Margaretta (2001), 'Ilse Singer', Obituary, *The Guardian*, 13 March.

Jolly, Richard (1998), 'Redistribution without Growth', in Sapsford and Chen, eds (1998: 172ff).

Laughland, John (1997), *The Tainted Source: The Undemocratic Origins of the European Idea* (London: Little Brown and Company).

Mason, E.S. and R.E. Asher (1973), *The World Bank since Bretton Woods* (Washington DC: Brookings Institution).

Meier, G.M. and Dudley Seers, eds (1984), *Pioneers in Development* (Oxford: Oxford University Press).

Oakeshott, W.F., A.D.K. Owen and H.W. Singer (1938), *Men without Work: A Report Made to the Pilgrim Trust* (Cambridge: Cambridge University Press); reprinted in 1968 by Greenwood Press, New York.

OECD (1985), *Twenty-Five Years of Development Cooperation – A Review, 1985 Report* (Paris: Organization for Economic Cooperation and Development).

Pearson, L.B. *et al.* (1969), *Partners in Development: Report of the Commission on International Development* (New York: Praeger).

Prebisch, Raúl (1950), *The Economic Development of Latin America and Its Principal Problems* (New York: United Nations).

—— (1959), 'Commercial Policies in the Underdeveloped Countries', *American Economic Review*, 49 (2): 251ff.

—— (1976), 'A Critique of Peripheral Capitalism', *CEPAL Review*, 1: 9ff.

—— (1984), 'Five Stages in My Thinking on Development', in Meier and Seers, eds (1984: 175ff).

Raffer, Kunibert (1994), 'Disadvantaging Comparative Advantages: The Problem of Decreasing Returns', in Renée Prendergast and Frances Stewart, eds, *Market Forces and World Development* (London and Basingstoke: Macmillan): 75ff.

—— (2004), 'The Debt Crisis and the South in the Era of Globalization', in Max Spoor, ed., *Globalization, Poverty and Conflict* (Dordrecht: Kluwer).

Raffer, Kunibert and H.W. Singer (1996), *The Foreign Aid Business, Economic Assistance and Development Cooperation* (Cheltenham: Edward Elgar).

—— (2001), *The Economic North–South Divide: Six Decades of Unequal Development* (Cheltenham: Edward Elgar).

Reid, Escott (1973), *Strengthening the World Bank* (Chicago: Stevenson Institute).

Reinhart, Carmen and Peter Wickham (1994), 'Commodity Prices: Cyclical Weakness or Secular Decline?', *IMF Staff Papers*, 41 (2): 175ff.

Sapsford, David (1985), 'The Statistical Debate on the Net Barter Terms of Trade between Primary Commodites and Manufactures: A Comment and Some Additional Evidence', *Economic Journal*, 95 (379): 781ff.

Sapsford, David and John-ren Chen (1998), 'The Prebisch–Singer Terms of Trade Hypothesis: Some (Very) New Evidence', in Sapsford and Chen, eds (1998: 27ff).

——, eds (1998), *Development Economics and Policy, The Conference Volume to Celebrate the 85th Birthday of Professor Sir Hans Singer* (London and Basingstoke: Macmillan).

Sapsford, David, Prabirjit Sarkar and H.W. Singer (1992), 'The Prebisch–Singer Terms of Trade Controversy Revisited', *Journal of International Development* 4 (3): 315ff.

Sarkar, Prabirjit and H.W. Singer (1991), 'Manufactured Exports of Developing Countries and Their Terms of Trade since 1965', *World Development*, 19 (4): 333–40.

Sen, Amartya (1983), 'Development: Which Way Now?', *Economic Journal*, 93: 745ff.

Shaw, D. John (2002), *Sir Hans Singer: The Life and Work of a Development Economist* (Basingstoke: Palgrave).

Shaw, D. John. ed. (2001), *International Development Cooperation, Selected Essays by H.W. Singer on Aid and the United Nations System* (Basingstoke: Palgrave).

Singer, H.W. (1935), 'Can Overcrowding Automatically Disappear?', *Review of Economic Studies*, 3: 130ff.

—— (1940), *Unemployment and the Unemployed* (London: King and Son).

—— (1943), *Can We Afford 'Beveridge'?* (London: Fabian Society Research Pamphlet).

—— (1950), 'The Distribution of Gains between Investing and Borrowing Countries', *American Economic Review*, 40 (2): 478ff.

—— (1984), 'The Terms of Trade Controversy and the Evolution of Soft Financing: Early Years in the UN', in Meier and Seers, eds (1984: 275ff).

—— (1986), 'Raúl Prebisch and His Advocacy of Import Substitution', *Development and South–South Cooperation*, 2 (3): 1ff.

—— (1989a), 'Lessons of Post-War Development Experience 1945–1988', IDS Discussion Paper no. 260 (Sussex: University of Sussex).

—— (1989b), 'Terms of Trade and Economic Development', in Peter Newman, Murray Milgate and John Eatwell, eds, *The New Palgrave: Economic Development* (London: Macmillan): 323ff.

—— (1989c), 'The Relationship between Debt Pressure, Adjustment Policies and Deterioration of the Terms of Trade for Developing Countries (with Special Reference to Latin America)', Institute of Social Studies Working Paper Series no. 59, Den Haag; reprinted in Singer and Shaw 2001.

—— (1991), 'Food Aid: Development Tool or Obstacle?', in H.W. Singer, Neelambar Hatti and Rameshwar Tandon, eds, *New World Order Series 9: Aid and External Financing in the 1990s* (New Delhi: Indus): 109ff.

—— (1993), 'Prospects for Development', in S. Mansoob Murshed and Kunibert Raffer, eds, *Trade, Transfers and Development, Problems and Prospects for the Twenty-first Century* (Aldershot: Edward Elgar): 7ff.

—— (1994), 'Problems and Future of Food Aid in the Post-GATT Era', *Newsletter, Bruno Kreisky Dialogue Series*, 10: 42ff.

—— (1997), 'The Influence of Schumpeter and Keynes on the Development of a Development Economist', in Harald Hagemann, ed., *Zur deutschsprachigen wirtschaftswissenschaftlichen Emigration nach 1933* (Marburg: Metropolis): 127ff.

——(1998a), 'Beyond Terms of Trade: Convergence/Divergence and Creative/Uncreative Destruction', *Zagreb International Review of Economics and Business*, 1 (1): 13ff.

—— (1998b), 'How Relevant is Keynesianism Today for Understanding Problems of Development?', in Soumitra Sharma, ed., *John Maynard Keynes – Keynesianism into the Twenty-First Century* (Cheltenham: Edward Elgar): 104ff.

Singer, H.W. and D.J. Shaw (1995), 'A Future Food Aid Regime: Implications of the Final Act of the GATT Uruguay Round', in Helen O'Neill and John Toye, eds, *A World without Famine?* (Basingstoke: Macmillan): 305ff.

Spraos, John (1983), *Inequalizing Trade, A Study of Traditional North/South Specialization in the Context of Terms of Trade Concept* (Oxford: Clarendon).

Stolper, Wolfgang F. (1998), 'Joseph A. Schumpeter: The Man and the Economist', in Sapsford and Chen, eds (1998: 513ff).

Streeten, Paul (1981), *Development Perspectives* (London and Basingstoke: Macmillan).

—— (1994), 'A New Framework for Development Cooperation', in *Benessere, equilibrio e sviluppo, Studi in onore di Siro Lombardini*, a cura di T. Cozzi: C. Nicola, L. Pasinetti, A. Quadrio Curzio, con la collaborazione di G. Marseguerra, I (Milano: Vita e Pensiero): 111ff.

Thirlwall, A.P. and J. Bergevin (1985), 'Trends, Cycles and Asymmetries in the Terms of Trade of Primary Commodities from Developed and Less Developed Countries', *World Development*, 13 (7): 805ff.

Toye, John and Richard Toye (2003), 'The Origins and Interpretation of the Prebisch–Singer Thesis', *History of Political Economy*, 35 (3): 437ff.

UNICEF (1984), *The State of the World's Children, 1984* (Oxford: Oxford University Press).

Williamson, John (1996), 'Lowest Common Denominator or Neoliberal Manifesto? The Polemics of the Washington Consensus', in Richard M. Auty and John Toye, eds, *Challenging the Orthodoxies* (London and Basingstoke: Macmillan): 13–23.

Index